TALES OF
THE ROSE TREE

JANE BROWN

HARPER PERENNIAL
London, New York, Toronto and Sydney

In Memory

PAMELA GORDON

1920–2004

Harper Perennial
An imprint of HarperCollins*Publishers*
77–85 Fulham Palace Road
Hammersmith
London w6 8jb

www.harperperennial.co.uk

This edition published by Harper Perennial 2005

1 3 5 7 9 10 8 6 4 2

First published in 2004 by HarperCollins*Publishers*

Copyright © Jane Brown 2004

Jane Brown asserts the moral right to
be identified as the author of this work

A catalogue record for this book
is available from the British Library

Grateful acknowledgement is made to the following to reproduce copyright:
Messrs. John Murray Ltd for John Betjeman's 'Pot Pourri from a Surrey Garden'
and 'Subaltern's Love-song' (*Collected Poems 2001*); and Charlotte Zolotov's
'Pink Azalea' from *River Winding* Scott Treimel of New York

ISBN 0-00-712996-3

Set in Postscript Linotype Minion and Spectrum display by
Rowland Phototypesetting Ltd, Bury St Edmunds, Suffolk

Printed and bound in Great Britain by Clays Ltd, St Ives plc

CONTENTS

FOREWORD

It is St George's Day, Shakespeare's birthday, 2002, and Late Spring Show day at the Royal Horticultural Society in Westminster. There is a crush of people and plants, and so breathing in I slither and 'Sorry' my way around the tables of woodland displays (somehow reminiscent of old film-set fantasies of English springtimes with everything in flower at once), making for the far back corner. Behind a dazzling chorus line of frilled peonies are the rhododendrons; whether show etiquette deems the back of the hall the dunce's corner or the Holy Grail I do not know, but it is certainly uncommercial. Here is old-fashioned horticultural competition. Three particular kinds of people filter around these tables, pinstripe-suited gentlemen of a certain age who make notes, and masses of equable matrons accompanied by young men in T-shirts, many of whom wave their hands, murmuring 'they won't do for me' as they steam onwards to the miniature meadows. I loiter with intent along the rows of regulation green vases holding the pastel-coloured heads of upturned bells or branches of fluttering pinks and mauves. A golden orb of *falconeri* rests on its rosette of leaves like Tutankhamen's decapitated mask; a pink and frilly number is butchly called 'Wally Miller'. The creamy bells of 'Roza Stevenson' would seem more aptly named, and 'she' has won a Gold Medal. Such awards are still prestigious, but there is a forlornness about these flowers in the alien and stuffy hall, plucked from their breezy woodlands to die alone. Once the whole hall would have been filled with treasured and cosseted rhododendrons and their worshippers; now these few occupy a shabby corner behind all those herbaceous upstarts and 'weeds'. There is such an incongruity in their presence here, in their faded magnificence, in their frivolous names, in their eastern inscrutability and mystery. I come away, muttering 'What are they doing here at all?'

Whilst the Royal Horticultural Society may have an A for effort in the rhododendron world, the Blue Riband is undoubtedly held by the Royal Botanic Garden in Edinburgh. Less than ten days after the London show I was heading northwards for that famous grey portal on the Inverleithen Road, for the *Rhodo'02* conference, an international gathering of more than 200 rhododendron buffs from the farthest reaches of the planet. They talked solely of rhododendrons for three days and more; of gardens from Bremen to Portland, Oregon, by way of Pukeiti, New Zealand, of taxonomy endlessly and of vireyas (the newest section of the genus) obsessively, of the unfathomable mysteries of leaf waxes, anatomical traits and molecular phylogeny to the blissfully nostalgic restorations of old Scots gardens and the regeneration of China's lost botanical heritage.[1] Breaks from the talking were taken in the garden, walking around the historic living collection which (with the Younger, Dawyck and Logan Botanic Gardens) holds more than half the known species of rhododendrons, many as collectors' numbered original plants. Additional treats included the glasshouse of treasured vireyas and an exhibition of botanical drawings of rhododendrons. For me it was a feast, a fantastic overview of the thoroughly modern world of the rhododendron through the eyes of its experts and heroes and plainly passionate gardeners. It was an invigorating world-view that balanced the prevalent despondency amongst some British gardeners that their precious genus is becoming tarred with the black brush of the bad press about 'rogue' species.

The conference, properly titled 'Rhododendrons in Horticulture and Science', was so packed with innovations and enthusiasms (and there is a limit to the number of speakers than can be fitted into three days) that I am embarrassed to admit I was left with more questions than answers. Why was all the scientific effort so obsessively horticultural, geared only to the garden-centre production line? Do horticulturists not exist amidst fellow humans who have other – medical, cultural or ecological – needs from such a great genus of plants? Why were there no considerations of biochemistry or phytogeography? And why this apparently shrinking history of rhododendrons? It is 250 years since the mid-eighteenth-century introductions into English gardens, or 150 since Joseph Hooker's expedition to the Himalayas, but now the conference referred to 'over 100 years' of importance in temperate horticulture. Does the rhododendron, one of the oldest plants on earth, have no history unless it is in a garden border?

At this point I knew that I had a book to write, and it was going to be an enormously difficult task. I wanted to construct a history for the genus *Rhododendron* that paid tribute to the mystery and majesty of these plants, and was less obsessed than is usual with the intrepid plant hunters (who were mostly looting after all). To find that the rhododendron's botanical family, Ericaceae, was so named because the ancient Greek shepherds had no use for such plants other than as their bedding was not an auspicious start. Then, dipping into Richard Dawkins' *Climbing Mount Improbable* (because that is what I was going to be doing) I found the following:

> The attitude that living things are placed here for our benefit still dominates our culture, even where its underpinnings have disappeared. We now need, for purposes of scientific under-standing, to find a less human-centred view of the natural world. If wild animals and plants can be said to be put into the world for any purpose ... it is surely not for the benefit of humans. We must learn to see things through non-human eyes. In the case of the flowers ... it is at least marginally more sensible to see them through the eyes of bees and other creatures that pollinate them.[2]

A tall order, but it points to the dignity of the genus Rhododen-dron as something more than a horticultural plaything. And the bee's eye-view might be rather appropriate as the most notorious rhododendron legends concern the poison honey. However, I cannot turn myself into a bee, and can only attempt this more rhododendron-centric history out of such writer's objectivity that I can muster, and an ingrained respect learnt long ago for a plant so much larger than myself.

Rhododendrons have always been present in my life, invariably as great green-skirted ghosts. Green ghosts that guarded a miniature cottage in a New Forest garden, where my favourite aunt once sat sewing petticoats out of parachute silk, guarded by a giant yellow teddy bear, all fascinating to an under-five. By the time both garden and cottage were lost beneath a road-widening scheme I was growing up in bleak, chalky north Hampshire. The sun rose in the east, along the road to life and London town. Swathes of magenta and pink rhododendrons lined the old A30 through Sunningdale and Virginia Water as if to celebrate rare excursions for London shopping. In those days of few gardens open for visitors, and even fewer visits in my case, the rhododendrons of Surrey and in parts of the New Forest around Lyndhurst were free gardens, flowery benedictions on favourite and forbidden landscapes.

Naturally when I married I went to live in Surrey, at Abinger in the greensand hills with rhododendrons in every garden. They were the long-lived natives, we peripatetic humans were just passing through. A favourite place was the scented copse on Leith Hill, planted with rhododendrons in memory of Dr Ralph Vaughan Williams. The road up the hill, fringed with beech trees, was one of the most magical of roads, which I was lucky enough to travel in all lights and seasons. The beech woods were devastated in the 1987 great storm, but nature and the National Trust have restored the greenery and the rhododendrons are thriving. At Abinger I found out about Gertrude Jekyll and her young architect friend, Edwin Lutyens, and began to write the story which made my first book, *Gardens of a Golden Afternoon* (1982). Their rhododendron connections appear later in this book.

Most of my subsequent books had some rhododendron content.

Lanning Roper,[3] the American who made some of the most beautiful twentieth-century gardens in England, found his inspiration at Exbury in wartime, when serving in the US Navy. He cultivated an encyclopaedic knowledge of the genus and believed their effect on gardens had been 'electrifying', and planted them prolifically. Rhododendrons give way only to roses for the number of mentions in his classic *Sunday Times Gardening Book*.[4] My other American subject, Beatrix Farrand,[5] learnt her plant expertise from Professor Charles Sargent at the Arnold Arboretum and could not but become an addict and an expert. Sargent and the Arnold play conspicuous roles in this rhododendron history, and I have just come across Beatrix's 1936 plant list for the wilderness at Dartington Hall in Devon. It contains no less than 80 different species and hybrids, undoubtedly planted in threes or fives.

Most recently I have consciously turned my back on sandy Surrey and taken refuge in fairly rhododendron-free Huntingdonshire, which allows me perspective. Perhaps that is why they have nudged my elbow and said 'write about us'. *Tales of the Rose Tree* falls a long way short of Professor Dawkins' scientific idealism but at least shows that some members of the family Ericaceae have been rated worthy of more than shepherds' bedding.

CHAPTER ONE

A Rose by Another Name

RHODODENDRONS ARE A RACE OF GIANTS on a global scale, at home in the snows of the Himalayas and the swamps of Carolina, in the jungles of Borneo and the island inlets of Japan. They are too complex a genus for single truths, and many of the 1,025 species that we know are of a manageable size, for all azaleas are rhododendrons, and 'the smallest rhododendron in the world', the ground-hugging mite, *Rhododendron caespitosum*, now sits snugly on a bench in the vireya house at Edinburgh Botanic Garden, recently found by Dr George Argent and his colleagues growing amongst tree ferns in the Central Highlands of Irian Jaya.[1]

At the other extreme must be the 'colossus' of the Burmese hills that made Frank Kingdon Ward, that most urbane and articulate of plant hunters, stop in his tracks, spellbound. The rhododendron, aptly named *magnificum*, had a trunk a yard in girth at five feet from the ground and it was covered in rose-purple flowers – he guessed a thousand – all in bloom at once. He believed that this plant was already old when George I was on the throne of England.[2]

The beauty of rhododendron flowers is self-evident, but is there something more? The giant species have longevity and a nobility, they dwarf our puny human scale, they have an oriental mystique – for most of them come from China – and more than a tinge of that fabled inscrutability. They certainly make no concessions to life in the West. They are anathema to the cosiness of the 'English' garden.

Travellers' tales of their voluptuous and perfumed flowers have incited waves of horticultural passions for over 250 years. They have been hunted in the name of scientific curiosity, for the booty of empires, to gloss reputations and make fat profits and for sheer greed; for a rhododendron a pot is hardly adequate and acreages have been bought for them. This curious and short history (for what is 250 years to a genus that has been on earth for 50 million?) of men and rhododendrons is full of violence, death and destruction, ravaged homelands, failures, heartbreaks and bitter disappointments; in fact, it is much like other stories of exodus and migration, a passage to survival. The rhododendron, blithely and beautifully continuing to flower, becomes the heroic exile.

Imagine yourself a rhododendron. Imagine you have been kidnapped, plucked from home, imprisoned in dark and sulphurous airs, prinked and poked by ugly hands, mated with strangers and given an alien name. No one knows anything about you, nor seems interested in finding out, except by mutilation and experiment. When your new masters have lost interest your frail limbs will be discarded, and if not burnt, thrown to the winds. The dregs of yourself, warmed by the sun, healed by the rain, might just find the determination to survive.

Was this the treatment that inspired survival at all costs?

'Those ruddy rhododendrons,' scream the headlines, 'they are ruthless triffids, strangling our wild flowers, choking our woodlands.'

'Cutting them down does not work,' whines the conservationist, 'because they just grow again from the stump.'

'They are invaders, capturing our Snowdonia!' and for Snowdonia read also Exmoor, Derbyshire, Norfolk and the Western Isles of Scotland. 'Kidnap victim bites back' would be a better headline, for the 'triffids' are partly natives of the Asian Pontic mountains, and partly Americans, the latter collected by the eighteenth-century botanists John and William Bartram who had openly recorded how their Cherokee guides had led them to the 'slicks' and impassable 'hells' of native rhododendron thickets in the Appalachians. Nevertheless the forced migrants with their frankly doubtful habits were used as grafting stock for garden hybrids and also planted in shelter belts (always in the windiest places) and game coverts throughout the nineteenth century, and they have found the determination to survive.

It took a different kind of approach, a gardening revolution, really to understand rhododendrons: 'The real art of gardening,' wrote Lionel de Rothschild, 'is to make a plant that has come from distant lands not only look at home but feel at home'.[3] Was it purely coincidental that the maker of Exbury, the doyen of rhododendron gardeners was the great-great-grandson of a Jew from the Frankfurt ghetto?

Could it be the 'otherness' of rhododendrons that fundamentally attracts or repels? Even the xenophobes of the Celtic fringes (I know of no other nations having rhododendron wars) have to admit that the visitors to Exmoor, Snowdonia, the Western Isles, 'the public', love the mauvy-purple masses of flowers. Spend a fine Sunday in May or June at Exbury, or in the Valley Garden of Windsor Great Park, or at Lea Gardens at Matlock, and you will meet with even stronger passions. All kinds and conditions of people will be simply falling in love, over and over again, with the glorious and scented strangers, the Asian species and their descendants, who make up most of our garden rhododendrons. These are the real charmers, for their mouth-watering candy colours, their cascades of waxy bells or iridescent globes proffered in ruffs of leaves. But after the sniffs and sighs, perhaps even falling to your knees as I did before the fabulous 'Fortune' at Exbury, what next? Are you happy to accept the generality of *rhododendrons*? Or does this wonder plant have a name? If you are lucky enough to find a label (and keeping the labels going is most gardeners' nightmare) you will be lucky again if it is a famous hybrid, such as 'Fabia' or 'Naomi', which hopefully you will be able to buy from a good nursery. More likely it will be tongue-gobbling Latin – in the case of 'Fortune', *Rhododendron sinogrande x falconeri* – which will be pretty meaningless unless you happen to have the Exbury stud-book to hand where it says that the *sinogrande* pollen came from a particularly good plant at Trewithen in Cornwall, and the hybrid first flowered in 1938. An additional source tells me that 'Fortune' was thought the 'finest hybrid' produced by that date. This makes the Exbury plant the floral equivalent of a painting by Augustus John or Stanley Spencer, a plant of museum quality. But why 'Fortune'? Who, or what, is *sinogrande*? Let alone *falconeri*?

The chief difficulty with these beloved aliens is their name, or names. Even the Royal Botanic Garden in Edinburgh, the College of Arms of the rhododendron world, has allowed 'rhodo' (or at least *Rhodo'02* as a conference logo), and devotees in private may use 'rhodie', but any diminutive becomes infuriating throughout a long book. Rhododendron it has to be.

The first 'rhododendrons' came into Western gardens during the working life of Carl von Linné (1707–78), the Swedish naturalist we know as Linnaeus. Linnaeus made a tour of England in 1735–6 and met the London merchant Peter Collinson (1694–1768), the pioneering connoisseur of new plants from the American colonies, who told him of the 'swamp honeysuckle' and 'Great laurel' or 'Rose Bay', some of which were already flowering in Collinson's garden at Peckham or in the gardens of his friends. Linnaeus, an unusual young man, had already published his thesis setting out his system for arranging and naming plants and animals according to their reproductive organs: 'It expiated in a learned way on stamens and pistil, pollen (sperm), seeds (ova), castration and infertility. Also on polyandry, polygny, incest, and concubinage and marriage-beds of petals, with a strong erotic charge.'[4]

This was naturally the subject of much debate between those in the know during his English tour. 'The *Systema Naturae* is a curious performance for a young man,' wrote the Quaker Collinson to his

Quaker collector John Bartram in Philadelphia, '. . . his coining a set of new names for plants tends but to embarrass and perplex the study of Botany. As to his system, on which they are founded, botanists are not agreed about it. Very few like it. Be that as it will, he is certainly a very ingenious man and a great naturalist.'[5]

The sex life of plants and perhaps the even more heated debates on Linnaeus' conviction that swallows spent their winters in the depths of lakes and rivers, a belief that remained unshaken for the rest of his life, gave him an attractive notoriety that did no harm to his cause. Though many eighteenth-century botanists continued to be both embarrassed and perplexed, Linnaeus' *Species plantarum*, the bible of plant taxonomy, published in 1753 became universally, though not immediately, accepted. *Species plantarum* (a small and modest book in its original edition) names vegetable creation. Linnaeus proposed binomials, double names, the first to indicate the plant's family or genus, the second to denote a defining feature, the specific epithet. Labouring away in his narrow room in Uppsala he dissected the myths of Greece and Rome, the Greek and Latin dictionaries and, some say, gossip on the clandestine relations of the Swedish court, for his names. 'The whole family of ferns, mosses, algae, fungi, he called Cryptogamia (plants that marry secretly).'[6] Linnaeus saw scholarly derivation as one of the virtues of his system, and he tried to conjure his generic names from a plant's past. For 'rhododendrons' he had the alpenrose, as well known and loved in Alpine villages as the eidelweiss; from Collinson he knew of the American rosebay, great laurel or sometimes sweet mountain rose; he took into account Pliny's lilting oleander (a name it was a pity to lose) and suggestions of kinship with cistus, ledum and euonymus. He might have chosen Chamaecistus or even Chamaerhododendros (this was used for a time) so small mercies must be acknowledged. Even so, it must have been a particularly bad day when he cobbled together the Greek *rhodon* (rose) and *dendron* (tree) to create, *voilà* – *rhododendron*!

The rose seems to have been inevitable, but surely a mistake.

Was he so occupied peering into ovaries that he never looked at the whole flower? How can the clustered trumpets of a rhododendron be anything like the proffering petals of a rose? The reclusive Linnaeus, with his early travels a dim, fantastic memory and no desire at all to see the living specimens he was launching into futurity, could not have known that the wide world would produce such a bounty of rhododendrons, or perhaps he would have given us another name, one with the charm of magnolia or camellia. He had no notion that Frank Kingdon Ward's aptly named *Rhododendron magnificum* of the Burmese hills was flaunting her thousand rose-purple flowers as he wrote. Linnaeus became a martyr to his great system; his harassed youth and poverty yielded only domestic troubles and ill health and his single-mindedness was a burden: the glamorous rose tree was half a world away from his chilly garret. The great genus Rhododendron can afford to forgive him.

Other families, even human ones, have unwieldy names and yet achieve happiness and distinction. Rhododendrons are not alone with their difficulty, and it could be worse – tsusiophyllum, margyricarpus, crataegomespilus are just three picked randomly from modern taxonomy, though thankfully foisted on to very minor genera. In mildly accepting these botanical mouthfuls we have sanctioned a barricade between ourselves and plants, especially when, as with rhododendrons, there is no common alternative. I know only one challenger: 100 years after Linnaeus, John Ruskin (1819–1900) would not utter or write the botanical name for his beloved 'rubied crests of Alpin roses', one of his favourite flowers of Switzerland, *Rhododendron ferrugineum*. Ruskin challenged 'Rose-tree', as 'the botanists have falsely called the proudest of them', and suggested 'Aurora' – 'That shall be our name for them, in the flushed Phoenician colours ... And the queen of our own Alps shall be "Aurora Alpium".'[7]

If Ruskin would not use the word at least he celebrated the flowers; one of his alpine poems, 'Splügen', revels in the mountain flora:

And round, beneath, beside, there grew
The alpine roses' heathery hue,
That blushed along the mountain head.
Was never flow'r so regal red!
It climbed the scathed old rocks along, –
Looked out, the cold, white snow among,
And, where no other flower would blow,
There you might see the red rose grow.[8]

In 1767 the 'Rhodora' was brought from Newfoundland by Joseph Banks (oh, that it had been known fifteen years' earlier and I might be writing about rhodoras); it is an ancient but comparatively rare plant, low-growing, deciduous, with small oval leaves with a white indumentum, and pale purple flowers, fond of a boggy mountain habitat. It was called by various names for well over a century, most often *Rhodora canadensis* until *Rhododendron canadense* was settled upon. Ruskin liked 'Rhodora', and included it with Azalea and Aurora in his private nomenclature. Most significant of all, Lionel de Rothschild, the chief rhododendronophile of the twentieth century, named his yachts 'Rhodora' 1 and 2, unable to bring himself to use 'Rhododendron'.

Not surprisingly the word *rhododendron* has proved difficult for poets, and the nineteenth-century Russian romantic Afanásy Fet is a hero for taking it head on:

Rhododendron! Rhododendron!
The splendid flower of the orangery,
How beautiful and how elegant
Thou art in the hands of the flighty fairy!
Rhododendron! Rhododendron!

Rhododendron! Rhododendron!
But in the hands of the flighty fairy
Beautiful are not only roses,
Beautiful also are large volumes
Of poetry and prose!
Rhododendron! Rhododendron!

Perhaps Fet's real fancy was his 'flighty fairy' with green fingers, but his loud singing of the name 'rhododendron' is endearing, and encouraging, and I cannot insult him by leaving his work unfinished. Here is the third, and last, verse:

> Rhododendron! Rhododendron!
> Beautiful too are all attacks
> On poets, advertisements,
> Beautiful too are misprints,
> Beautiful too are supplements.
> Rhododendron! Rhododendron![9]

John Betjeman, being a poet of Surrey, had to take the name in his stride; here is Pam, his 'great big mountainous sports girl' in full flight:

> See the strength of her arm, as firm and hairy as Hendren's;
>   See the size of her thighs, the pout of her lips as, cross
> And full of pent-up strength, she swipes at the rhododendrons,
>   Lucky the rhododendrons,
>   And flings her arrogant love-lock
> Back with a petulant toss.[10]

But, of course, *rhododendron* is not the only difficulty, for there is the second half of the Linnaean binomial, the specific epithet. The species can also be named for their homeland, habit or character: *Rhododendron sinogrande*, for a lucky human being; *Rhododendron falconeri*; or for their growth pattern, *Rhododendron arboreum*, which strictly translates as 'a tree-like rose tree'. These are inevitably long and difficult names, and when further distinguishing details are added, they get even longer.

Frank Kingdon Ward (1885–1958) gave nicknames to his finds, used with his collectors in the field, and to allow his prose to fly, as in this dazzling description from his *Riddle of the Tsangpo Gorges*:

> It is impossible to do justice to the rhododendrons at the Doshong-la as we saw them in June; the valley, flanked by grey cliffs, roofed by grey skies, with the white snowfields above, spouting water which splashed and gurgled in a dozen babbling becks; and everywhere the rocks swamped under a tidal wave

of tense colours which gleam and glow in leagues of breaking light. 'Pimpernel' whose fiery curtains hang from every rock; 'Carmelita' forming pools of incandescent lava. 'Yellow Peril' heaving up against the floor of the cliff in choppy sulphur seas breaking from a long low surf of pink *lacteum*, whose bronzed leaves glimmer faintly like sea-tarnished metal.[11]

'Scarlet Pimpernel', classified *Rhododendron forrestii* (for George Forrest, who first collected it) *repens*, and Kingdon Ward's 'Scarlet Runner', both became popular garden 'carpeting' varieties; 'Carmelita' was a 'racy carmine' *Rhododendron var. chamaethauma*; and 'Yellow Peril', a *Rhododendron campylocarpum* variety, was named for its 'aggressive abundance'. Kingdon Ward called his 'dreamed of, but scarcely hoped for, treasure, a real orange-flowered Rhododendron' – the prince of oranges – 'Orange Billy'. Clearly the nicknames were much better for shouting about the mountain, but once the precious plants reached home they were loaded with their Latinised Linnaean epithets. We may long for the simplicity of the Bhutanese, who managed for centuries with *takpa* for white flowered plants and *takma* for the red, and be glad that popular hybrids such as 'Beauty of Littleworth', 'Lionel's Triumph' and 'Goldsworth Orange' slip easily into everyday speech. But the Latinised epithets are the basic language we have; there is no detour to be taken around *Rhododendron periclymenoides* (which George Washington collected from the wild for his garden at Mount Vernon in Virginia, calling it Pinxterbloom), no escape from *Rhododendron griffithianum* nor *Rhododendron campylocarpum*. An acquaintance with rhododendrons gives regular exercise in verbal gymnastics.

Plant taxonomy is intended to be logical, and the rhododendron hoops and hurdles usually have a pleasing clarity and reason. The epithets are less daunting when their flowery personalities become familiar – it is rather like picking out a friendly face in a crowded room, and working on successfully from there! For instance, *Rhododendron grande* (known for a time to the Victorians as *argenteum* because of its silvery young shoots and backs to its leaves) is quite simply 'grand', the most imposing plant with shining dark-green leathery leaves and bell-mouthed ivory flowers held in spectacular clusters. *Grande* was introduced into Western gardens from Sikkim by Joseph Hooker in 1849, but she has an even more splendid botanical counterpart ('differing in the eglandular ovary and pedicels and the shorter and stouter style' according W. J. Bean) in *Rhododendron sinogrande*, found by George Forrest in 1912 in the mountain borderland of China, Tibet and Burma. *Sinogrande* has a cult status; she (for rhododendrons are indisputably 'she') ruled her fortress heights above the valley of the Salween and westwards to the Mishmi Hills and beyond, long before her human neighbours and demigods established their forbidden cities. She was, and is, remote and imperially despotic, preferring an altitude of about 10,000 feet and dominating dark forests and impassable jungles with her gnarled and twisted branches. She lives to a great age, grows into a substantial tree; everything about the plant is hugely impressive – its leaves are the largest of all rhododendrons, great deeply veined, dark green ovals sometimes two feet long, sagging under their own weight as they hang by thick stalks from an even thicker stem, surrounding great spear-headed buds. She flowers with an imperial insouciance, when she feels like it but not every year; when they come the flowers are pale yellow, translucent globes springing from the ruffs of glossy leaves, lighting the dark woods like the lamps at the feast table.

Sinogrande has an imperial cousinage, the inevitable relatives and pretenders that put something of a strain on the supply of epithets. As well as her western counterpart, *grande*, in Sikkim, the crimson-purple flowered *giganteum* was found by Forrest in south-west Yunnan in 1919, seven years after he found *sinogrande*. The cousinage includes three of Kingdon Ward's introductions: rosy-purple *magnificum*, *montroseanum* (for the Duchess of Montrose) and Mr McCabe's rhododendron, the pale yellow *macabeanum*. McCabe was a deputy commissioner for the Naga Hills in Assam where it was originally discovered in 1882.

If John Ruskin had written more on botany, and less on art and architecture, perhaps he could have carried his case, but the name 'rhododendron' has never been seriously challenged, evidence of the Svengali-like hold that Linnaeus has on the botanical world. Azaleas, vireyas and others have been gathered into the rhododendron's fold, and a string of botanists and gardeners have struggled to order and reorder new species and their natural variants as they have been presented by triumphant and mischievous plant hunters. Taxonomy is a rolling sea of knowledge, entered at great peril; the lists and classifications are the bulk tankers of the rhododendron world, necessary but ugly and best left to go about their business unheeded. It is enough here to mention briefly a few terms which might unsettle the unwary. There is a 'natural' divide amongst rhododendrons into lepidotes, those with scaly buds, and elepidotes, with non-scaly buds. This was thought critical to hybridisers as the two kinds did not mate, but this genetic rule has already been breached at least twice, and presumably has a shaky future. Leaf sizes are self-evidently variable, from 3 to 30 centimetres; some are pointed (lanceolate, elliptic, ovate) and others have rounder ends (oblanceolate, oblong, obovate) but the most critical factor is the indumentum, the hairy covering of the undersides which can vary from silvery-white to rusty-cinnamon. These velvety undersides, so delicious to stroke, and their obverse faces of polished dark green or deep-veined grey-green, are indicators of the plant's welfare, drooping miserably in the cold or drought, gradually lifting – sometimes with a chorus-like co-ordination – to meet the rain. Unseen, or only under the microscope, are the diverse structures of the indumentum hairs, which are used to classify subgenera, sections and subsections, but need not concern us here.

Rhododendron taxonomy is a path to lonely sainthood, pursued in chilly garrets and overheated laboratories. The names that linger in lists and catalogues have a cosmopolitan eccentricity – Don, Planchon, Maximovicz, Rehder, Tagg and Sleumer. George Don the Younger, who followed his father as superintendent of the

Chelsea Physic Garden, was the first to divide the genus into sections in the 1830s, and he confirmed that azaleas were rhododendrons. Jules Emile Planchon grouped the azaleas into evergreens and deciduous species in 1854. Carl Johann Maximovicz of St Petersburg Botanic Garden was a field botanist, collecting through Siberia, Manchuria and Japan, and he redefined species according to the leaf buds and flower buds. Dr Alfred Rehder of Harvard University's Arnold Arboretum, H. F. Tagg of Edinburgh Botanic Garden and J. Hutchinson of Kew divided the genus between them, azaleas and elepidote and lepidote rhododendrons respectively, for a combined classification of all the new species collected in the late nineteenth and early twentieth centuries. Sir Isaac Bayley Balfour (1853–1922), the great Regius Keeper in Edinburgh, had initiated the grouping into Series as he worked to classify the Chinese species sent home by George Forrest. Dr Hermann Sleumer 'continued the long process of refining the recognized groups within the genus' and analysed the genus within the family Ericaceae, publishing his system in 1949. Within the last 50 years Edinburgh has ruled the waves of reclassification via the work of J. M. Cowan, H. H. Davidian, James Cullen and David Chamberlain, the last two, especially, working increasingly from their observations as field botanists.[12]

These taxonomists dealt only in the aristocratic species who sired the first hybrids, although immediately gardener-induced crosses were made between species and hybrids, and then hybrids and hybrids, producing an abundant race. There are also the spontaneous hybrids, the uncertain but often wondrous works of nature, that sprout and flower in the woodland gardens (as they do in the wild). In theory the naming of hybrids, like the naming of roses and racehorses, is controlled by registration, when pedigrees and evidence of uniqueness have to be provided, but in practice, on a worldwide scale, this is but a fine remove from the chaotic. Hybrids come and go in unnumbered thousands, beauties with a brief trajectory. The world of the rhododendron is actually limitless.

If the poets quailed and the botanists have bored us, then painters have done justice to the glories of rhododendrons. Georg Dionysius Ehret (1708–70), the gardener's boy from Heidelberg whose talent for botanical drawing took him around Europe, was the first. He could have seen the American azalea (*nudiflorum*) now called *Rhododendron periclymenoides*, painted in 1734 with her alluring pink ribbon, either at Leiden Botanic Garden or the Jardin des Plantes in Paris. Two years later Ehret settled in London at the very moment that the first big American, *Rhododendron maximum*, arrived, at least as seedlings and seeds, from John Bartram in Philadelphia. *Maximum*, under her pre-Linnaean name, *Chamaerhododendros lauri-folio semper virens* (literally 'like a rose tree with laurel foliage, ever living, evergreen'), made her debut in Mark Catesby's *Natural History of Carolina, Florida and the Bahama Islands* (1731–43) in a curious double portrait (see page 1 of the first picture section). Ehret had drawn the beautiful flower head from a dried specimen sent by Bartram, and Catesby, 'a conscientious amateur artist', has added his copy of Ehret's kalmia (*Chamaedaphne semper virens*) bending over the stem to fit the page.

Rhododendron ponticum, painted by Peter Henderson, made her debut as a plate in Robert Thornton's *Temple of Flora*, between 1790 and 1807, when she was merely a junior migrant of some 30 years' standing, or growing. The *Temple* was a select company of 28 flowers, including cereus, kalmia, canna, passion flower, aloe, tulips, hyacinths and *Lilium superbum*, all painted in their natural settings.

Almost half a century later they had a flora to themselves: Joseph Hooker's (1817–1911) *Rhododendrons of Sikkim-Himalaya* was hailed as 'one of the marvels of our time' when the first part was published in 1849, eighteen months after Hooker had first set foot in India and long before he returned home. The explanation was in the *Athenaeum*'s jibe: 'But it is not every botanist who has such a father at home as Sir W. Hooker.'[13] Hooker senior (1785–1865) was working hard to publish for Kew's reputation as well as his son's, and a third person must also share the congratulations on this splendid volume, the illustrator Walter Hood Fitch. Fitch had been apprentice in a firm of Glasgow calico printers when William Hooker discovered him, and he brought him south when he became director of Kew Gardens. Fitch had, and needed, an uncanny ability to visualise a live plant from a sketch and dead specimen. He could have seen only a *Rhododendron ponticum* or an American species at Kew, and here he was faced with 30 quite different Asian wonders, to be envisaged at second hand, and across half the world, through Joseph Hooker's eyes. He had the courage 'rather to treat his originals as sketches than to work them into finished pictures' so that the life and liveliness of his imagined plant were carried through the engraving process, then enhanced with bold hand-colouring.[14]

Consequently *Rhododendrons of Sikkim-Himalaya* (the hyphenated title was because Joseph Hooker's permission to enter Sikkim was delayed so the actual species found there were in Part Two, published in 1851) introduces some fantastic rhododendron characters. None more so than Fitch's image of *Rhododendron falconeri*, found in the shadow of Kangchenjunga, which unleashes a prehistoric monster of a plant, fleshily stemmed, with primitive leathery prehensile tails for leaves and club-like inflorescence of white trumpets (see page 8 of the first picture section). At Glenarn in Argyll, Michael and Sue Thornley see their *falconeri*, grown from Hooker's seed, sitting 'like a huge buddha, a reincarnation from another continent and time, whose vast flesh-coloured limbs have grown into an oriental pattern against the grey Scottish sky'.[15]

The rare, epiphytic, delicately scented *Rhododendron dalhousiae* is illustrated as Hooker found her, tumbling from on high, her white trumpets clustered on the ends of branchlets firmly rooted in the trunk of a blasted oak (see page 3 of the first picture section). Her ladyship is honoured with a second appearance, seven great white trumpets filling the page. Joseph Hooker knew she was a special find, but she was elusive, and when he returned to collect seed in the summer of 1849 he wrote: 'this is difficult for you cannot see the plant on the limbs of the lofty oaks it inhabits except it be in flower and groping at random in these woods is really like digging for daylight'.

Rhododendron dalhousiae.

Hearing, at least in his head, his father's urgings for more seeds, he wrote again two weeks later: 'if your shins were as bruised as mine with tearing through the interminable rhododendron scrub of 10–13 feet you would be as sick of the sight of these glories as I am'.[16]

Hooker found home comforts from the trials of plant hunting with the Archibald Campbells, he the political agent in Darjeeling, she the giver of splendid dinners. When he was in the mountain passes of north-east Nepal, the snow falling relentlessly, he was reminded of Mrs Campbell for she had given him one of her crêpe veils to shield his eyes, which he cut up to share with his Lepcha guides, also troubled with snow blindness. For Mrs Campbell's wisdom and hospitality, and to keep a promise he had made, he named one of the ten species collected on this snowy journey for her, *Rhododendron campbelliae*. In plate six of *Rhododendrons of Sikkim-Himalaya* Fitch portrays the neat posies of pink bells, flushed mauve on their outsides, of Mrs Campbell's rhododendron.

Joseph Hooker kept and published a detailed diary of his journey but, as is now becoming clear, the plates of *Rhododendrons of Sikkim-Himalaya* are the true memorial. Hooker was dispensing immortalities to his friends and supporters, and more than half the plates illustrate these rhododendron people. The fabulous *falconeri* was named for the lucky Hugh Falconer (it is a good job he had such a noble name), superintendent of the Calcutta Botanic Garden. Hooker had journeyed to India with free passage in the party of the new governor-general, Lord Dalhousie, hence Lady Dalhousie's rhododendron. Were the lovely white trumpets made for mourning? The gentle James Mangles wrote in the *Gardeners' Chronicle* many years afterwards: 'What shall I say of *R. Dalhousiae*, named after the unfortunate Lady Dalhousie, who died of sea-sickness on her voyage home from India?' How could anything unseemly be said? But the hopes for this most lovely flower, a dream combination of a white lily and an orchid, were never fulfilled. 'The habit of the plant is frequently so bad, so leggy and so shapeless', mourned

Mangles, 'that people tire of growing it.'[17] Even to the present day *dalhousiae* seems to have been overlooked and resides only in a few greenhouses. Why was her habit never treated as a virtue to mother a race of rambling rhododendrons?

In contrast, the vigorous red-flowered *thomsonii* was named for Hooker's travelling companion in Assam, his fellow student and friend from Glasgow University days, Thomas Thomson (181/–/8). Thomson was an assistant surgeon for the East India Company, captured during the Afghan campaign of 1838–42 and imprisoned at Bukhara, he then escaped and returned to active service, whereupon he was sent to survey the Ladakh/Tibet border and climb the Karakorams. *Rhododendron thomsonii* has become one of the most popular rhododendrons, its blood red bells, as many as twelve on a flower head, and a generosity to flower to exhaustion, as well as being a good parent, all ensuring this. Hooker and Thomson found it in the Khasia Hills but its territory extends to Yunnan and Burma, and it retains a legendary connection with the song of the hawk-cuckoo (*dujuan* in Chinese) in its name *ban tuan ye dujuan*, 'semicircular leaved rhododendron'.

Which raises the question, why all these opportunist English names? Did these evidently ancient plants have none of their own? Hooker must have heard the opinions of his Lepcha guides and collectors – was his imperialist arrogance such that he took no notice? (He certainly gained a reputation for aloofness in later life, and was not like his father, the genial Sir William.) Or was it simply that as a scientist his creation was an ordered, Latinised universe and 'common' names had no value? Sometimes it must have seemed that a plant's existence was only valid after it had been tabulated in London. Some 40 years after Hooker's journey, Augustine Henry was to realise that the Latin binomials were something of a nonsense if they did not correlate to an identifiable native plant. That rhododendrons are virtually nameless before Linnaeus' 1753 *Species plantarum* is a most intriguing facet of their history.

Joseph Hooker's haul from the Himalayas, distributed as seeds and seedlings around Britain and the world during the 1850s, spurred the later nineteenth-century rhododendron craze, which even affected the fashionable artists. *Azaleas* by Albert Moore was exhibited at the Royal Academy in 1868. (See page 2 of the second picture section.) The beautiful 'Grecian' woman and the azalea, which fills half the canvas, together with the Japanese patterning on the pot and the bowl holding the petals were motifs beloved of the Aesthetic Movement. Algernon Swinburne thought *Azaleas* good, to say the least: 'The faultless and secure expression of an exclusive worship of things formally beautiful . . . The melody of colour, the symphony of form is complete: one more beautiful thing is achieved, one more delight is born into the world; and its meaning is beauty; and its reason for being is to be.'[18] James Tissot's *The Morning Ride* (1872–4) is filled with a glade of hybrid azaleas, their life and colour contrasting with the black-clad figure, the consumptive woman in her donkey cart whose pale hand reaches for a flower. Henri Fantin-Latour's *Azalées et Pensées* is an exquisite study of a miniature white azalea in a pot, with a basket of tumbling pansies. This painting was for a long time in the collection of Queen Elizabeth the Queen Mother, a passionate and knowledgeable devotee of all rhododendrons.

Somewhere between Tissot and Walter Hood Fitch, in graphic terms, comes the high priestess of the Victorian passion for rhododendrons, Marianne North (1830–90). Marianne was a prime example of Victorian womanhood of the more adventurous kind. She was born into a distinguished and affectionate family who loved to travel. She was tomboyish and musical and took lessons in sketching and painting; her family name was 'Pop'. Her rather ailing mother died when she was fifteen, having made Pop promise never to leave her father. Marianne was unperturbed, for she adored her father, she was fairly robust in body and mind, and had a dread of the 'upper servant' status of a wife who was snubbed and 'to be scolded if the pickles are not right and then she will have to amuse herself by flirting with the most brainless of the Croquet-

Badmintons'.[19] Father and daughter travelled all over Europe and the Mediterranean for a dozen years, sharing their enthusiasm and knowledge of plants and places, and Marianne was never without her sketchbook. When they were at home her painting progressed from watercolours to oils – the latter 'a vice like dram-drinking, almost impossible to leave off once it gets possession'.[20] She had the most talented artistic mentors, including Edward Lear (who wrote 'The Owl and the Pussycat' for Marianne's niece), and impressive friends, including Sir William Hooker who introduced her to the tropical treasures of Kew. Marianne was bereft when her father died in October 1869. She was 39, financially secure, used to her freedom, passionate about her painting and most of all determined to get out of stuffy England and see for herself the exotic countries and plants she and her father had never reached. And so, careless but not immune to the difficulties of a lone woman, she travelled. She went to North America, the West Indies, Brazil, Japan, Singapore, Borneo, Ceylon, India, Australasia, South Africa, the Seychelles and Chile, an astounding itinerary which produced the 832 paintings that crowd the walls of her gallery at Kew Gardens. The rhododendrons – blowzy and billowing just like *de rigueur* Victorian crinolines – responded warmly to Marianne's lavish oil technique (which the ungenerous thought garish and heavy-handed); painter and flower seem especially united in Victorianness. She painted most of them in their native habitats and this adds to the imperial splendours. The mighty snow-capped Kangchenjunga is framed in *Rhododendron arboreum*; none of the English young ladies of Darjeeling ever got up early enough to see the mountain unclouded, Marianne painted for a week at sunrise. A red-flowered species is seen draping the Nilgiri Hills in southern India, and the vain and poignant vapours of the Raj seem to rise from her luscious creams and yellows of *cinnabarinum* and *formosum*, and from the ivory trumpets of the epiphytic *Rhododendron dalhousiae* (see page 4 of second picture section).

In 1917 John Guille Millais produced *Rhododendrons*, the first important book devoted to the practicalities of cultivating rhododendrons, but it was still, like *Sikkim-Himalaya*, a large volume for book rests and library tables, and it had plates of the flowers by well-known garden artists of the day, Beatrice Parsons, Winifred Waller, Eunice Brennand (distinguished by a 'Miss' and presumably an amateur) and Archibald Thorburn. The last name is most interesting because Thorburn (1860–1935) is perhaps the most famous British painter of birds and mammals and *Rhododendrons* is his only purely botanical work. It came about out of a friendship, for he had illustrated previous books by Millais, for instance *The Natural History of British Surface-feeding Ducks* (1902), and he lived in rhododendron country, at High Leybourne in Hascombe in Surrey, just down the road from Gertrude Jekyll, and Millais himself was not far away at Compton's Brow near Horsham. Thorburn always painted from life and invariably gave his winged subjects their favourite plant food in sprays and branches of berries and leaves; he also loved working in his own garden at Hascombe so may we presume his plates were painted there? Gardens as subjects for themselves were legitimised by George Samuel Elgood (1851–1943). Elgood painted the 'old' gardens of England and Scotland – Crathes, Compton Wynyates, Berkeley Castle, Penshurst – for the heyday of the Arts and Crafts Movement. He painted in Italy in springtime, portraying azaleas in Florence and Rome; however, there are no more than six views with azaleas in all Elgood's vast output. By the time he returned to paint *en plein air* at home the rhododendrons were long over and lilies, phlox and Michaelmas daisies (these massed at Munstead Wood) were his favourites.

Rhododendrons were never particularly photogenic and there seem to be more bad photographs of them, in black and white and colour, than of any other flower. They really belonged to the botanical artists who were constantly lured on; every 50 years or so has seen a splendid rhododendron flora. Some 50 years after Millais, Beryl Urquhart financed the publication of two folio volumes, *The Rhododendrons*, in memory of her late husband Leslie Urquhart

(1874–1933). Connoisseurs think these plates by Carlos Riefel some of the finest ever painted. Most recently Marianna Kneller, one of the most bemedalled botanical artists of our day, sometime artist in residence at Exbury gardens, has painted over 60 glorious plate illustrations for *The Book of Rhododendrons* (1995). Finally it is back to Walter Fitch and his friends and successors; so splendid were the *Botanical Magazine* plates for rhododendrons that 121 plates have been recently reprinted into a single volume, *The Illustrated Rhododendron*.

Marion Dorn (1896–1964), a design diva if ever there was, whose carpets and fabrics were beloved of the 1930s beau monde and featured at Claridges and the Savoy Hotel, was photographed by Horst P. Horst in 1947 with a table runner covered with her design, a scattering of enormous rhododendron leaves. At about the same time, the Danish modernist Carl Theodor Sørensen (1893–1979) wanted to demonstrate how the English, and perhaps specifically London city square with trees could be applied to mid-twentieth-century Denmark. The result was Vitus Bering's Park in Horsens, a triangular site with an arc of lawn (easily mown in continuous circuit) that 'bends elastically, like a steel spring' through a woodland edge of oaks and rhododendrons. There are perimeter paths, within protective berms, and cross paths, or the freedom to march directly across clearings, oak groves and through the rhododendrons – 'no matter how busy you are, you end up crossing through a forest edge at least six times: into the shadow, from shade into sunlight, over a piece of meadow, towards a dense wall of rhododendrons on the opposite side of the clearing, into a grove again ... It is a living rhythm one never tires of.'[21] The park is named for a local hero, the explorer Vitus Bering, and the Bering Strait is pivotal in the geography of the genus as later pages (page 30 and chapter 7) will show.

Even as I write, rhododendrons are appearing in swish settings. At Buckingham Palace the garden's very own hybrid 'London Calling' is in flower, appropriately a child of the famous 'Loderi King George', named for George V. Across at Chelsea Harbour Design

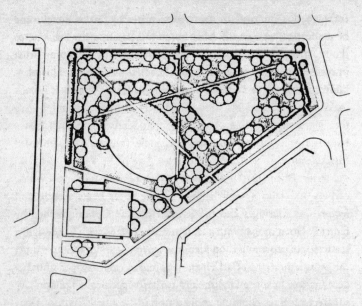

Carl Theodor Sørensen (1893–1979), design for the rhododendron grove,
Vitus Bering's Park, Horsens, Denmark, 1954–6.

Centre there are fabulous fabrics 'Frampton' and 'Rhododendrons'
being sold by Titley & Marr (see page 8 of second picture section);
Kate Marr, whose own garden in Hampshire is full of ancient
rhododendrons planted by former owners, has unearthed these
nineteenth-century designs to give them new life. And I can almost
hear the universal sigh of relief amongst sports photographers as
they gather for the US Masters golf tournament at Augusta, Georgia,
that rhododendron and azalea-girt golf course, frequently dubbed
'the most beautiful in the world'. Let us be honest, it is the rhododendrons in flower that splash their photos across double-page
spreads, not the golf. (See page 1 of third picture section.)

But in a way, the glory of the rhododendron does not *need*
exquisite representation, for it is a plant – in whatever subgenus
or section one chooses – of such *character* that a few skilfully drawn

lines will do. The glory of the rhododendrons is that they refuse to be demeaned, as even the most mundane of their genus will show. 'Pink Azalea' is the title of a poem by Charlotte Zolotow, first published in 1970 but given new life and space by the illustrator Simon James in his children's anthology, *Days Like This*:

> I feel as though
>   this bush were grown
>   especially for me.
> I feel as though
>   I almost am
>   this little flowering tree.

This pink azalea, a determined survivor of the small commercial kind, especially grown for flower stalls and supermarket racks, has been planted out in a small circle of earth in the centre of a square of sallow lawn in a city garden. The house is end-of-terrace, the street is filled with cars, the black plastic bags gather at the back gate; this is Anytown in almost all of what we call Western urban society, in the cool season. But there are signs of kindliness in this little garden within high walls; the washing blows cheerfully, someone has actually planted the azalea and other pot plants are about, and there is a tree with other green things growing from the ground. For a moment grown-ups are absent, and alone in the garden is a small person in a blue duffel coat with a hood and an orange scarf, possibly two years old, having her moment of communion with the miraculous pink flowers.

Consider the miniature azalea, for it has a small magic, the air of a sympathetic alien, a vegetable ET, with its delicately frilled petals defying the harshest cold, the façade for a woody sturdiness, a bonsai-like compression of energy, as though it has privately determined to grow up into a tree. Little Bluehood and her pink azalea are but the smaller representatives of their respective races, at the head of a long cavalcade of the enchanted and the enchanters that fill the following pages.

CHAPTER TWO

Sinogrande's Story

T HE TROUBLE WITH HISTORY IN GENERAL, and rhododendron history in particular, is not when something happened, but when we knew it had happened. Aeons of ignorance, or wilful blindness, can confuse the scheme of things. Having introduced some characters and characteristics of this fabulous genus, faced up to the name problem, and accomplished the verbal gymnastics, where next? The doings of rhododendron fanciers since the eighteenth century are densely documented, but clearly the plant with no name (at least before 1753) has a much older history. How to find it? I propose to start, as all histories do, in myth and legend, add a little geography and see where it leads.

One familiar legend has a twist, suggesting that the dove returning to Noah's Ark was carrying rhododendron leaves rather than an olive branch. In Genesis 8:11 'Noah knew that the waters were abated from off earth' after the flood by this sign. Noah, more of a zoologist than a botanist, however, could well have mistaken an olive twig for a rhododendron, or vice versa, and almost certainly Old Testament scribes and translators will have got it wrong. The Ark was supposedly grounded on Great Mount Ararat, 16,945 feet high and close to the present Turkish and Armenian borders. The nearest high land within the dove's range would be the Caucasian peaks to the north, where Armenia and Georgia meet the Euxine. Here

Rhododendron caucasicum grows higher than any other shrub – it is a tough, slow-growing monoculture, carpeting the snowy mountainsides, with aromatic leaves and rich milky-cream-coloured flowers. The flowers are edible, for man, beast and bird, so presumably the dove knew her target?

Further north, beyond the shores of the Black Sea, the four other native species of Turkey grow at lower levels, among the mountains of the old kingdom of Pontus. Mount Savval Tepe (11,074 feet), close to Artvin, presides over a countryside that botanists still call a paradise. *Rhododendron ponticum* grows as 30-feet high bushes in woods of pines and beech, with the smaller aromatic evergreen species (*ungernii* and *smirnovii*, named for Russian botanists) with apple-blossom pink flowers and velvety cinnamon backs to their leaves. Most individual of all, loved and hated with equal passions, is the sweetly scented *Azalea pontica, Rhododendron luteum*, from the Latin for 'yolk of egg' (*luteus* = yellow), the scourge of hungry soldiers, the basis of 'deli bal', the 'mad' honey that tempted Xenophon's weary Ten Thousand, after they had crossed the Armenian plain on their long retreat from Baghdad. Those that ate a small amount went wild with vomiting, lurching and rolling in intoxication; the greedier ones died. Little wonder that the survivors went equally 'mad' with joy and relief when they breached the Pontic Gates and saw the sea that paved their way home from the Zigana Pass.[1]

Something like 2,300 years later, Rose Macaulay's fractious party of Aunt Dot, the camel wearing ostrich plumes, Father Chantry-Pigg, the lady doctor Halide and the absconding student Xenophon in his jeep, set out from Trabzon for Ararat in *The Towers of Trebizond*: Soon 'we were among the rhododendrons and the azaleas which had supplied the madding honey to the Ten Thousand, and the May breezes blew about, sweet with the tang of lemon trees and fig trees and aromatic shrubs; and pomegranates and cucumbers and tobacco plants and gourds and all the fruits you would expect flourished in the woods we went through, and I thought the Garden of Eden had possibly been situated here'.[2]

Later the troubled heroine/storyteller, now alone with the camel, collapses with exhaustion on the mossy, shaded woodland floor, and the legends filter into her dreams. She dreamed she had come ashore from the *Argo*

> and had wandered up from the coast into these woods that climbed the mountain sides, and had eaten myself full of ripe cherries and of azalea honey, so that I lay in a swoon, pretending to be dead, because the barbarous Pontic natives, the Mossynoici, were all about, and I saw the boys they kept, fattened up on boiled chestnuts and tattooed all over with bright flowers, just as Xenophon had said eight hundred years later, and I saw that the Mossynoici did not change at all, for they were still having loving intercourse with women in public as they lay about the woods, and I thought, this would never do if it was Hyde Park.[3]

Strabo, the Greek geographer who was born in Pontus, wrote of the Mossynoici (named for the wooden houses, mosynes, in which they lived), who were wise in tree and plant lore, living on fruits and nuts and wild animals: 'for they mixed bowls of the crazing honey which is yielded by the tree-twigs, and placed them in the roads, and then, when the soldiers drank the mixture and lost their senses, they attacked them and easily disposed of them'. This time it was 600 men of Pompey's army that were caught.[4]

Another familiar myth of the rhododendron world is that they were seen by Marco Polo on his late thirteenth-century journeys to the land of the Great Khan. Modern studies of Polo's itinerary agree that he passed through the homelands of the most common native species on an erratic progress eastwards from Venice; through the territories of *caucasicum*, *afghanicum*, *campanulatum* and *arboreum* (these petals long used for chutneys and drinks, the flowers and leaves for festival decorations in Kashmir). Further north in the Karakorams and the Pamirs they grow, and there are native species in the north, in Gansu and Manchuria and even eastern Siberia. Marco Polo then journeyed south across the Yellow

River to the Yangtze, crossing Yunnan to Burma and beyond. He must have seen so many rhododendrons as to think them a universal weed.

Marco Polo is far from a long-dead traveller; he is the patron saint of modern travel writing. The scholarly arguments dig deeply into the meaning and veracity of his original account – even the original language of Gothic French is 'by no means a settled question' – and the pitfalls of Asian and Chinese place names are eternal. A devout sceptic, Professor John Larner[5] finds errors galore in checking Polo's version against Chinese sources, but finds that he at least included (as other travellers did not) some flora and fauna – the banana and the rhubarb, tigers, elephants, the gazelles of Gansu, giant wild sheep of the Pamirs and the hairless chickens of Fujian. Polo was looking for, or remembering only, the spectacular and the strange. He had his reputation to secure and a book to sell. Much was put in but more was left out. Why would he even notice that the Chinese tree peony was called 'Powdered Slave Aromatic' (white flower), 'Purple Dragon Bowl' or 'Beyond Description Yellow', when he was besieged with tales of slaves and dragons? Gentle flowers, even the azaleas glowing against the green of the hills, were hardly food for medieval European appetites, which salivated for the monstrous and lurid as in a modern movie spectacular.

Another famous traveller, Ibn Batuta (1304–68), spent 30 years wandering through Asia and Africa in the fourteenth century. In 1344 he visited Ceylon and climbed Adam's Peak (7,357 feet), the site of the sepulchre of the Buddha, Gauntama Siddhartha (Sakya-Muni), where he was fascinated by, but struggled to describe, a nameless flower. He thought it so beautiful that it must have been touched by the Hand of God. Only in 1817 was this wondrous plant identified as *Rhododendron nilagericum*, which has soft, rather fleshy, pink tubular flowers.[6] As Ibn Batuta, so surely Marco Polo – neither would have had a name for the rhododendrons except the many local dialect names, easily forgotten and meaningless to Europeans.

There is a Venetian story that when Marco Polo eventually returned from his long absence in Xanàdu, changed from a youth of seventeen into a middle-aged man, his old friends and even his family did not, would not recognise him. He was foreign in so many ways, had difficulty with his native language and had apparently returned from the dead. There are elements here of the famous Chinese myth, 'Peach Blossom Spring', credited to T'ao Chi'ien (372–427) but reinterpreted many times. Two men go to the sacred mountain to collect herbs, a virtuous activity, where they meet two alarmingly beautiful women 'blowing breath like orchid fragrance' who keep them enthralled. Protesting that they must return home the men go to collect their ponies and ride down the mountainside, only to find that everything and everybody at 'home' are changed, they are unrecognised, treated as suspicious strangers. Time and the wiles of the women, handmaids of the Immortals, have played tricks with them and so, puzzled and unhappy, they return to the mountain and disappear. No one knows their fate – 'the peach blossom trees tell nothing – they only put forth blossoms,' wrote the eighteenth-century poet Yuan Mei (1716–98).

The peach and plum blossoms, near and belovedly fruitful familiars, were from the earliest times the aesthetically correct symbols for Chinese poets and painters. The more mysterious rhododendrons grew higher up the mountains; it was they that belonged closest to the homes of the Immortals and would more likely have 'observed' the fate of the two lost souls.

Present day China can claim as natives over half the 1,025 species that we know; her south-western provinces of Sichuan and Yunnan and the Autonomous Region of Tibet are especially rich in rhododendrons. As political boundaries are meaningless to flowers, northern Myanmar (Burma), Arunachal Pradesh, Bhutan, Sikkim, Nepal, Himachal Pradesh and Kashmir, all the states along the southern fringes of the Himalayan massif, are also rhododendron-rich. That some species are given geographical names – *sinogrande*, *bhutanense* (*indicum* is misnamed, it is actually a Japanese native), *afghanicum*, *caucasicum*, *ponticum* or *dauricum* – reveals that they have evolved especially in response to their particular habitats, and yet these names string a necklace of rhododendrons across Eurasia. Others can be added, *carolinianum*, *californicum*, *canadense*, *japonicum*, to extend the necklet around the earth. Not a mere word game, but evidence that the species have a distant cousinship?

When Joseph Hooker explored Sikkim in 1849 he botanised through a mixture of tropical and temperate plants – 'birch, willow, alder and walnut competed with plantain, palm and giant bamboo; figs, balsams, peppers and vigorous climbers consorted with brambles, speedwell, forget-me-not and nettles'[7] – as he climbed towards the gentians, saxifrages, primulas and ferns and rhododendrons in abundance. He came to believe that he had found some kind of ecological grail, that tiny Sikkim held the key to the flora of the world. He reached the Tibetan border, and by mistake crossed over it, so that his guides and porters were terrified that they would be captured as slaves. Hooker, preoccupied with his great idea, calmly sat down beside the fire and wrote to Charles Darwin: 'I am above the forest region, amongst grand rocks and such a torrent as you see in Salvator Rosa's paintings, vegetation all a scrub of rhodods. With pines below me as thick & bad to get through as our Fuegian Fagi . . .' (Darwin and Hooker had separately experienced the dense evergreen beech forests of Tierra del Fuego) '. . . and except the towering peaks of P.S. [permanent snows] that here shoot up on all hands there is little difference in the mt scenery – here however the blaze of Rhod. Flowers & various coloured jungle proclaims a differently constituted region in a naturalists eye & twenty species here, to one there, always are asking the vexed question, where do we come from?'[8]

In rhododendron terms, it was a third person, the American botanist Asa Gray (1810–88) in frequent correspondence with Darwin, who suggested an answer. In 1859, the same year as *The Origin of Species*, Gray published his conclusions on the apparent similarities between the flora of Japan and of eastern North America, suggesting that 'before the glacial epoch the flora of the North Temperate Zone had been relatively homogenous, extending in a more or less undisrupted belt across North America and Eurasia'. 'Rhododendrons', being tough survivors of some 50 million years, had happily circled the globe during this time, or at least they existed across the extent of the great Laurasian landmass of the northern hemisphere. Gray further proposed that with the advances of the glaciers the temperate flora was pushed southwards; when the ice finally retreated other complications – 'mountain building in particular' – made life difficult for the 'rhododendrons' trying to regain their former territory, remaining communities found they had to adapt or die, and others had to adapt in order to recolonise. But in eastern North America and eastern Asia (including the Great Plain of China), Gray suggested, the ancient flora had survived or was able to recolonise without drastic change: 'thus the similar flora in the two regions today constitutes relics of the preglacial flora that once encircled the globe'.[9]

Gray's theories slumbered for a long time but have found confirmation by a new breed of phytogeographers, discovering their inspiration in Armen Takhtajan's *Floristic Regions of the World*, published in translation from the Russian in 1986.[10] Takhtajan identifies flowering plants in six distinct 'kingdoms', then regionally by genera and species, then by specific combinations of species unique to a given area, and in this way the eastern North American/eastern Asian similarities are reasserted. (These theories have influenced plantings at Wakehurst Place, notably the Tony Schilling Asian Heath Garden that includes rhododendrons.) Even more recently Russian and American scientists studying the Beringian ice, i.e. the confluence of the American and Eurasian plates, have identified rhododendrons amongst the Tertiary relict floras. In his *Flora Britannica*, the naturalist Richard Mabey believes that the 'triffids', the *Rhododendron ponticum* that has 'gone native' in western Britain, are in fact reclaiming old territory. Findings of pollen and other remains in Austria and Ireland lead botanists to confirm that rhododendrons were native to much of central and western Europe during interglacial periods, but only recolonised in pockets. A relative, perhaps a relict, the trailing azalea, *Loiseleuria procumbens*, survives in the Scottish Highlands.[11]

Old as they are, rhododendrons are descended from the more ancient magnolia (Magnoliaceae) and tea (Theaceae) families and so have ancestral connections to the tulip trees (liriodendron), camellias, stewartias and the franklinia. The rhododendron's family is a cadet branch, the Heaths (Ericaceae), giving them cousinage to other heaths, including kalmia (mountain laurel) and *Menziesia ferruginea*, known as the false azalea. The menziesia, named for Archibald Menzies (1754–1842), who found it on his first expedition to the Pacific north-west in 1788, looks exactly like an azalea, but the horticultural grandees in London would not allow it to be in the family because of its insignificant cream flowers and consequent lowly status.

All the plant collectors from Hooker in the mid-nineteenth century to Frank Ludlow (1885–1972) and George Sherriff (1898–1967) almost a hundred years later came to believe in a rhododendron 'heartland' – 'Rhodoland' as Frank Kingdon Ward called this utopia – where the greatest variety of species were to be found in abundance. In his biblical *Trees and Shrubs Hardy in the British Isles*, W. J. Bean, having said that this heartland cannot be precisely defined, comes up with the best definition, supposing

> its eastern limit along a line that stretches from the Tali range in Yunnan north-west to the great gorges of the Mekong and Salween, and its western limit in Sikkim and bordering Nepal. In India the southern limit is of course the plains of Assam; in Burma and Yunnan the southern border is less definite since mountains high enough to support a temperate flora extend far to the south, and many harbour rhododendrons ... but the boundary could be taken as a line drawn from Tali in Yunnan to Myitkyina in Burma, near the confluence of the two upper branches of the Irrawaddy.[12]

74992

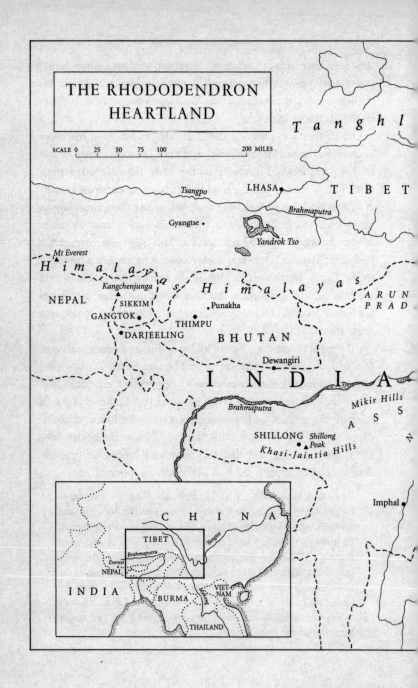

THE RHODODENDRON HEARTLAND

SCALE 0   25   50   75   100   200 MILES

Tsangpo   LHASA   T I B E T

Brahmaputra

Gyangtse

Yandrok Tso

Mt Everest

H i m a l a y a s   H i m a l a y a s   ARUN
                                       PRAD

Kangchenjunga

NEPAL   SIKKIM   *Punakha*

GANGTOK   THIMPU

DARJEELING   BHUTAN

Dewangiri

I N D I A

Brahmaputra   Mikir Hills

A S S

SHILLONG   *Shillong Peak*

Khasi-Jaintia Hills

Imphal

C H I N A

TIBET

Brahmaputra   *Yangtze*

Everest
NEPAL

INDIA   VIET-
        NAM

BURMA   *Mekong*

THAILAND

T a n g h l

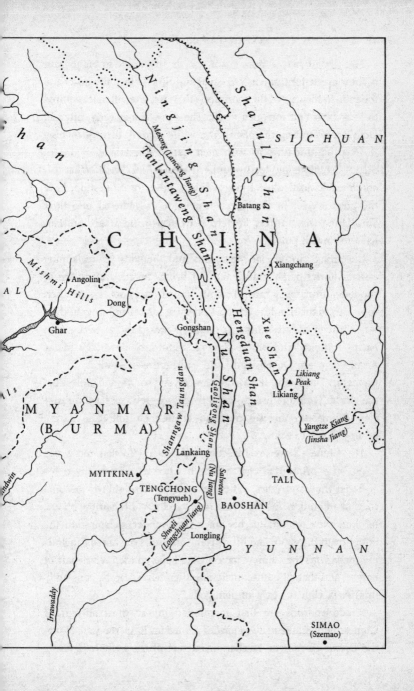

The climate here – Bean again – 'is as favourable to plants as it is abominable for humans'.[13] Leaves and flowers love the mists and the rain-sodden air of the monsoon (they are, after all, not required to look their best for open days). The snow comes early, often in October, protecting the plants in a white shroud, then quenching their spring-thirsty roots with melt water. 'Rhodoland' is one of the most remote and least populated areas of the Earth. What this comfortable horticultural talk avoids is the critical question: have the great species in their ancient splendours gathered into their Sino-Himalayan fortress, in retreat from a world where humans have too much power?

Imagining post-glacial migrations and thoughts of 'reclaiming lost territories' is an indulgence – it brings to mind an image of rhododendrons as a race of snow-capped ancestors, easing their roots out of the mould of their Himalayan forests and singing their way through eastern China, to Japan, Korea, and via Beringia to North America, and others singing southwards down the Malay Archipelago to Queensland, and still more westwards to the Caucasus, Turkey and the Mediterranean and so 'rhododendroning' the world. Or is the process actually now in reverse; have forestry clear-felling and tourism overload taken their toll? The testing ground is surely China.

The Chinese have an attractive creation myth, that the world began in a primordial egg, 'which hatched a god who lived for eighteen thousand years. When he died his head split to become the sun and moon, his blood the rivers and seas, his hair the plants, his limbs the mountains, his voice the thunder, perspiration the rain, breath the wind' and his fleas the ancestors of animals, including man. Thus the Chinese have always believed themselves part of nature, and that all nature, including themselves, can be constantly improved, with the help of demigods.[14]

Rhododendrons are first mentioned in the most ancient of Chinese herbals, the *materia medica* named for Emperor Shen Nong, the Divine Farmer or Husbandman, one of the five pre-dynastic rulers, and the demigod who gave his people the plough and hoe and taught them to grow cereals. Shen Nong is believed to have lived in the Yellow River area of China's Great Plain, in what is now Henan province, at sometime in 2800 BC, in a time of paradise. He led a pastoral and unpretentious life, collecting herbs and divining their uses and distilling his potions and mixtures, all in a wild and lovely landscape innocent of rice terraces or rampaging warlords, where rhododendrons were widespread.

His people put the plough and hoe to good use; China prospered and expanded southwards to the Gulf of Tongking and westwards through the Hindu Kush and Parthia to meet the Roman Empire at the Caspian Sea. The Great Wall was built and rebuilt to keep out the Mongolians from the north. A Han Dynasty census of AD 2 recorded 58 million people in China, making its empire somewhat larger than the Roman Empire at that time. Most of these millions laboured eternally in their fields:

> Farming is encouraged, secondary pursuits, discouraged,
> All the common people prosper;
> All men under the sky
> Toil with a single purpose;
> Tools and measures are made uniform,
> The written script is standardised;
> Wherever the sun and moon shine,
> Wherever one can go by boat or by carriage,
> Men carry out their orders
> And satisfy their desires.[15]

The Chinese history that we know reels fast forward, passing *The Book of Songs*, the earliest book of Chinese poetry, the age of Confucius, the rise of vast metal-working and silk-weaving industries, the manufacture of paper from bamboo stems, past the Qin Emperor Shih Huang Ti and his Terracotta Army, the Han agrarian revolutions and the invention of the wheelbarrow, and the coming of Buddhism and Daoism, to the sunlit Tang Dynasty (618–907). From the Great Wall in the north to the South China Sea the toiling millions had created the greatest man-made landscape in the world; fields filled every valley, tiers of rice terraces covered the hills, dams and canals controlled the water supplies, forests and copses had been consumed in domestic and industrial fires. The herbs and flowers that Shen Nong had gathered for his lotions and tinctures were no more in the lowlands. They had retreated to the mountains.

Everything in China is learned tangentially. Landscape painting has a far greater status than in the West, and a thousand years ago it had already been elevated to a spiritual and aesthetic esteem above other arts, and far above any earthly landscape. (The status of Chinese gardens was to follow the same upward path a few centuries later.) The delicate scrolls and silk paintings that have survived are overwhelmingly of the mountains, the homes of the Immortals, exquisite idealisations of deep and high distances, and the differing textures of rocks, trees and waterfalls. Bamboos are always distinctive, being supremely symbolic, but the painting of the landscape was far above any other realities. The utilitarian landscape was not painted at all.

The earliest persisting Chinese name for the yellow azalea (*Azalea mollis/Rhododendron molle*) is *Yang chi chu*. This is a combination of *yang* meaning sheep, and *chi chu*, to reel or stagger, as it was common knowledge that sheep eating azalea leaves would fall over and die. Thus the Chinese, as an agrarian people, had already come to recognise the yellow azalea as a dangerous toxic weed and had purposefully destroyed it wherever they could. Clues to what they cannot tell, in the silence of their dumb centuries, are provided by the ancient script symbols for rhododendron and azalea. The symbol for *Yang chi chu*, sheep stagger, also means 'embarrassed' or 'bewildered'; the second symbol means to make a disturbing uproar, a troubling boisterousness (and also bowel troubles); the third is simply a mountain, a mountaineer or a rhododendron (these are the same); the fourth symbol has contrasting double connotations – it either implies being shut out, excluded or impeded (by the rhododendron thicket?) or simply the benign red azalea (*Rhododen-*

dron simsii), bracketed with the russet pear and other blossoms. This last symbol cannot have served the rhododendron well, for history depends upon generations of translators, and given the choice between a flower dangerously close to the toxic sheep-stagger and the bland and friendly pear or peach blossom, they opted for the latter. This might explain the mystifying shortage of references to such a famous plant in so much Chinese poetry and literature.

The yellow azalea's toxicity to beast and man entered the peasant folklores throughout China to India, Tibet, Afghanistan, west to the Caucasus and the shores of the Mediterranean and the well-remembered toxic honey. All these areas had a native species that was poisonous in some way – apart from the losses of valuable sheep, humans suffered nausea, diarrhoea, intestinal cramps, dizziness and disorientation. If the leaves were mistaken for tea by children they caused severe poisoning. Rhododendrons – most usually the infamous yellow azalea – entered the oldest books for reference, the materia medica, as remedies to be used with great care. They were officially a drug of the third class, along with aconite, euphorbias, *Rheum palmatum*, veratrum and peach kernels; they were *tso* (assistants) and *shi* (agents of healing and of the earth), but poisonous and not to be used continually. But always there was that fine distinction between malady and cure; some herbals recommended the leaves pressed to the forehead for headaches and migraines, or made into a poultice, and the orange and red flowers could be crystallised or ground into soft drinks. As a homoeopathic remedy the powerfully hallucinogenic rhododendron produces a long and blood-curdling list of symptoms and uses. In Tang Dynasty China, so long ago, folklore had wreathed around rhododendrons and azaleas, which deemed them best left to the sages.

And, of course, such warnings would have appealed to the sophisticates. As the azaleas became rarer they became more prized, even by imperial gardens of the early Tang, along with wisteria and tree peonies for the courtyards of the capital Chang-an, then the greatest city in the world, a city of a million souls:

Hundreds of houses, thousands of houses – like a great chessboard.
The twelve streets like a huge field planted with rows of cabbage.
In the distance I see faint and small the torches of riders to Court,
Like a single row of stars lying to the west of the Five Gates.[16]

The words are those of the young Po-chu-I (772–846), a most
endearing character as well as a great poet. Po loved flowers, especially
azaleas, and the countryside, and in his life, lived so long ago, these
things were almost unattainable. Like all educated young men he was
bound to strive for a high place in the prestigious literary examin-
ations, and so be destined for great things in the service of his masters.
When he was about thirty he was posted to Chang-an, which he found
overwhelming; on another occasion he took a walk to escape the city
and wrote his poem called 'Ant's Nest': 'I turn my head and hurry
home ... A single grain of rice falling into the Great Barn.'[17] He is
acutely conscious that most of his fellow citizens are so engulfed in
the struggle for existence that they are blind to nature: 'A thousand
coaches, ten thousand horsemen pass down the Nine Roads; Turns
his head and looks at the mountains – not one man!'[18]

Po's niche in the 'Great Barn' is a pleasant one, for he was able
to rent the pavilion in Chief Minister Li Te-yu's town garden in
the An-I quarter of the city, just south of the Eastern Market.
Minister Li[19] is the first famous garden owner of the rhododendron
story. In the country garden of his villa in the hills south of Luoyang
he collected plants as a signature of his 'poetic worthiness' even
though he was a man of great business. He had bamboos, magnolias,
osmanthus, tamarix, cassia, box, myrtle, juniper, lotus, camellias,
peaches, lilacs, hibiscus and cherries (though, of course, he called
them by other names). He especially prized his red azaleas, *Rhododendron simsii*, which he called *Tu chuan* or *dujuan*, or another
name meaning 'reflect mountain red', which he had brought back
from his travels in the south, in the presently named Guangxi
Autonomous Region. It had retreated to the mountains, though
also survived, and has done so until comparatively modern times,
in the Yangtze Gorges.

The name *tu chuan* or *dujuan* also means 'hawk-cuckoo flower' and comes from a legend that the Qin Dynasty king of Sichuan, Du Yu, had taken shelter in the mountains with his people at the time of a great flood, and with the help of the spirit of a soft-shelled turtle had opened a gorge, causing the flood to subside. In return he gave his crown to the turtle, but then this saviour of his people took flight with the Immortals. His people, missing him, believed his soul transformed into the hawk-cuckoo, which they named *dujuan* and the rhododendrons that flowered as the cuckoo began to call *dujuanhua* – *hua* meaning flower. This association was much celebrated in literature. The poet-gardener Bai Juyi wrote: 'When rhododendron flowers begin to fall off, cuckoos begin to cry. The red rhododendrons, however, are still in bloom.'[20] And Cheng Yanxlong: 'Rhododendrons and cuckoos, What's the relation between them? Perhaps the bleeding mouths of cuckoos have dropped blood onto the rhododendron branches and it turned into red flowers.'[21] While Li Bai wrote: 'I have heard the cry of cuckoos in Shuguo (Sichuan) and now I have seen the rhododendron flowers in Xuancheng, the cry and the flower make me homesick, in such late spring.'[22] And yet another, Han Yu: 'I once travelled to a mountain area in March; the red rhododendrons were over hills and down dales.'[23]

In this way the red azalea became symbolic of the warm south, of the eternal poetic longing for the mountains, and the compensating warmths of fiery and beautiful women. Only the poets of the rhododendrons were not great travellers, except in their imaginations; Po-chu-I and Bai Juyi both rose to high office as city governors, but their lives were so strictly regulated as to leave no time for pleasurable or aimless travelling. Hence they dreamed, poetically:

> The south was fine.
> [I] could remember its scenery
> At sunrise the red river flowers were brighter than fire;
> In spring the green river water was darker than indigo.
> How can I not recall the south?[24]

With the yellow azalea undesirable and the red ones unreachable, Po-chu-I offers an acute insight into the tastes of the more ordinary people of Tang China. Their desperate preoccupation with the practicalities of life had found an outlet in a love of flowers, the already domesticated flowers that could be grown and marketed for quick profits and fitted conveniently into crowded city lives. From 'The Flower Market', one of his most famous poems, we know that human nature was little different then, almost 1,200 years ago:

> We tell each other 'This is the peony season';
> And follow with the crowd that goes to the Flower Market.
> 'Cheap and dear – no uniform price;
> The cost of the plant depends on the number of blossoms', calls
>   the seller,
> adding the helpful tips –
> 'If you sprinkle water and cover the roots with mud,
> When they are transplanted, they will not lose their beauty.'
> Each household thoughtlessly follows the custom,
> Man by man, no one realising.
> There happened to be an old farm labourer
> Who came by chance that way.
> He bowed his head and sighed a deep sigh;
> But this sigh nobody understood.
> He was thinking, 'A cluster of deep-red flowers
> Would pay the taxes of ten poor houses'.[25]

Po balanced his long life between his state service and his love and understanding of country ways, and of the mountains and flowers. He gardened modestly whenever he had the chance, bringing his favourite roses and azaleas in from the wild, coaxing them into growth; at one time, perhaps his, provincial governors were required to send well-tended native flowering plants as tribute to the imperial gardens.

I come to the conclusion, with Po-chu-I's guidance, that what we so blithely call the Chinese culture of flowers was bought – in that great country of turbulent histories and transient names – at great price. Po had an interesting life, he rose to be a provincial governor of Suzhou, that elite city of lovely gardens, for a while; he suffered banishments, was constantly shifted about, but that was the way things were. In the end he retired as governor of Honan province, to his house and garden in Luoyang; when he was 70 he wrote 'A Dream of Mountaineering' (remember that one of the script symbols for mountaineer is the same for rhododendron):

> A thousand crags, a hundred hundred valleys –
> In my dream-journey none were unexplored
> And all the while my feet never grew tired
> And my step was as strong as in my young days.
> Can it be that when the mind travels backward
> The body also returns to its old state?[26]

He lived out his 'palsied and tottering' days, striding strongly in his dreams at night, out among the paradise of flowers that he had seen in the Yangtze Gorge country in the west, and on his retreat visits to remote Buddhist monasteries, where ancient species of rhododendrons were often grown inside the walls for temple decorations. Po must have seen, as Augustine Henry was to see, again more than a thousand years later, the rock ledges covered in primulas and saxifrages, the extravagant landscape that teemed with roses, lilies, honeysuckles and rhododendrons that fringed the roof of the world.[27]

The fate of Minister Li's villa garden in the hills south of Luoyang was symbolic; it was almost destroyed in one of the interminable post-Tang rebellions, only junipers and waterways surviving, and then entirely given over to fields of millet by the twelfth century. As China forsook its natural paradise of flowers under pressures from turbulent dynasties and increasing population, so the need and demand for those flowers became ever stronger. At the popular level were the flower markets, and the lovingly tended backyard tubs of mud for the lotus (covering the roots with mud was the sage advice for red azaleas, too), but the voices we hear at long centuries' remove mostly speak of the culture of flowers as a court and city fiefdom, expressions in poetry and paintings by and for a society that had no connection with the utilitarian landscape.

The four seasonal deities, 'the four gentlemen of flowers', are usually named as plum blossom for spring, bamboo for summer, orchid for autumn and chrysanthemum for winter. These are market friendly and much more amenable to propagation than the difficult rhododendrons but their chief virtues are symbolic; the plum blossom, forced for the markets, blooms on bare branches heralding the first hope of spring; the chrysanthemum is simply the last:

'It is not that you are dearer to me than many another flower, But only that when you have faded, there will be no more flowers.'[28]

The early Ming poet, Wang Xing, described how a Mr Hua had named his pavilion 'Picking Chrysanthemums Pavilion' as an allusion to (his own?) gentlemanly qualities: 'Only the chrysanthemum comes into blossom after it has reached maturity. That which is unique to something is an expression of that which is worth preserving. Hence the gentleman emulates such qualities . . . Moreover, when it is windy and frosty, and all the other plants are blown about and lose their flowers and foliage, the chrysanthemum stands resplendent, it alone in blossom . . . the gentleman as one who also has the discipline to withstand the winter.'[29]

The famous twelve flowers or 'guests' – most popularly cassia (*kuei*), plum (*mei*), orchid, lotus, tree peony (*mu-tan*), daphne, rose, jasmine, herbaceous peony, camellia, cherry and chrysanthemum – leave no room for the red azalea.

And there are subtle sexual connotations: the bamboo was thought to display humility, perseverance, flexibility and an 'upright appearance which matches the gentleman's demeanour'.[30] From Tang times the red azalea of the warm south had become synonymous with the fiery, passionate women that were supposed to reside there. The painted handscrolls of 'one hundred flowers' must have included azaleas, but not simply to make up the number; these handscrolls were often painted by beautiful and talented courtesans as a pastime. In the precise and mannered Chinese society no high-born lady would dare or deign to be seen painting or wearing a red azalea.[31] Perhaps this colourful reputation kept them out of so much poetry by women otherwise attuned to flowers. The magnificent anthology *Women Writers of Traditional China*, has no azaleas (though it does have courtesan poets) in over 800 pages, just one very early, third- or fourth-century anonymous glancing reference to 'spring flowers' and the *dujuan*, here translated as 'nightjar':

> Last month of spring:
> As the boat floats through the curved pool
> We lift our eyes to the spring flowers
> The cry of the nightjar threads the woods
> Here's a willow bough
> They come two by two, fluttering here and there
> My love and I shall have each other.[32]

The evidence of surviving handscrolls and paintings produces parallels to the literary tradition in the search for rhododendrons. Mountain landscapes were painted to nourish the spirit of a people who could no longer reach the reality: valleys vanish into the horizon between jagged peaks clothed with contorted trunks and branches conjuring the very homes of the Immortals in fantastic rather than botanical detail. Sometimes the spectre of reality is informative: Xu Daoning was an eccentrically free spirit, who even drank wine while he painted, and his *Fisherman on a Mountain Stream*, painted *c*. 1050, is 'a visionary's image of high mountain valleys in autumn'. 'If paintings of landscape', writes R. M. Barnhardt, 'reflect the actual appearance of the time, then Xu's virtually denuded earthen slopes confirm the textual evidence indicating that most of north China was already deforested by this time.' A whole world is condensed into this fragile handscroll of rippling thin-peaked mountains and tufted trees 'only a magician could have worked such a miracle of illusion by which ink is transformed into pure space'.[33]

Painters, whether of landscape or 'bird and flower' styles, *were* magicians. Their very artistry was in conjuring the familiars – the distant mountains, 'the four gentlemen of flowers', 'the twelve guests' – into well-understood images. The rhododendrons, which had so long since retreated into the southern mountains, were neither familiars nor essentially of the flowery traditions, which must explain their absence in surviving paintings.

It is much later, with the great Ming Dynasty (1368–1644), that the rhododendrons begin to appear in literature and garden history, but even so they come as a fluttering, not an avalanche. When I began to search the auguries were not good: amongst British garden historians the true light on Chinese gardens – as opposed to the willow-pattern plate image of pagodas, stone lanterns and Chinese Chippendale bridges – came as recently as 1978 with the publication of Maggie Keswick's magnificent *The Chinese Garden: History, Art and Architecture*, which she wrote from her family's century-old connections with China and her own love for the country, with the help of many Chinese friends. The apparently complete absence of any rhododendrons in her book and her confident assertion that they were a late-coming British taste and not important in traditional Chinese gardens were disconcerting. Equally so was Joseph Needham's comment, after his encyclopaedic trawl of Chinese culture, that the 'only time' rhododendrons 'got into disquisitional Chinese literature' was in a Ming document by Chang Chi-Shun of notes on two 'ornamentals', camellias and rhododendrons, being cultivated in Yungchang (now Baoshan) in Yunnan. The 'rhododendrons' were the various shades of yellow and red azaleas – 'the whole mountain turned red, but this,' said Chang, 'was to forget the splendid yellows and greens'.[34] At least some Chinese botanists and gardeners appreciated rhododendrons before modern times.

Chinese gardens are still full of mysteries to Western understanding. The most recent researches are being conducted at the Garden Library at Dumbarton Oaks in Washington DC, where scholars from East and West work in the empathetic glow of a century and a half of horticultural courtesies between America and China and Japan, a tradition traced in chapter 3. Oriental texts are being re-examined objectively, revealing the evidence for a Chinese cultural society committed to life in cities, even as early as the sixteenth century, and completely in opposition to the mindset of the feudal, land-gathering English aristocracy. Scholars and philosophers, the most likely garden makers, had neither the hope nor the desire for large estates and were happy to retire to a 'suburban'-sized garden in a southern city, with a view of the mountains, as Po-chu-I had done. There was a political dictum against occupying too much marginal land outside cities for defensive reasons, or hindering the subsistence farming of the people, and a Buddhistic objection to digging for fear of disturbing the *qi*, the vital breath of the earth. Hence the piled rocks on the earth to make miniature water courses and the prevalence of herbaceous flowers and shrubs in pots.

These restrictions fostered the garden as a symbol of elsewhere, an *aide-mémoire* to a beloved though distant wild landscape, of the mountain regions as the shrines of the Immortals and spiritual enlightenment, or to another fondly remembered place. The aim was to create a garden full of illusion and allusiveness, where nothing was quite what it seemed: the rock must bring to mind the mountain, the brimming bowl the lake, and the lantern smoke the evening mist.

The fabled Ming gardens of the southern city of Suzhou were thus given allusive and metaphorical names: 'Drinking on a Summer's Day at Yike's Pond Pavilion', presumably a happy memory; 'In the Gu Clan's Xiangying Hall there is a Flowering Plum Planted by my Grandmother's Hand', for a family connection; or simply celebrating ownership or inheritance – 'Twenty-eight Poems on the Returning-to-Possession Garden'.[35]

Beyond the names and the piled rocks and contrived water courses, the plants formed another layer of symbolism. The elite Suzhou garden owners prided themselves on 'reclusion in the city' and in being utterly unlike other parts of their city, particularly 'the commercialized promiscuity of the market place'. The rules of planting were very strict, the status of the flowers was an immediate give-away. Rhododendrons were listed as suitable but they would have been treated as rarities, and only welcomed in subtle colours: Suzhou sensibilities saw camellia and magnolia together as 'vulgar', and similarly peach and willow, and red and white of anything together were far too dazzling. The lovely, local 'cloud-brocade rhododendron', which we know as the blushing *fortunei*, would surely have passed muster? Roses on arbours were in doubtful taste – sitting beneath them in flower was hardly better than dining in the market place. Roses were just about acceptable around the women's quarters, planted where the maids could pick them. The 'West Lake Willow', *Tamarix chinensis*, was condemned for having 'an effeminate air'[36] – and so what chance had the rose-red azalea from the south, which was synonymous with a passionate woman?

And yet she did creep in, as horizons lifted in the later Ming period and the most prized rarities were those that came furthest away from exotic pines, the Japanese quince and sophora and the gingko. 'Pear flower' is quoted and we know this can be an alternative translation for a rhododendron, and what could 'the great embroidered red ball flower' – not native but brought by boat from Thailand to Suzhou – be but a species rhododendron? Possibly one of the *arboreum* or *barbatum* series, or more likely *Rhododendron delavayi*, known as the lantana rhododendron, *ma ying dujuan*, which was recorded by the Ming geographer Xu Hongzhu.[37]

Rhododendrons were rare and were difficult to transplant, they would only ever have been planted in small numbers, but they must have had a fleeting presence in gardens which were themselves ephemeral. In their native landscapes we have to presume they were hardly ever seen, since the Ming Chinese, so absorbed in their administrative or scholarly lives, did not explore or travel for pleasure. Too much nature was thought detrimental to poetic style: their man-made landscape was perfection. The writer Hsu Hung-tsu (1586–1641) thought differently and was the unique exception. He came from an old Suzhou family, he was wealthy and well educated, and yet a cultural outcast because he refused to conform and loved to travel. He began in 1607 when he was 21, regularly returning to visit his widowed mother who encouraged him on his travels (Confucius had taught that a son must never stray too far from his widowed mother), and he wandered over all the provinces of China keeping diaries and records until the year before his death. His observations are minutely detailed:

> As our boat wound its way through the peaks of the rocky area, it was like a shuttle going through the threads, confronted with more scenery than we could leisurely absorb. Moreover, at this point not only were the rocky mountains beyond comparison but also the stone cliffs presented themselves with endless variations. All this is caused by the river water smashing at the mountains. The mountains after continual washing take the form of sharp cliffs. As the water winds its way and carries with it the sandy sediments, steep rocks protrude where they are least expected, some presiding over the center of waves and others looking as though they were thrown across the water's surface . . .'[38]

Hsu had found the gorges of the Yangtze; he travelled on to discover that the legendary River of the Golden Sands that washed the gold dust down from the mountains of Tibet was actually the Upper Yangtze, putting his findings into a detailed dissertation, which was promptly buried in a local archive. More than half a century afterwards French Jesuits sent out on a mapping expedition for the emperor claimed the discovery. But it was Hsu who had found rhododendron land.

Other Jesuits revealed Chinese gardens to the eyes of the west: Father Jean Denis Attiret's (1702–68) famous letter from his studio inside the walls of Emperor Qianlong's summer retreat was first published in Paris in 1749. He described a secret, walled paradise of lakes and palaces, the Garden of Perfect Brightness of Yuan Ming Yuan, where clear streams wound 'at will' through gentle valleys, where paths lazed along linking pleasure houses and grottoes, and 'as if by chance' willows and blossom trees grew in profusion.[39] Those conditioned to the despotic glare of broad terraces and screaming vistas at Versailles and Hampton Court scoffed at a ruler who could allow himself to be compromised by Nature; the garden-minded, who were themselves inclining to the delights of grove, dell and copse, were amazed that some eastern barbarian had anticipated their sophistication. It was best to grasp at certainties. William Chambers (1723–96) sailed with the Swedish East India Company as a young man, and on the strength of a visit to Canton, the only port open to Europeans during the eighteenth century, he published his *Designs of Chinese Buildings, Furniture, Dresses, etc.* in 1757, which led to him designing the Pagoda and other Chinese illusions at Kew Gardens. It was an oriental 'foot in the door' where the rhododendrons might follow.

It was not until the 1860s, well over two centuries after Hsu's trip up the Yangtze, that the Basque Lazarist brother Jean Pierre Armand David (1826–1900), a teacher at the mission school in Peking, travelled up river to I-chang and continued westwards into Sichuan and to the Tibetan border. Père David reported on the big tree rhododendrons – one of them, with lilac-spotted flowers, is named for him *Rhododendron davidii* – to the Jardin des Plantes, where there was apparently more excitement over the rhododendrons than over David's famous first sight of the giant panda.

In Canton, an ingenious East India Company tea inspector John Reeves (1774–1856) had started shipping live plants home to his friends in England. These included tree peonies, camellias, roses, chrysanthemums and azaleas, but he despaired of the 'difficult' azaleas when not one of a shipment of 500 reached England alive. Reeves came home himself in 1816, personally tending the plants on board, and only lost ten out of a hundred; he persuaded the captains of the Indiamen to learn from his experience and with some success for the Horticultural Society of London made an award (of a medal!) to nine such captains in 1820 for bringing their plants home safely. The very best minds were bent on this matter:

Professor William Hooker at Glasgow University penned a popular pamphlet 'Directions for Collecting and Preserving Plants in Foreign Countries' (1828) and Joseph Hooker and Charles Darwin (1809–82) contributed to the *Navy's Manual of Scientific Inquiry*, which ran into several editions, and hoped 'the honour and advantage of the Navy' would be served if 'facilities and encouragement' were given to the causes of botany, zoology, astronomy and other earth sciences. The Lords of the Admiralty even went as far as 'producing a carrot out of a lace cuff', suggesting a cash prize or promotion for 'eminently useful results'.[40] The critical invention was Nathaniel Bagshaw Ward's (1791–1868) small, portable greenhouse, a sealed glass case in which the plants could reuse their own condensed moisture. The Wardian case revolutionised the transport of plants and came into general use in the 1830s.

All this was not, of course, for the Chinese azaleas, but for seriously economic crops such as tea and cotton. John Reeves, as keen a gardener as he was a progressive tea inspector, suggested to his friends in the (not Royal until 1861) Horticultural Society that a collector should be sent to China, ostensibly to look into tea planting but also one with a good eye for garden plants. The Society chose a Scot trained in Edinburgh but working for them in London, Robert Fortune (1812–80). It was a good choice.

The Treaty of Nanjing, concluded at gunpoint at the end of the First Opium War in 1842, forced the Chinese to keep open the five Treaty ports for the British trade in Indian-grown opium, a vital part of the Raj economy. Robert Fortune was on a kind of mercy mission, instructed to find tea plants and learn the production techniques in order to encourage tea growing in northern India and reduce the reliance on the opium poppy harvest. (Machiavellian market forces were alive and well in the China trade, though sadly beyond the scope of this book.) Fortune set foot in Hong Kong (ceded as a Crown Colony under the 1842 treaty) in July 1843 and went north to Shanghai, from where he made several trips exploring the coastal territories, to which he was confined, sailing to Assam

in the intervals for tea planting, and remaining in China until the
Taiping rebels from the south reached Shanghai in 1860.

Fortune wrote of his adventures, making the most of his esca-
pades – dressing up as a Chinaman with a pigtail, scuffling in the
alleys of Canton, and being chased and reviled as a 'foreign devil'
– but slowly his repugnance at the crowded cities gave way to his
acute and sympathetic observations of the landscape. Fortune had
a good eye for plants: he found the glorious 'cloud brocade rhododendron' with lilac-blushing-pink scented and nodding flowers
and its elegantly pointed leaves, which was named *Rhododendron
fortunei*, growing at 3,000 feet in the hills inland from Ningbo in
Zhejiang province south of Shanghai. He marvelled at the flower-
covered hills of the Chusan peninsula (now Zhoushan) – he
remembered azaleas at Chiswick fêtes – 'but few can form any idea
of the gorgeous and striking beauty of these azalea-clad mountains'
with their masses of flowers 'of dazzling brightness and beauty' –
and with clematis, roses and honeysuckles as well as the azaleas.
This was why he named China 'the central flowery land'.[41] He
returned to the Ningbo hills for the seed of the 'cloud brocade
rhododendron', but this was later also collected in other places
further inland and in the south, suggesting that the fabulous *fortunei*
was a beautiful ghost from a past when the large species rhododendrons had grown all over central and southern China.

Fortune haunted the Fa-tee – 'flowery land' – nursery, the former
East India Company's nursery from where John Reeves had shipped
his plants, some two miles up river from Canton, now operated by
Chinese nurserymen. One old gardener who spoke English and did
a lot of business with Americans and English residents was notorious
for boiling his seeds so that his trade was not spoiled by some
enterprising English or American propagator. Fortune thought it
more likely that the seeds were a year or two old before they were
dispatched – 'besides the long voyage round the Cape – during
which the seeds have twice to cross the tropics – is very prejudicial
to their germination'.[42] Surely a strange belief for a botanist?

Fortune has left a lovely vision of the old Fa-tee gardens: 'the plants are principally kept in large pots arranged in rows along the sides of narrow paved walks, with the houses of the gardeners at the entrance through which the visitors pass to the gardens'. The pots contained azaleas, magnolias, oranges, roses, the 'cum quat' – a small oval-fruited plant which made excellent preserves – and peonies, many of them scenting the small enclosures.[43] Fortune makes Fa-tee sound not unlike one of our garden centres, a hundred years before their time. He noted that most of the customers were foreigners; the Chinese bought their flowers for festival decorations from dealers who gathered in the wild and brought blossom branches, enkianthus, camellias and magnolias by the boat load into the city.

In 1981 a Garden History Society party, visiting a horticultural commune outside Canton, came across an old walled garden, with enormous tubs of aged bonsai ranged beside the paths and an ancient frangipani in flower. They were told it was a 200-year-old nursery and realised that they had found part of Fa-tee, still working.[44]

Robert Fortune's 'cloud brocade rhododendron', *fortunei*, was a refugee and as far as we know the last of the large flowering species to be found in south-eastern China. At the time he left the 'central flowery land' was engulfed in turmoil. The Taiping Rebellion of 1850–64, moving up from the south to Peking, spread to sixteen provinces, destroying 600 cities and killing unknown millions. Largely thanks to the British, opium smoking was endemic by the later decades of the nineteenth century, and it was estimated that 10 per cent of the 400 million people were smokers, and half of these addicts. Post-rebellion China suffered the indignity of being unfit to run her own Customs Service, which was parcelled out, contracted jointly to the Americans, French and British; soon the first two had decamped, the French to Vietnam, and things were left to the British. Many sent to work for the Chinese Imperial Customs Service became themselves China-addicts, devoted to the country and her lost history, and one of these was Augustine Henry (1857–1930).

Henry did not even like rhododendrons, but he was to save *sinogrande* and her fellows, or at least alert the world to their existence. He was an Irish Catholic, born in 1857 and brought up in the glens of Antrim, where the landlords gave out *Rhododendron ponticum* to poor cottagers as a kind of 'plantation', a brand mark. Henry was a medical student at Queen's University in Belfast when the doyen of the Chinese Customs Service, Sir Robert Hart, came back to his Alma Mater looking for likely recruits; Henry was hooked and after finishing medicine at Edinburgh he set out for Shanghai. Sir Robert must have noted the qualities of an Arctic explorer or a mountaineer in this young man of 24, for the Service gave him the roughest postings in social terms – no partying in Canton or Hong Kong for Henry – for most of the next 20 years.

His first posting was to the remote Treaty Port of I-chang (now Yichang), downstream from the Yangtze Gorges. Consumed with loneliness, feeling cut off from his known world, he took to sightseeing and botanising. Like Hsu Hung-tsu he was confronted with more scenery than he could readily absorb – the numberless tributaries cutting their own gorges, waterfalls, rocks water-sculpted into fantastic forms, caves with stalagmites and stalactites, pagodas perched on impossible heights, and always the limestone cliffs towering above the torrential river. But Henry also saw the ledges encrusted with saxifrages and pale lilac and pink primulas; he realised that the extravagant landscape teemed with flowers, roses, lilies and rhododendrons, and creepers flinging themselves from rocky heights – and all still there simply because they were out of reach.

Henry became interested in forestry because he could see how ruthlessly the Chinese had cut down their trees and destroyed every plant without obvious economic value. He ventured further on long forays, one of these to 'wild' Hubei, north of I-chang, in the spring of 1888. He travelled in a sedan chair for status; he was the first foreigner many of the people had seen, the very image of a demon – tall, fair, blue-eyed and with a fine red beard – and one party of travellers dropped everything and ran at the sight of him. But he was also welcomed; he saw virgin forest, which began three days out from I-chang, and bears, monkeys, wild boar and exotic pheasants. The mountains of Hubei were the home of the vegetable drugs for which he was officially searching the opium, betel nut, dendrobium orchid and *Liquidambar formosana*, together with wild chrysanthemum, lilies, clematis, vines, roses, rhododendrons and the Chinese tulip tree (*Liriodendron chinense*), more modest in size and flower than its American cousin and introduced into Britain – at Henry's prompting – by Ernest H. Wilson in 1901.

Augustine Henry struggled to match the local names of plants to the botanical names he knew; he patiently numbered specimens and sent them home to Kew, asking that they be identified and correlated with their native names, without, it has to be said, much response. The following year he left I-chang for the south, for tropical Hainan Island, where he contracted malaria and so was sent home for sick leave. Whilst at home Henry made a happy but tragically brief marriage, his wife Caroline dying after a few months; broken-hearted, he returned to China, this time to Mengzi in the far south of Yunnan province. He found himself in a Graham Greene kind of situation comedy, with an American couple, the Spinneys (she had brought her piano, had smartly decorated rooms and hardly went outdoors), a nervous little French doctor and other assorted recluses and drug addicts. To keep his sanity he went for a long tramp every Sunday away from the Mengzi madhouse into the exotic hill country of fabulous lilies, magnolias and rhododendrons, the haunt of vermilion birds,[45] wild cats and beautiful snakes.

Evidence of Henry's loneliness must surely be that he even yearned for letters from Kew and from Professor Charles Sargent, director of the Arnold Arboretum. Henry wrote to Sargent: 'Letters are the only stimulant of a healthy kind an exile has to cheer him up in moments of depression, and to remind him that there is a fair world on the other side of the globe where men and women live . . .'[46] Out of his isolation he squeezed his passion for the flowers and their country. Kew and the Arnold both pleaded for the evidence, and so Henry, with the help of a Lolo 'man of the woods', Old Ho, set about collecting specimens, drying them and sending them home. When Henry was moved to a new customs post at Szemao (now Simao), further west in Yunnan towards the Burmese border, Old Ho and his proud wife, whom Henry was not allowed to address, went with him – and in the much happier community at Szemao, where Henry made many friends, they continued botanising and sending home.[47]

Rhododendron augustinii, the delicately flowered blue-mauve species, a prize in herself but also valued as a parent in the search for a blue rhododendron, was one of Henry's discoveries; also *auriculatum*, sweetly scented and late flowering. Besides rhododendrons, so many other flowers were to be named for him as the 'discoverer' – the orange, turkscap *Lilium henryi*, a scarlet, long-tubed honeysuckle, a single white large-flowered clematis, a large-flowered hypericum and the colourful vine, *Parthenocissus henryana*. How wonderful his walks must have been.

Henry's story ends happily. He left China in 1900, returned to find himself rather a botanical celebrity, married again and set up the department of forestry at Cambridge University, before returning to Ireland to promote reafforestation. He died in 1930.

In the months before he left China the letters flew from Szemao to Boston, and London to Boston and all around. Henry felt an effort should be made to send a botanical expedition to Yunnan. At Kew, where the post-Hooker regime probably felt that enough had been done for rhododendrons, and the new focus was on economic botany, they feared it would be too expensive.

'Money is not what is wanted, but time, oceans of time,' retorted Henry. 'Nothing astonishes people at home so much as the fact, a real fact, that in countries like China, you cannot do everything with money. Patience is more valuable.'[48]

At the Arnold, Sargent was hoping for an expedition in partnership with James Herbert Veitch, whom he had met plant hunting in Japan, and who was still on a world tour; but James's uncle Sir Harry Veitch put his foot down on more travelling. James must come home to mind the shop: the Veitch Royal Exotic Nurseries in Chelsea. But there was a tree that Henry had found, the ghost tree, with fluttering white bracts, the legendary 'pocket handkerchief tree' (*Davidia involucrata*) that Père David had first seen some 30 years before, and Sir Harry wanted that tree. At Kew, the director Thistleton-Dyer had a promising young man named Ernest Wilson (1876–1930), whom he passed on to Veitch, who paid Wilson £100 and sent him to see Sargent in Boston. There it was arranged that Augustine Henry should wait at Szemao and show Wilson the pocket handkerchief tree. So, in October 1899, having crossed the United States and sailed from San Francisco, Wilson arrived in Szemao. Henry, who was by now rather irked by the unimaginative responses from both Kew and the Arnold to the urgency of rescuing the fabulous Chinese flora that he had found, gave Wilson a sketch map of a country the size of Newfoundland, and waved him goodbye.

Wilson set out up the Yangtze in a picturesque riverboat with a sedan chair, bearers and guides; after ten days of threats and ambushes he arrived at the village where Henry was remembered, only to find a spanking new house and the stump of the pocket handkerchief tree which had been felled for its timbers. Three weeks and many miles later Wilson found another, and then a whole grove of the unbelievable trees, and he was able to gather the seeds. He finally returned in triumph to London in the spring of 1902; the Veitches gave him a gold watch, engraved 'Well done'.[49] Besides the *Davidia involucrata*, dove tree or 'ghost tree' as it became known, Wilson brought back some marvellous rhododendrons and was keen to return for more, and for lilies and the mystical blue poppies.

However, the danders were up, as they say, and the irrepressible Arthur Kilpin Bulley (1861–1942), scion of prosperous Liverpool cotton brokers and an outspoken socialist who hated the secretive tendencies of the plant world, was not going to let the Veitches get away with their triumph. Bulley had bought 60 acres for his botanic garden at Ness on the Wirral, which was open for all to enjoy, and started his seed co-operative, 'All to Gather – All Together', which was to become the famous Bees' Seeds.[50] He was intrigued by the possibilities of the Chinese plants and in April 1904 he wrote to Professor Isaac Bayley Balfour (1853–1922), Regius Keeper of the Edinburgh Botanic Garden, to know if he had a likely collector. Oddly enough Balfour did, a young man of 'the right grit' by the name of Forrest.

George Forrest (1873–1932) was Edinburgh's own, their 'Prince of Collectors'; he in turn, for all his wonderful haul of primulas, gentians and meconopsis, which so delighted Bulley, was a rhododendron man – they 'above all others captivated his enthusiasm'.[51]

Forrest was born in Falkirk in 1873, a Kilmarnock Academy boy who started working in a chemist's shop, studied botany with his pharmacy, and then toughened himself up in that finishing school for would-be adventurers, the Australian outback. He was home, in that spring of 1904, working in the Botanics' herbarium and chafing for action, when Balfour and Bulley sent him to China. He sailed to Rangoon, then went by rail to Mandalay and Myitkyina, crossed the 'open' Burma–Yunnan border to Tengyueh (now Tengchong), which he made his base and his 'home'.

George Forrest was the definitive hunter, a man's man, stocky, muscular, shaven headed, dressed in khaki with puttees strapped around bulging calf muscles and with a gun slung on his shoulder. He was a broad-minded naturalist, interested in all living things, including the mountain peoples and their traditions (a trait by no means common amongst British plant hunters). He learned Chinese and the local dialects, and was good at training his native collectors, who were devoted to him in return. He was self-disciplined and hard working, but patient and kindly at dispensing medicines and helping the sick. He needed all his attributes for he had been sent into a maelstrom. Henry had warned that 'a lot of killing' would be needed before the bandit-riven Chinese–Burma border country would be passable. Forrest went straight into it.

On his infamous first trip north to the Tibetan border country he stayed with the French missionary, Father Dubernard. The border was inflamed, the Tibetans' furious at Colonel Young-husband's march into Lhasa and a Chinese infiltration into Batang, and the mission was stormed, Father Dubernard was murdered and the mission staff and Forrest and his party fled for their lives.

About eighty of them were hunted through the foothills on the west bank of the Mekong, by lamas armed with poisoned arrows and double-handed swords and Tibetan mastiffs, until almost all were killed or captured; of Forrest's own party of seventeen collectors and bearers only one escaped. After eight days, Forrest was on his own, he had ceased to care whether he lived or died; his clothes were in shreds, his feet swollen out of shape, hands and face torn with thorns, he had eaten only a few ears of wheat and some parched peas, but in attempting to get food at a tiny Lissu village, he found the headman was to prove one of the best friends he ever had. Being saved, however, was even greater misery; in pouring rain, the way to safety was upwards, 'struggling through cane-brakes, cutting our way through miles of rhododendrons, trampling over alps liter-ally clothed with primulas, gentians, saxifrages, lilies etc., till we reached the snowfields' at the top of the Mekong–Salween divide, at about 17,500 feet.[52] They travelled along the summit for six days, over glaciers, snow, ice and tip-tilted limestone strata (that rhodo-dendrons grew on limestone was carved into Forrest's brain for later reference), until it was safe to come down into the valley again; after one or two further alarms Forrest was delivered to a border town with Chinese troops, welcomed 'as one returned from the dead' and taken under armed escort to Tali.

Though none of his later expeditions were quite so hair-raising, none were easy. He was to find *Rhododendron sinogrande* on his third expedition, from February 1912 to March 1915, this one financed by

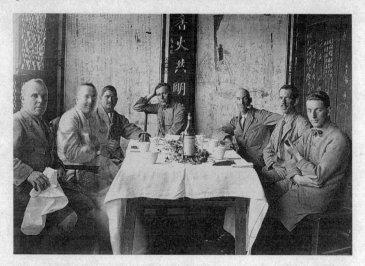

The Boozels Club at Tengyueh, George Forrest is on the extreme left.

J. C. Williams of Caerhays in Cornwall. Forrest took a wonderful photograph of stacks of cases ready for dispatch, labelled 'J. C. Williams Esq., Cornwall, England via T. Cook & Son, Rangoon'.[53]

At Tengyueh revolution was in the air – the last Qing emperor had abdicated in early 1912 – 'living in China just now is like camping alongside an active volcano,' wrote Forrest. But, un-stoppable, he went plant hunting to the east, crossing the Shweli, the local river, to the ridge – or divide – between it and the valley of the mighty Salween (which comes all the way from the Tanghla Range in the Tibetan Plateau, and reaches the sea in the Gulf of Martaban in Burma. *Sinogrande* was a last-minute find. That August of 1912, he had seen it in fruit, carefully noting where it was grow-ing, but on returning home found rioting in Tengyueh so decided it was best to leave. Forrest returned in mid-November when things had settled down, immediately heading up to where he had left *sinogrande*: 'seems to be a magnificent species. The cap-sules are two to two and a half inches long, slightly curved and

Boxes of seeds and plants ready for dispatch from Burma to
J. C. Williams in Cornwall.

thick as one's thumb. The foliage runs from one foot by six inches
to as much as two feet by ten inches, dark green and glossy on
the upper surface, ash coloured beneath. Very handsome tree of
20–30 feet. More later.'[54] These first seeds must have reached J. C.
Williams at Caerhays. There were more later, many more, Forrest
sending nine different batches in 1919. Williams' generosity first
flowered in 1919 from seed or a young plant that he had given to the
Tremaynes at Heligan; Edinburgh Botanics had *sinogrande* flower in
their glasshouse on 6 April 1920, and a month later, on 5 May, it
flowered for another lucky recipient, Dame Alice Godman, at South
Lodge near Horsham in Sussex (in her cool greenhouse). Williams
had to wait until 1922 for his flowers at Caerhays and George
Johnstone at Trewithen and Trengwainton also claimed flowers that
year. Dame Alice exhibited her *sinogrande* in 1922 and it was given
an RHS Award of Merit; Johnstone took the more prestigious First
Class Certificate in 1926.

But there was (at least) one other success: *Rhododendron sinog-rande* flowered in the spring of 1933 and thrived in a quiet garden on the west coast of Scotland, at Larachmhor near Arisaig, and from there she made her real début into society. Patiently waiting for the next spring – perhaps innocent then of *sinogrande*'s spasmodic habits in flowering? – Mr John A. Holms must have been delighted at the prospect of her second flowering, as delicate and nerve-racking a time as for any father-to-be; when the moment came he carefully cut off (oh, sacrificial moment!) the flowering truss, bedding the stalk in wet moss and wrapping it carefully, and set out on the long journey to Edinburgh. Next morning he walked down Princes Street, carrying his *sinogrande* like a huge, magnificent umbrella; it became a royal progress, he was stopped by the curious, questioned, *sinogrande* was examined and admired, she undoubtedly picked up a following, as Mr Holms turned north, lengthened his stride along Dundas Street, crossed the Water of Leith by the Clock Tower, and entered the Botanics on Inverleith Row. Here he, and *sinogrande*, were received in triumph – even those dour Scots gardeners must have looked up from their work to applaud. The Regius Keeper, whom Holms had come to see, was so delighted that he recorded this story for posterity.[55]

And what of John Holms, who so gleefully laid his *sinogrande* flower on the Regius Keeper's desk? It was the triumph of his rhododendron garden at Larachmhor, which he had been making throughout the 1920s, in a sheltered glen beside the Road to the Isles. Soon after his Edinburgh trip – perhaps it was his last fling? – he was bankrupted, and the bailiffs were sent to clear out his house and garden at Formakin at Langbank by Port Glasgow, and even to get the rhododendrons from Larachmhor. The big species, including *sinogrande*, were loaded on a train for sale in Glasgow, but they got stuck in the first tunnel, and so were returned to Larachmhor, where they flower still. Rhododendron 'John Holms', from an *arboreum x barbatum*, was raised and named by Archie and Sandy Gibson of Glenarn in honour of Holms, who had started their enthusiasm for gardening and given them many plants for Glenarn.

The time of *sinogrande*'s 'leaving' for the West should have presented the opportunity to open a twentieth-century dialogue between Chinese and Western botanists. Instead, the trickle of Westerners continued by the back, Burmese, door, and China once again slipped into turmoil with the fall of the last, Qing, dynasty and the long struggle of revolution and counter-revolution which ended in the Communist party-state. It was not until the 1940s that Dr Wen-pei Fang of the National Sichuan University was able to publish the first volume of his Mount Omei flora and lead the rediscovery by Chinese botanists of their own rhododendrons.

CHAPTER THREE

The King's Botanist's Tale

ABOUT 800 YEARS after rhododendrons flowered in the high-status gardens of Luoyang, the London apothecary John Parkinson (1567–1650) suggested that they might be suitable for English gardens. Parkinson's garden in Long Acre was a store of curiosities; he had acquired plants from the Pyrenees, knew European botanists and it is easily supposed that his eminent gardening friend, John Tradescant the Elder (*c.* 1570–1638) may have brought him the pink flowered *Rhododendron hirsutum* home from one of his European expeditions. Whether *hirsutum*, the hairy Swiss named for its bristly shoots and leaves, flowered in Long Acre in the days of Charles I remains supposition; it is usually credited to the Tradescants' own garden in Lambeth, on the strength of John the Younger's (1608–62) catalogue of his rarities, *Musaeum tradescantianum*, published in 1656. If it flowered there, then after John the Younger's death in 1662, the small *hirsutum* found itself part of a lawsuit in which Elias Ashmole claimed, and won, his rights to the Tradescant collections. Ashmole, less interested in the plants than in the stuffed animals and birds, the shells and relics, which he wanted for his planned museum in Oxford (the Ashmolean opened in 1683), let visitors into the Lambeth garden and it was completely destroyed. For the first rhododendron in England it was a lamentable end.

The story begins again in the late 1680s with the disappointed

Bishop of London, Henry Compton, (1632–1713), too much a Protestant for the Romanist faction and suspended by James II (though allowed to remain as tutor to his daughters, the Princesses Mary and Anne), passed over as Archbishop of Canterbury, and so semi-retired in his palace on Fulham riverside, with a cool responsibility for all the souls in the new colonies and a warm passion for botany. Bishop Compton's priests, ministering to souls in Virginia, also collected plants, and one of the consignments from the Revd John Banister (1654–92) that arrived at Fulham contained the first *Magnolia virginiana*, and the first American rhododendrons, the spice-scented *viscosum*, called the swamp honeysuckle or clammy azalea, and the Pinxterbloom, *Rhododendron periclymenoides*. Banister, now hailed as one of the first field botanists of distinction, compiling his flora of Virginia, was accidentally shot whilst plant collecting along the Roanoke River in May 1692, the first rhododendron martyr. The Bishop's Palace garden at Fulham became famous for 'a greater variety of curious exotic plants and trees' than any other garden in the England of its time; besides the azaleas and magnolias these included the first dogwoods, red hawthorn, the sweet gum (*Liquidambar*), the box elder (*Acer negundo*) and *Aralia spinosa*, the viciously prickly 'Hercules club', also known as the 'devil's walking stick'. It retains some of this curious atmosphere even today.[1]

The fashion for American plants was fuelled by a transatlantic partnership between a 'down right plain country man', as John Bartram (1699–1777) called himself, and a prosperous Quaker haberdasher in the City of London, whose name has become mossy with time, Peter Collinson (1694–1768). It was a partnership in letters and boxes of seeds and cuttings that lasted for about 35 years, in a window of time when the eastern fringes of North America were mostly painted pink on the map, and gentlemen in London, especially Quakers, were kindly disposed to scientific correspondences with their colonial cousins.

John Bartram had been born in 1699 to a farming family from Derbyshire who had settled at Darby, Pennsylvania, the year

The King's Botanist, John Bartram (1699–1777), a likeness drawn
by Howard Pyle for *Harper's New Monthly Magazine*, February 1880.

Philadelphia was founded, 1682. He had a Quaker Meeting School education and started working on the farm as soon as he was strong enough, but continued to school himself in Latin and medicine so as to be a competent amateur doctor. He was prime settler material, strong, wise and self-reliant, he built up his own farmsteading on land at Kingessing on the Schuylkill River, and he was a family man, twice-married, and a stalwart of the Quaker community. He was a good, improving farmer – he dumped horse manure and wood ash into a special reservoir and watered his meadows with a liquid manure, so doubling his hay yield over his neighbours – and was ever interested in improving his soils and trying new crops. But for John Bartram there was always, it seemed, the wonder of his new found land – he botanised, and kept the margins of his fields and woods for propagating plants he brought in from the wild, and was always the keen observer of wild animals and birds and was concerned about signs of soil erosion and about the whole-sale felling of forests.[2] Posterity has found him rather quaint, folksy, though none the less loved, caricatured (for he was never portrayed in life) as a lean, tall man in a beaver tricorn hat, long apron and buckled shoes as 'The Botanist' – a being from a *Tristram Shandy* world. His garden has become a national shrine, and still harbours one of his rarest plants, the franklinia or franklin tree from Georgia, with large cream cups for flowers and crimson autumn colouring, which was named for his friend Benjamin Franklin, and which has never been seen in the wild again since Bartram's day.

Bartram's Quaker connections led to his recommendation as a reliable supplier of seeds and young plants to the London merchant Peter Collinson. When Collinson began corresponding with Bartram, in 1733 or thereabouts, he was approaching 40 and working with his brother James in the family's successful textile trading firm, his desk making an excellent perch for a go-between. An early success seems to have been with American cranberries – 'of grand use for Tartts' wrote a grateful Dr John Fothergill, one of Collinson's gardening friends.[3]

Collinson escaped to his garden in Peckham, south of the Thames, whenever he could: this had been his grandparents' garden, he had loved it since he was two years old and this love had made him a gardener. Between his city desk and his garden Collinson filled his exceedingly elastic days with unpaid activities; he was a member of the Royal Society, a copious correspondent with wide scientific interests, a bibliophile, a constant supporter of the Society of Friends and – of most importance here – the agent for Bartram's boxes of seeds and plants, the linchpin of a botanical brotherhood who both commissioned and paid for Bartram's collecting.

The general plan seemed to be that Bartram went botanising after his harvest, setting off alone on his good horse, with capacious saddlebags for his bounty, and he returned when these were full. By Christmas he had patiently packed everything for dispatch to the waiting ship that Collinson had arranged for the crossing to Bristol or Liverpool. This packing was critical and evolved into an exact process which Dr Fothergill brought to perfection over the years:

> Acorns, nuts, kernels of fruit or stones of fruit and all the larger seeds come very safe in moss. It should be rather dry than moist, as it imbibes a good deal of moisture from the air. When the seeds, acorns and so forth are got together, make a shallow box of any dimensions. Cover the bottom with moss, then lay the seeds and so forth in little distinct patches. Lay a covering of moss, then a layer of seeds, and so fill up the box. A few gimlet holes may be bored in the lid and sides, to let in some air; [the box] may be kept in the cabin and will come safe.

Bulbs, said Dr Fothergill, taken up after flowering and dried, should be wrapped in paper or dry sand, then put in the boxes; small seeds were wrapped in brown paper laid in sand. Plants and shrubs 'of any kind' were to be lifted in the autumn. 'Wrap the roots with the earth adhering to them in moss. Cut off some of the branches, or long tops, and lay them close in a box, and so close . . . as they shall not be shaked loose by carriage. If the moss is a little wet, it will be no worse. The seams between the boards of the boxes need not be very close, just to keep out mice and other such-like vermin. Carefully packed in this manner, they will preserve their vegetative powers many months . . .'[4]

The boxes were for spring planting, so they had to ride out the winter gales; the most precious were kept under the captain's bunk, some were lost overboard, others doused in salt water and sometimes the rats made a picnic of both packaging and seeds. Once Collinson wrote tetchily: 'to my great Loss some prying knowing people looked into the Cases and out of that No. 2 took the 3 roots of Chamaerhododendrons, Red Honeysuckle, Laurel, Root of Silver Leafed Arum and the Spirea'.[5]

But more often the boxes arrived intact, in splendid condition, with everything as 'fresh and Lively as if that Minute taken out of the Woods'. With practice the system worked so well that insects, eggs (snapping turtles were successfully hatched in Collinson's garden pond), shells, fossils and even wasps' nests were sent. 'I am like the parson's barn. I refuse nothing,' wrote Collinson.[6]

It was on an expedition in the autumn of 1736 that Bartram found his first rhododendrons. He had heard that they grew beside the Delaware River in the Blue Mountains, but he was following the course of his own river, the Schuylkill, up into the mountains, and there he found them in impressive groves, growing not quite so tall as himself. These were *Rhododendron maximum*; as it was autumn he must have pulled up young plants and wrapped their roots in wet moss, and these very plants or some collected soon afterwards found their way to London and Peter Collinson's Peckham garden.

Kalmias, named for Linnaeus' assistant Peter Kalm (1715–79), whom Collinson sent over to meet Bartram, magnolias, robinias, maples, viburnums, the witch hazel, pines, thorns, American box varieties, as well as rhododendrons, all these and more came in Bartram's boxes. The seeds and seedlings came in vast amounts and numbers, for the box customers were ambitious planters on a large scale. By 1756 Collinson called it a prodigious influx: 'England must be turned upside down and America transplanted Heither'.[7]

So what happened to the plants, who were the botanical brotherhood and what did they do with their bounty? Collinson left various lists of some 60 or so who were customers at one time or another, a bevy of dukes and lords figured prominently and there were many nurserymen of the day whose names are forgotten. Lord Weymouth, for whom the Weymouth pine was named, made plantings of pines and other Americans at Longleat. Some of the lordly parks are gone, some are still famous and if any gnarled and aged *Rhododendron maximum* still lurks in the depth of the woods at Woburn or Blenheim or Syon, Arundel or Windsor, then she may be the offspring of a Bartram plant. Others of the botanical brotherhood can speak for themselves.

In Upton Lane in east London, the City Corporation still maintains West Ham Park, once the home of Collinson's Quaker friend, Dr John Fothergill. The park has a camellia dell, cherry avenue, an iris and peony garden, a tribute grove of modern rhododendrons and azaleas and one ancient live oak, *Quercus virginiana*, which just may have survived from the eighteenth century.

Fothergill (1711–80) was a busy London doctor, a former Sedbergh grammar schoolboy who trained at Edinburgh and St Thomas's; he was studious and kind, a serious Newtonian interested in rocks and the cosmos, and he told Bartram, 'I love the vegetable Creation. I love its varieties and cultivate it as an amusement – with not the leisure to become a perfect botanist'.[8] His 30 acres (13 ha.), with greenhouses and hothouses, were packed with treasures (and later greatly admired by Sir Joseph Banks) but Fothergill had a disarming modesty: 'I have a little wilderness, which when [I] bought the premises [1762] was full of old yew trees, laurels and weeds. I had it cleared and well dug, and took up many trees, but left others standing for shelter. Among these I have planted kalmias, azaleas, all the magnolias, and most other hardy American shrubs. It is not quite eight years since ... So that my plants must be considered but as young ones. They are, however, extremely flourishing.'[9]

Leave Upton Lane for the Romford road, passing the roar of the West Ham football crowd at Upton Park, and about eleven miles to the north-east at Thorndon Hall, Brentwood, the youthful, rich, Catholic Robert James, 8th Lord Petre (1713–42), was Collinson's star customer. The Petres were his clients for silks and blue damasks and it seems likely that a chance conversation set the whole business of Bartram's boxes in train. Was it a partnership of persecuted minorities inclined to help each other? Petre was absorbed in his planting, and he was pioneering a new fashion for the landscape, as Collinson reported to Bartram on 1 September 1741:

> Last year Lord Petre planted out about ten thousand Americans, which, being at the same time mixed with about twenty thousand Europeans, and some Asians, make a very beautiful appearance: – great art and skill being shown in consulting every one's particular growth, and the well blending the variety of greens. Dark green being a great foil to lighter ones, and bluish green to yellow ones, and those trees that have their bark and back of their leaves of white, or silver, make a beautiful contrast with the others.
>
> The whole is planted in thickets and clumps, and with these mixtures are perfectly picturesque, and have a delightful effect ...
>
> His nursery being fully stocked with flowering shrubs, of all sorts that can be procured, – with these, he borders the outskirts of all his plantations: and he continues, annually, raising from seed, and layering, bedding, grafting – that twenty thousand trees are hardly to be missed out of his nurseries.[10]

Collinson, a frequent visitor to Thorndon, loved its reclusive luxuries – walking in the park made him feel he was in North America – 'but to be at his table, one would think South America was really there – to see a servant come in every day with ten or a dozen Pine Apples – as much as he can carry. I am lately come from thence, quite cloyhed with them.'[11]

At his own garden's progress he grumbled wryly, 'The Chamae-rhodendendrons move very slow. They seem to like Lord Petres Soil Better – they seem to Die *Dayly* with Mee and I have tried them in different Methods.'[12]

The rhododendrons and azaleas were still 'difficult' and it seems unlikely they were planted in large numbers at Thorndon, but clearly they were planted successfully. It is hard to know, for the young Lord Petre died of smallpox in 1742, aged 29, and much of his innovatory planting knowledge died with him. Almost 40 years later his blendings of differing greens and 'outskirts' of flowering shrubs were shown diagrammatically in James Meader's *The Planter's Guide* (1779) using *Rhododendron maximum* in tiers of evergreens. This kind of planting, the beginning of the Victorian shrubbery 100 years before its time, has only very recently been unearthed from obscurity by planting historians. Lord Petre's early death, the ingrained privacy of the Catholic families, and the apparently different interests of his heir – who commissioned James Paine to build a Palladian mansion and Capability Brown to landscape his park (and probably fell all the overly varied straight line plantings) – all meant that Thorndon remained unrecognised as being different from anywhere else. The kindly Collinson, who continued to visit Thorndon, took indulgent pleasure in a letter to 'my dear John' Bartram ordering a ten-guinea box for the young Lord Petre, but the seeds and plants probably had short lives. Today Thorndon is Essex County Council's Country Park, and in the southern part, near the ruin of the old hall, in what is called Menagerie Plantation, a grove of ancient rhododendrons – just possibly Bartram's *maximum*'s offspring – survives.[13]

The spur to the unearthing of these early eighteenth-century shrubberies was the restoration, begun in the 1980s, of Charles Hamilton's (1704–86) pleasure park at Painshill in Surrey. Hamilton was a customer for Bartram's boxes. A list for a five-guinea box has survived, seeds and seedlings of as many as a hundred different varieties – pines, maples, cedars, birches, oaks, limes, ash, hickory wood, acacia (honey locust), alders, cherries and thorns, and shrubs – magnolias, hydrangeas, cornus, viburnums, kalmias, sumach and roses, as well as rhododendrons. Painshill has always been thought of as the first fashionable home of American rhododendrons, planted by Charles Hamilton in the 1730s or thereabouts as an exotic ingredient in his pleasure park. The restoration of Painshill's planting, masterminded by Mark Laird, author of *The Flowering of the Landscape Garden 1720–1800*, completely destroys the accepted notion that 'landscape' planting was dull; in a deep border around the Painshill amphitheatre trees and shrubs are lined up as taking their bows, tallest and sternest at the back with their long legs masked by the fluffy and flowery company in the middle ranks, blonde golden and silvery leaves contrasting with 'brunette' dark evergreens, and in front are the juveniles, touching hands, rows of fat box plants with dashes of purple and pinks, all kept in order by a sprinkling of freakish, columnar junipers.[14] It is an almost comic sight, a chorus line from the heyday of Sheridan and Goldsmith returned to play an encore after 250 years.

Lord Bute (1713–92), whom Collinson called the 'Maecenas of Gardening' after the patron of Horace and Virgil, added his colourful influence to the line-up of Bartram's box customers. The splendid Bute, as painted by Joshua Reynolds in his garter robes and short embroidered surcoat to show off his famously fabulous silk-stockinged legs, was lean and handsome, with deep-set eyes and wide sensual mouth, a swan amongst stout and waddling Whigs and Tories. As a boy Bute had spent his holidays from Eton helping his uncle the Duke of Argyll make the park at Whitton by taking in a part of Hounslow Heath in 1723–4 and planting 'by raising all sorts of trees and shrubs from seeds from our northern colonies and all other parts of the world' a collection, amongst which Philip Miller of the Chelsea Physic Garden reported there were rhododendrons. When the Duke died in 1761 it was Bute who arranged for the best plants to be moved to Kew for Princess Augusta. He owned, at various times, Caen Wood (Kenwood), Luton Hoo, Cardiff and Highcliffe Castles, all gardens where rhododendrons have settled.

In power or out he was always 'the minister behind the curtain', a great friend of George III, albeit one with a self-confessed passion for botany; he was certainly the cohesive force behind Bartram's ducal patrons, a company who easily forgot political animosities and turned the talk to gardening over their port wine. It was botany – 'My favourite studdys' – that kept him at Kew, rather than Princess Augusta's charms, as the caricaturists liked to suppose (he was happily married). He worked with a botanist, John Hill, on their 'Vegetable System' of taxonomy, which, needless to say, was never completed. In the end Bute left the scene because he did not like Joseph Banks; he retired to his Isle of Bute and died in late 1792, his death hastened by a fall from a cliff whilst reaching for a plant, a botanist's death.[15]

Lord Mansfield had taken over Caen Wood from Bute in 1754 and there is a painting by John Wootton done the following year, a view of the south terrace with his lordship's great niece, Dido Elizabeth Belle, the child of his nephew and a slave, with a fore-ground of waist-high bushes of deep green with pinkish flowers. We *assume* them to be roses, but were they not, more appropriately, American rhododendrons?

Peter Collinson's botanical hobby took over his life; when he thought about it he grumbled at the time it took 'keeping accounts, writing letters with orders, receiving and paying the collectors' money, difficulties and attendance at the Customs house to procure the delivery of the seeds and then dispersing the boxes to their proper owners'. And his motives were 'without the least grain of profit to myself in hope to improve or at least to adorn my country' – though he did write this at the end of his life, with a necessary reminder from his son that he was nearly 72, and felt gratitude at seeing the rewards of his labours 'in the numerous plantations spread over this delightful island' which gave him great pleasure.[16] But it still seems a Herculean labour, delivering Bartram's five- or ten-guinea boxes for nearly 35 years.

His friendship with John Bartram grew very warm, if rather

patronising on Collinson's part; he cared deeply for the welfare of Bartram and his family, sending them clothes and other presents, and constantly good advice. His proudest moment came on 9 April 1765 when he wrote: 'I have the pleasure to inform my good friend that my repeated solicitations have not been in vain; for this day I received certain intelligence from Our Gracious King that he had appointed thee his botanist, with a salary of £50 a year ...'[17]

Collinson's Mill Hill garden (now Mill Hill School), where he successfully cultivated so many of Bartram's rarities, became very famous, and he was proudest of his rhododendrons. In June 1761 his flowering kalmia was fine enough, 'but in a few days will the Glorious Mountain Laurel or great Chamaerhododendron appear with its Charming Clusters of flowers prethee Friend John look out sharp for some more of these two fine plants – for one can never have too many'.[18] And it was no mirage, for again he reported to Bartram that his magnolia and red acacia both made a glorious show, 'but above all is the Great Mountain Laurel or Rhododendron in all its Glory – this 10th June, what a Ravishing Sight will the Mountains appear when alive with this rich embroiderie. How Glorious are Thy works O Lord ...'[19]

Collinson was a good man, wishing little for himself but the time to carry on with his botanical correspondence. He did love his noble 'customers' though, and the peak of his enjoyment came in October 1761 when he was in a party from the Society of Friends to meet King George III and Queen Charlotte just after their coronation. Collinson talked 'almost entirely' botany and planting with the king, and purred with pride when Princess Augusta invited him to visit Kew. But even goodness failed to get its reward; five years later he was struggling at Mill Hill, his last years 'clouded by restricted means and by constant thefts' of his precious plants. Just a few weeks before he died in July 1768 a notice was issued from Bow Street police station offering a reward of ten guineas for information concerning the theft 'last Friday morning early' of 'exotick plants unlawfully plucked up'.[20]

In 1753 Bartram had taken his 14-year-old son Billy south to New Jersey with him; it was an induction, and William Bartram (1739–1823), with a great deal of advice donated by Collinson and Fothergill from their comfortable London libraries, grew up to be 'Billy the Flower Hunter' or 'Puc-puggy' as the Seminole Indians called him. He looked the part, he was stocky and habitually dressed in leather from top to toe, but William was not a nose-to-the-ground botanist, passing from flower to seed head, more of a head-in-air romantic with a talent for drawing. He was captivated by the wonders of the American landscape, especially the fabulous rhododendron treasures of the South, the flame azaleas and the big lilac-purple flowered *catawbiense*, named for the Catawba Indians, in whose country it was.

Dr Fothergill paid for William's trip which began in the spring of 1773 and lasted almost four years, but the impressive frontispiece of *Travels through the Carolinas, Georgia and Florida* (first published in Philadelphia in 1791 and London in 1792) was a magnificently befeathered portrait of the Long Warrior, Mico Chtucco, Great King of the Seminoles. William travelled with Long Warrior's safe-conduct amongst Cherokees, whom he found grave and steady in bearing and manners, and proud Muscogulges who were sprightly and talkative, and also the Catawbas and Choctaws of west Florida. His guides took him high into the Appalachian uplands, the heathy balds covered with close-canopied kalmias and rhododendrons so dense that they were known as 'slicks' or 'hells' and only passable by following the bear tracks. He followed the Savannah River to its birthplace, a landscape of pyramidal hills and fertile dales where the Cherokees grew fields of corn and beans, always climbing higher: 'the air feels cool and animating, being charged with the fragrant breath of the mountain beauties, the blooming mountain cluster Rose, blushing Rhododendron and fair Lily of the valley: having now attained the summit of this very elevated ridge, we enjoyed a fine prospect indeed; the enchanting Vale of Keowe, perhaps as celebrated for fertility, fruitfulness and beautiful prospects as the Fields of Pharsalia or the Vale of Temple'.[21]

In these 'charming, sequestered, prolific fields' William is shown the beautiful, prancing horses belonging to his guide (destined for market in Charleston), flocks of 'turkies', herds of deer – room for all in 'a vast expanse of green meadows and strawberry fields' – and more – 'companies of young, innocent Cherokee virgins, some busily gathering the rich fragrant fruit, others having already filled their baskets, lay reclined under the shade of floriferous and fragrant native bowers of Magnolia, Azalea, Philadelphus, perfumed Caly-canthus, [and] sweet Yellow Jessamine . . .'[22]

It was strawberries and cream all the way for William; Billy the Flower Hunter wandered hills wreathed in magnolias and rhodo-dendrons, aromatic groves of cornus, laurel and azaleas, he was certain he had found the floral treasure house of the 'west' (for he was as far west as the British remit went, in Indian country – he actually travelled as far as the Mississippi, the boundary with Spanish Louisiana). From the Blue Ridge above the Oconee River in northern Georgia he viewed a wilderness 'appearing regularly undulated as the great ocean after a tempest' with the undulations gradually depressing and 'yet as regular as the tiles on a roof'. The nearer ground was 'almost perfect full green', the next more glau-cous, and lastly 'almost blue as the ether with which the most distant curve of the horizon seemed blended'. His imagination 'thus wholly engaged' he managed to look down, finding 'charming objects' within his reach – including *Rhododendron catawbiense* 'foremost in the assembly of mountain beauties', the flaming azalea, *Rhododendron calendulaceum*, a 'snowy-mantled' philadelphus, a robinia and a perfumed calycanthus.[23]

William Bartram travelled a thousand miles in this floral wonder-land; when he was not marvelling at the view or the flowers he was learning from his Indian hosts, watching them play football and 'their most noble manly exercise', a kind of lacrosse, and after the sports their feasting and dancing. They told him of their festivals and hunting, the fiery rituals that cleansed their possessions in readiness for the first fruits of each new harvest; they talked of their

Rhododendron catawbiense, named for the Catawba Indians in whose Appalachian country it was found.

Great Spirit, their beliefs in the hereafter, and of their monuments – legendary pyramids and ceremonial avenues and other wonders of their ancient civilisations. By the time William set out for home, he – rather like the Chinese wanderers of the Peach Blossom Spring and Marco Polo – had lost his sense of time, having lived like the Indians with the rhythms of nature. He had seen the rhododendrons and flame azaleas, 'the most gay and brilliant flowering shrub yet known . . . the colour of the finest red lead, orange and bright gold, as well as yellow and cream'.[24]

When he arrived home in Philadelphia there were redcoat soldiers in the streets and talk of revolution and of a wave of battles in the north moving ever nearer. William's father, the King's Botanist, died in late September the following year, 1777, in his seventy-eighth year, and within a few days of the decisive British defeat at Saratoga; the flowery empire in the West was slipping away.

*   *   *

The rhododendrons came from their distant mountains, from the Alps, the Pontics, the Pyrenees and the Appalachians, and were settled, to find their futures, into nurseries in the villages that are now engulfed in greater London. The 'culture' in horticulture was never more apt, for the ecological gulf they crossed was vast, and the tenderest care was lavished on both seeds and plants. For the triumphs recorded so far and those for a while to come, there must have been thousands and thousands of losses. It was a fragile, sputtering progress, and most of the recorded histories have long mouldered away in damp potting sheds or been piled on the bonfires that followed the deaths of old nurserymen. It is a trade that constantly reinvents itself, with a disregard for last year's flowers and a belief only in imminent miracle and novelty.

The street names of Hackney still bear witness to the first flowering of the mauve *Rhododendron ponticum* in the early 1760s, when it was a novelty with no hint of its rampaging infamy to come: Sylvester (sic) Path and Road, just south of Hackney Central Station, are named for Dr John Silvester's garden, *ponticum*'s first English home. Dr Silvester had found himself a promising gardener, the grandson and son of a gardener to the Hanoverian court, Joachim Conrad Loddiges (1738–1826), while he was travelling in Europe, and brought Loddiges back to lay out his Hackney garden and fill it with foreign plants in 1761. It is thought that Loddiges had the *ponticum* seeds in his baggage, loot from one of the fashionable Harlem gardens from where Silvester had poached him. Both Loddiges and the *ponticum* were so successful that Dr Silvester helped the former to start his own nursery in Hackney and the latter became the first star. (The names Nursery Road and Loddiges Road survive, off Mare Street.)[25]

Loddiges proudly sold his first *ponticum* seedlings to the Marquis of Rockingham (1730–82) in 'about 1763', and the young *ponticums* found themselves immediately in high society. Rockingham was an energetic Whig grandee in his thirties, with his political life in crisis because of his sister's scandalous elopement with a footman, who found his solace in long retirements at his beloved Wentworth Woodhouse estate in Yorkshire. Did he take the *ponticums* north? His head gardener was a customer for Bartram's boxes, so did the *ponticums* join the *maximum* already there?

Another route for the *ponticum* stems from Hackney; some of Loddiges' nursery ground was taken over from Johann Busch (d. *c.* 1790), who could have had *ponticum* from similar continental sources. Busch, as plain John Bush, moved to Isleworth in rural Middlesex, close to Kew (where Lord Bute was so influential) and the Duke of Northumberland's Syon. Bush was in the Collinson/Bartram syndicate with both Bute and Northumberland, so may have had the American *maximum* as well. Did *ponticum* meet her American cousin at Isleworth? Certainly Bush supplied plants for Kew and there, about a century later, they were felling great thickets of rhododendrons to make way for more novel exotics.

Loddiges of Hackney became famous for their rhododendrons, carrying them through to their nineteenth-century popularity. In 1839–40 the nursery planted one of the pioneering garden cemeteries at Abney Park in Stoke Newington as an arboretum, including all the known rhododendrons. Abney Park Cemetery survives as a green oasis full of ghostly stone furniture, but with no rhododendrons. Loddiges moved on to feed the public fancy for ferns, palms and orchids, devising and planting the great ferneries that adorned the Crystal Palace in Hyde Park in 1851. Shortly afterwards the Hackney nurseries were sold for development and the stock was auctioned; much of it, including a gigantic palm tree, as high as a three-storey house, which was hauled through the streets by 32 horses with a police escort, going to the Crystal Palace's new home at Sydenham.

Mauve *ponticum*'s sweet cousin, yellow *luteum*, the poison honey azalea, first flowered in England at the Watson brothers' nursery in Islington in 1798; she too went into society, becoming the floral deb's delight in the illustrated *Curtis' Botanical Magazine*, the nineteenth-century equivalent of the *Country Life* portrait page. William

Curtis (1746–99) was a Quaker apothecary who had published a London flora (financed by Lord Bute) but decided that lavish hand-coloured engravings of the new garden exotics would have a greater appeal to the public. The Pontic azalea, *luteum*, was 'immortalised' as plate 433, drawn by Sydenham Edwards from the plant in Watsons' nursery, in volume 13 (see page 2 in first picture section).[26]

After Lord Petre's death in 1742, his gardener at Thorndon Hall, James Gordon (*c.* 1708–80), was able to set himself up as a nurseryman in east London, at Mile End. His nursery became one of the most important for the London trade (and was to survive for 95 years until it was built over in 1837)[27] and not only would it be nice to think Gordon and his successors carried on the Thorndon taste for 'Americans' in general and rhododendrons in particular, for once we have the proof that this was so. It is very rare for plans for an ordinary London garden to have survived and so those for 13 Upper Gower Street in the Bodleian Library in Oxford have caused something of a stir. Number 13 is the standard long thin garden planned for a gentlemanly antiquary, Francis Douce, and drawn up by his garden adviser and friend, Richard Twiss, with Gordon's Nursery supplying the plants. A box-edged rectangle is to be planted with an edging of roses (slightly higher than the box), single specimens of rhododendrons and azalea, kalmia, colutea (bladder senna), arbutus, phillyrea, laurustinus, hibiscus and cistus stand around like ladies in waiting, and the centre rises to a flurry of almond and cherry blossom from these delicate trees. There is a gravel promenade pathway around the bed and an outside edging of Lombardy poplars and other shrubs to keep the garden from prying eyes. In a letter of 28 November 1791 Twiss proposes that the 'great bed' should be mounded, eight to ten inches higher in the centre, to enhance the graduated effect of the plants.

'A London garden must be made to please the Eye only, fruit is out of the question, as it will not ripen well,' he continues. His chosen ornamentals will 'gratify the eye', only needing watering in dry weather and once-a-month attention. Most interesting are the

... The Poplars must be at least 6 inches deep, & should be as fresh as possible ...

A Walk of 4 feet to an inch.

23 feet wide.
100 feet long.

Door
A Square with 4 strings & contain a Rose or an Evergreen to run up against the wall.

* 4 Holes for the Linen posts with green Lids.
2 more such posts may be set at the sides

42 Poplars

Privet
Laurel
Holly
or evergreens against the wall mostly to look green

these Poplars are about 3 f...
when they grow too large

if I had the exact dimensions of the ground, I would ma...
which might be wholly, partly, or not at all, used. The ne...

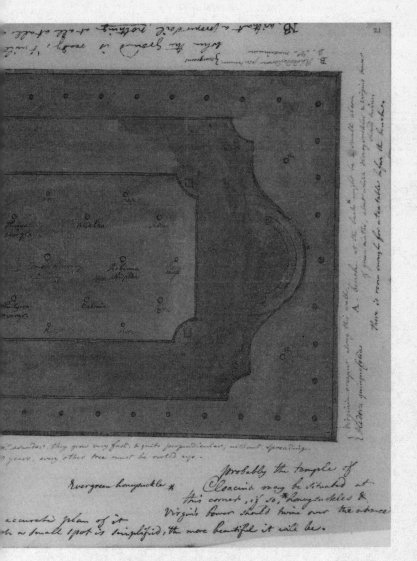

Richard Twiss (1747–1821), plan for the garden of 13 Upper Gower Street, London: a curious scheme for a late eighteenth-century town garden, surrounded with 42 poplars, with the central bed mounded to show off the specimen shrubs which include an azalea. The expensive rhododendrons would have been kept in two of the corner pots.

costs. The gravel, planting 'mould' (compost) and the screening poplars make up about half the total of £12 7s 6d; the plants the rest, the two *Rhododendron maximum* being the single most expensive at one guinea for the two (i.e. 10s 6d each), the azalea costing 3s 6d, and only the single kalmia and hibiscus being dearer at 5s.

In his biography of Beckford[28] James Lees-Milne noted the last word in American planting as seen by the arch-critic John Claudius Loudon (1783–1843) at William Beckford's Fonthill Splendens in 1833. 'To the south of the small plateau on which the Abbey stood ... the land dropped steeply. Below a terrace was ... a shrubbery of mauve rhododendrons, white magnolias, azaleas, arbutus, Portugal laurel and the Carolina rose. Here flourished also the Angelica tree (*Aralia*), the Andromeda shrub (*Pieris*) ... and the Carolina Allspice (*Calycanthus floridus*).'

William Beckford had chosen and placed the plants himself, and the shrubbery exotics were surrounded by predominantly native plants. When James Lees-Milne returned to the site of the vanished Splendens in the 1970s he found only 'rampaging ponticum'.[29]

In America, after the dust of revolution had settled, the French connection was more welcomed, and it was André Michaux (1746–1803), who began his tour as Royal Botanist and ended it as a Citizen of France, who collected seeds and plants of the southern azaleas and returned them to Europe. In the 1790s, John Fraser (1750–1811), a Scot who owned a nursery in Sloane Square, London, travelled both west to America, and east to the Russian Court, where he was part of a long string of British advisers and gardeners, including John Bush and James Meader, both already mentioned as rhododendron men. Empress Catherine had famously written to Voltaire, 'I now love to distraction gardens in the English style',[30] so undulating lawns and wooded walks were much in vogue; when Catherine died in 1796 her successor Tsar Paul and his Tsarina Maria were both keen gardeners, and appointed Fraser as their collector. In 1808–9 Fraser and his son (also John) returned to

America to follow William Bartram's footsteps into the Blue Ridge Mountains, from where they brought *Rhododendron catawbiense* to Britain, and presumably Russia. The craze for *le jardin anglais*, gardens of rural beauty and romantic freedoms, spread throughout the aristocracy returning to their estates in Russia and through the courts of Europe. The Dresden nursery of Traugott Jacob Seidel (1775–1858) and his brother Jacob Friedrich (1789–1860) was set up in 1813, firstly for camellias because they did so well in these cold gardens, but azaleas and rhododendrons were soon added.[31] The Seidel brothers began with *catawbiense*, and the European species *hirsutum* and *ferrugineum* (the alpenrose), but rapidly expanded; their 1846 list offers dozens of their own hybrids, many of which may be flowering still in the old gardens of Europe.

Bartram's boxes had instigated the first wave of rhododendron popularity; within 50 years from the coincidence of the old King's Botanist's death and the birth of the new America, they had started to reclaim their primeval territories. The Turkish *ponticum* had mated with the American Pinxterbloom (*periclymenoides*) to produce the bluish-mauve 'Odoratum', now acknowledged as the first hybrid in Britain and 'recorded' at Edinburgh Botanics 'by 1814'.[32] *Ponticum x nudiflorum*, the pink scented azalea recorded as a Collinson introduction of 1734 and therefore in one of the first of Bartram's boxes, produced 'Azaleoides'; both 'Odoratum' and 'Azaleoides' came from the Mile End nursery, now Thompson and Gordon's (the son of Lord Petre's ex-gardener James Gordon), who had supplied the plants for Francis Douce's Gower Street garden. (Both hybrids were also strictly azaleodendrons, two of a select company of hybrids before the term was abandoned.) Marriages were also arranged between *catawbiense* and *ponticum*, *ponticum* and *dauricum*, *maximum* and *ponticum*. No one was to be left out. Happily or unhappily the eternal triangle was formed when Francis Buchanan-Hamilton of Calcutta Botanic Garden sent seeds of the Indian giant, the blood-red *Rhododendron arboreum*, in 1810, and its white-flowered variety, some ten years later, to Britain. *Arboreum* crosses produced a stream of gorgeous plants. *Arboreum* crossed with a *catawbiense x ponticum* hybrid produced the celebrated 'Altaclerense' at Highclere Castle in Hampshire in 1831. But, besides the purposeful crosses, carefully made by gardeners with paintbrushes in private, to unite colour, scent and large flowers to hardiness, shiny evergreen leaves and variations in size, or any combination of all of these, out in the open the rhododendrons of East and West rather rejoiced in being together again. In other words, Mother Nature was rather good at hybridising, too; rhododendrons were soon dropping their seedlings like new-born lambs or baby rabbits, and gardeners and foresters were gleefully gathering them up and replanting them everywhere.

Any understanding of rhododendron habits – essentially, they are robustly promiscuous – which no one on this side of the Atlantic seemed to possess in this post-Bartram bonanza, should have been a warning. If a plant had been around for millions of years might it not just be a little persistent? Alternatively, now, less than 200 years later, are the places where rhododendrons thrive not harbouring the blood lines from Bartram's boxes and the other early introductions? At Highclere Castle, in 1834, observers drooled over hundreds of 'Altaclerense' massed in two large peat beds and a 'catherine wheel' bed of flame azaleas (the peat especially imported) as well as the massed rhododendrons around Milford Lake in Highclere Park; the coloured masses still flower around the lake and are a National Collection of azaleodendron hybrids. At Wentworth Castle, where Joachim Loddiges proudly sent his first *ponticum* seedlings, there are now 40 acres of species rhododendrons (and probably a few hybrids) including the National Collection of *falconeri* and her taxonomic relatives. At Clumber in Nottinghamshire the *ponticum x maximum x arboreum* hybrids are massed in cloudmountains of mauve-pinky-purples around the lake and along the walks near the ruined house; the 1st Duke of Newcastle was a Bartram box customer, and the 2nd Duke a great country sportsman, with his Clumber spaniels, who planted rhododendrons for

Chamaerhododendros lauri-folio semper virens (*Rhododendron maximum*) by George Ehret
(1708–70) from Mark Catesby's *Natural History of Carolina, Florida & the Bahama Islands*,
published 1731–43. The kalmia (*Chamaedaphne semper virens*) is by Catesby (1679–1749),
though copied from Ehret, and he 'broke' the stem to fit the page.

Azalea pontica (*Rhododendron luteum*), the poison honey azalea, by Sydenham Teast Edwards (1769–1819), 1799, for the *Botanical Magazine* no. 13, plate 433.

Tab. I.

RHODODENDRON DALHOUSIÆ, Hook. fil.

(in its native locality.)

Rhododendron dalhousiae by Walter Hood Fitch (1817–92), hand-coloured lithograph based on Hooker's sketch for *Rhododendrons of Sikkim-Himalaya*, 1849-51.

Rhododendron ferrugineum by Marianna Kneller for *The Book of Rhododendrons*, 1995.

OPPOSITE Larachmhor, Inverness-shire, the remains of John Holms' house, where his big species rhododendrons (*Rh. sinogrande* inset) still thrive and flower.

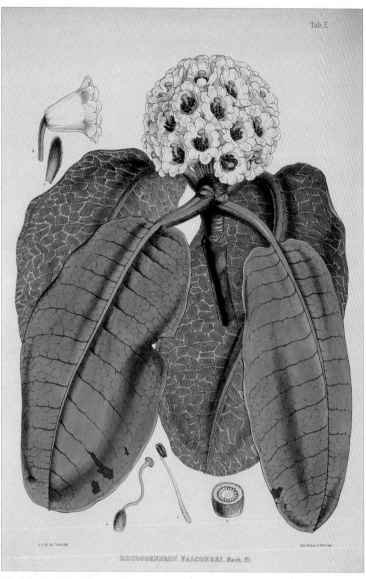

Tab. X

RHODODENDRON FALCONERI, Hook. fil.

Rhododendron falconeri by Walter Hood Fitch (1817–92), lithograph from Hooker's pencil and watercolour sketch for *Rhododendrons of Sikkim-Himalaya*, 1849-51.

PREVIOUS PAGE Alessandro Sanquirico (1777–1849), *Interno di una serra* (Inside a Hothouse) aquatint from *Raccolta di varie decorazioni*, published in Milan, 1829. Huge rhododendrons are flowering in pots on the left and reaching for the roof amongst the cacti, ferns and palms.

his game coverts. These mauve-pink giants of Clumber have great presence; they are the silent witnesses from the days of dreaming of an empire in the West.

America's first President, George Washington, was a gardener, though farming was 'his greatest pleasure': 'I think with you', he wrote to Alexander Spotswood on 13 February 1788, 'that the life of a Husbandman of all others is the most delectable. It is honorable. It is amusing, and, with judicious management, it is profitable.'[33] Washington led a breed of Americans who farmed with pride, loving their land and its native trees and flowers; it was as if honest John Bartram had been born again, a thousandfold. George Washington (as well as the other gardening president Thomas Jefferson) had gone to Bartram's Nurseries for plants and advice, and like the old botanist, both presidents were as interested in native plants as in curious imports. Washington had brought the Pinxterbloom into his garden; this flower, *Rhododendron periclymenoides*, was named by the Dutch settlers for its Whitsuntide bloom; it can have large, fleshy galls, pleasantly acid in flavour (at least to the early settlers), which were called Pinxter Apples.

The plantation owners of the South were the other great gardeners and rather a different breed: rich, sophisticated, inclined to send their sons to school in England, to make their formal gardens in the French fashion and improve the native plants, their whole economy and everything they did dependent upon their slaves. The Middletons of Middleton Place in South Carolina imported the evergreen, scarlet-flowered *Rhododendron indicum* (which the Americans continue to call *Azalea indica*, though it was sometimes thought to be Chinese but finally settled upon as a native of Japan) to enliven the deciduous flame azaleas that they gathered from the wild. This, and to a lesser extent other imports, was to have an amazing effect on the antebellum plantation gardens of the South; but first came Armageddon.

After the Civil War everything was different. There is a romantic story that General Robert E. Lee refused to turn his cannons on a beautiful Virginian house and garden during the battle of Fredericks-burg, even though the house was full of Union troopers, because it was the garden where he had proposed to his wife, Mary Randolph Custis.[34] But mostly neither side held their fire; the Civil War was the first war to be photographed, and one peculiar image, taken from the roof of Oak Island plantation house on Edisto Island in South Carolina, shows the Union soldiery going about their daily business amongst the ravaged flower beds, arbours and fountains of a once lovely garden. When peace came, in the spring of 1865, most of these signs of civilisation, and much more, had perished. Gardens may seem an inconsequent loss in war, but this is a story of gardens, and for America the Civil War severed the connection between the Bartrams' days and ours.

The South, where most of the rhododendron gardens were, was poor, and the plantation owners in their crumbling antebellum mansions ('too poor to paint, too proud to whitewash'),[35] who imagined themselves as beleaguered Cavalier gentry wearing 'Old South' as a badge of honour, were thrown back on their own resources. At Magnolia Plantation in South Carolina, the Drayton family mansion had been burned in the war, so the Revd John Grimké Drayton (who had inherited his 1,800 acre (750 ha.) plan-tation in 1836) sold off all but 50 (20 ha.) acres and moved into a cottage. The 50 acres became his magnificent garden, rhododen-drons and azaleas gathered in from the wild, as George Washington had done at Mount Vernon, but in Drayton's case he had hybridised the deciduous natives with the evergreen, scarlet *Rhododendron indicum*, known as Satsuki-tsutsutsi, the Fifth Month Azalea, for its June blossom, the fifth month of the old Chinese calendar. (The first Indian azaleas in the South are claimed to have been planted by Hamilton Boykin at his garden, The Terraces, in La Grange, Georgia, in 1841.)[36]

The hybrid azaleas and the moss-hung live oaks have persisted as the starring images of the Carolina Low Country gardens that are now world famous. Middleton Place added a 'mere' 35,000 azaleas to its green terraces, butterfly lakes and camellias in the 1920s; Cypress Gardens, 'a sort of Miltonic hymn to wilderness', had 'floating islands of pale or fiery azaleas, [the] dizzying sweetness of *Daphne odora* in the air, thick fringes of daffodils, and extraordinary birds – white owlets peering soberly down from nests in the cypress crowns' – and, all-pervasive, 'the play of reflections in the water, and the pleasure of wandering silently by boat on the surface of black streams lit by those bright mirrored flowers'.[37]

Magnolia Garden (no one would call their home Rhododendron!) was seen by the garden-traveller, Marion Cran, in 1930, despite her better judgement. She did not particularly like rhododendrons and azaleas, but felt thoroughly browbeaten by everyone – from New York to California – saying that she must see them, so she made her way back to Charleston. 'Azaleas had filled the town', but she had pre-booked so there was no escape; she felt garden indigestion coming on, maybe she would be disappointed. Her host Mr Schuyler Parsons mused:

'Some people like Middleton best; but I advise you to see Magnolia first.'

'Magnolia?'

'Yes, – it is called Magnolia garden, but it is famous for its azaleas' . . .

I girded up my loins and went.

I could hardly have approached one of the great emotional experiences of my life in a more ungracious mood . . .

All that there is of rebel in me – all that tugs against the everlasting *laid-out* gardens, against the coerced corseted beauty of formal terraces . . . found kinship here . . . I stood at last in a garden of form purely informal – in that which I had longed for always and never found perfectly expressed . . . imagination of a delicacy and of a strength, in perfect sympathy with the spirit of its surroundings . . .

One has to imagine green lawns and winding paths, banks of camellia Japonica thirty feet high, towering trees hung with long trails of the green moss with golden Banksian roses, mauve and white wisterias, yellow jasmine and Cherokee roses sprawl-

ing and scrambling . . . blood red camellias, snow drifts of dogwood, tender foliage of tulip trees, slender crepe myrtle and
garlands of bridal wreath spirea, are there out-dazzled by the
blazing banks of azaleas – and all reflected back from the clear,
black water of the cypress ponds[38]

John Drayton's garden was made from the inspiration of a tour
of England and Europe and the works of Repton and *le jardin
anglais*, but the warm South contrived an un-English potency.
Marion Cran was shown around in the evening light by Drayton's
grandson, a host 'who knew when to turn away and leave me alone'.
She was, she said, 'not expecting furnaces of red twenty feet high'.
Nor perhaps the 'wild tranquillity', the 'passionate peace'. Magnolia
was 'made by a poet out of the stuff of dreams . . . the Mecca of
all my garden wanderings; it is the place to which unknowing but
obstinate I have striven all my days; among the great green oaks
and seven veils of floating Spanish moss shines the Holy Grail. The
heart of a man burns steadily there, on a furnace of colour in a
garden shade.'[39]

Others were equally enthralled; here is Owen Wister, a friend of
Edith Wharton and Henry James, taking his deep azalea-draught:

in the grey gloom of those trees veiled and muffled in their long
webs and skeins of hanging moss, a great magic flame of rose
and red and white burned steadily. You looked to see it vanish.
You could not imagine that such a thing would stay. All idea
of individual petals or species was swept away in this glowing
maze of splendour, this transparent labyrinth of rose red and
white through which you looked beyond, into the grey gloom
of the hanging moss and the depths of the wild forest trees . . .
Burning, glowing, and shining like some miracle, some rainbow
exorcism . . .[40]

In 1906, with the publication of *The Man of Property*, the first
part of his *Forsyte Saga*, John Galsworthy gave Magnolia a fictional
fame. He sent Irene's architect-lover Philip Bosinney there, and
made Bosinney feel that all the great gardens of Europe, the Boboli,
Versailles, Hampton Court, the Alhambra and even La Mortola,

took second place to 'this kind of paradise which has wandered down' with its brilliant azaleas 'around a pool of dreamy water overhung by tall trunks wanly festooned with the grey Florida moss'. Bosinney sat there, day after day 'drawn as by visions of the Ionian Sea – paralysed by the absurdity of capturing it with his paintbrush'.[41]

Magnolia's 'rainbow exorcism' was launched on to the tourist map, and the 1937 Baedeker Guide gave the garden double stars for its beauty. Only three places in America were honoured with such high praise, and the other two were the Grand Canyon and Niagara Falls.

Which brings us back to the less enchanted subject of eastern America's ravaged landscape, the natural home of the rhododendrons, in the post-Civil War years. The plantation gardens were as a silken fringe on a moth-eaten tapestry; from Maryland to Georgia the Appalachian edens that William Bartram had seen were vanished, his friendly Creeks and Seminoles had been cheated of their lands with false promises and hounded westwards into plains America, their woods and groves left to the mercy of the lumbermen. The lumbermen returned with renewed vigour after the war and the giant oaks, chestnuts, hickories, maples and walnuts were felled and dragged away in the mud, to be converted into davenports and wardrobes.

The (very) British naturalist, Henry John Elwes (1846–1922) (a Victorian combination of the Davids Attenborough and Bellamy), travelled through the Blue Ridge country in 1895; he found 'slovenly and neglected' farms, bare-footed and sickly looking white women hoeing the corn and he shared boiled pork and corn mush, served by a gaunt woman to an old man and his surly grandson. When they realised he was a 'bug-sharp' they accepted him as harmless; the old man's son and two other grandsons had just been killed in a family feud. This poor white farming countryside, peopled by 'a very peculiar race' in Elwes' opinion, quite unlike any other Americans he had met, also yielded a timber merchant's agent rubbing his hands with glee over a parcel of 160,000 (70,000 ha.) acres of virgin forest he had the option to buy. There were still patches of lovely woods, even if the valuable walnuts had been hauled out, which reminded Elwes strongly of the Himalayan temperate forest; he climbed the Ridge 'to a beautiful open top with groves of spruce, azaleas, and other trees and shrubs'.[42]

Elwes, who found his journey worthwhile for the rare butterflies, had heard of the rhododendron country of the South from Charles Sprague Sargent (1841–1927), director of Harvard's Arnold Arboretum. Sargent is the linchpin in America's rhododendron story, because they were his favourites and he was in the best position to forward their interests.

Sargent was actually a man of three great passions: for his family, the Arnold Arboretum and rhododendrons, though I cannot vouch for the order. He was born in 1841, to the wealth and privilege of a great Boston Brahmin family (John Singer Sargent was his cousin), Harvard, of course (where he graduated 88th in his class of 90), then to the Civil War in the Union army, spending most of his time in New Orleans. After the war he travelled in Europe; when he returned he was given the job of managing his father's Brookline estate outside Boston and, having no other ambitions, in a short time he became deeply interested in botany and horticulture. It was *where* he was that was special.

A home-grown genius, Andrew Jackson Downing, author of *A Treatise of the Theory and Practice of Landscape Gardening* (1841), in his 6th edition of 1859, wrote: 'the whole of the neighbourhood of Brookline is a kind of landscape garden, and there is nothing in America of the sort, so inexpressibly charming, as the lanes which lead from one cottage, or villa, to another. No animals are allowed to run at large, and the open gates, with tempting vistas and glimpses under the pendent boughs, give it quite an Arcadian air of rural freedom and enjoyment.' Downing singled out the 20 acres around the Lee family 'cottage' as 'not only a most instructive place to the amateur of landscape-gardening, but to the naturalist and lover of plants': 'Every shrub seems placed precisely in the soil and aspect it likes best, and native and foreign rhododendrons, kalmias, and other rare shrubs are seen here in the finest condition.'[43] The Lees' house and land were added to the Sargent estate – which became Charles Sargent's Holm Lea, complete with rhododendrons – and the 'foreign' plants included the first to come from Japan.

Behind this euology the villas and 'cottages' of Brookline sheltered an ecological elite, into which Sargent slipped as of right, an elite which was to spin the thread of pastoralism across America from Walden Pond to Yosemite. They included Harvard's Professor of Natural History, the botanist Asa Gray, Darwin's correspondent, who had received his package of Hooker's rhododendrons from the Himalayas, and the man who created the history of the young America, Francis Parkman (1823–93), a keen botanical gardener whose garden overlooked Jamaica Pond, where he tended some of the first plants from Japan. These came as a result of Commodore Matthew C. Perry's gunboat 'persuasion' of the Japanese after he had sailed his flotilla, his steam frigate *Susquehanna* in the lead, into Tokyo Bay. Commodore Perry's winning of the Treaty of Kanagawa on 31 March 1854 opened Japan to Westerners after her two centuries' isolation. Immediately 'Westerners' included American botanists: the dogwood (*Cornus kousa*), *Rhododendron brachycarpum* (good for hardiness, evergreen with large creamy-white flower heads), crab apples and umbrella pines were amongst the first plants to reach Brookline, just as everyone's eyes turned to the Civil War. Lee and Parkman tended them safely until it was all over.

Where Sargent conceived his passion for rhododendrons I cannot say, but they were a plant on the right scale and opulence for his tastes. In November 1873 he married his domestic goddess, the sweet and sentimental Mary Robeson, and they settled into their long and devoted family life in all the comforts of Holm Lea – now an enormous and rambling house full of rooms, each overstuffed with polished mahogany sideboards, bowls of flowers, chintz-covered chairs, velvet-tasselled sofas, stools for feet, tables for books and stands for pots and pots of exotic and exciting plants. Two days prior to his wedding, Sargent, at 32, had been appointed director of Harvard's new Arnold Arboretum at nearby Jamaica Plain, with the support of President Eliot of Harvard and his distinguished cohort of the landscape 'doyen', Downing, the botanist, Asa Gray, Professor Parkman and other Brookline relations and friends. (Sargent had already succeeded Parkman as Professor of Horticulture, but it was a role he soon shed; he never gave a lecture, but his family always called him the Professor.) To his staff at the Arnold he was their 'Chief'.

The arboretum, still only rather muddy farmland, was to be designed by Frederick Law Olmsted (1822–1903), the designer of New York's Central Park and Boston's 'emerald necklace' park system. It, too, was to be park-like, and open to the public, but the first purpose was to grow living collections of trees and shrubs arranged in their systematic orders to emphasise their similarities and differences, and especially to celebrate the American native plants and show them to their people. Sargent's work was driven by two great visionaries, George Perkins Marsh (1801–82) and Asa Gray. The ecologist Marsh warned that the greedy and uncontrolled felling of forests would have dreadful consequences for the river systems, and contribute to flooding and soil erosion. Forestry as a science did not exist in America and botany was exclusive to Asa Gray, Sargent and a few others at Harvard; they feared that the botanists' lifeblood, 'diversity', was threatened and whole species might disappear before anyone knew that they even existed. Gray, asked by the Secretary of the Interior to suggest someone to take on a federal project to identify the trees of America, named Sargent. In January 1880 Sargent wrote to George Perkins Marsh: 'I have undertaken to prepare . . . a monograph of our forests. This seems a hopeless undertaking and will keep me very busy, but it is not without advantages to the Arboretum as it will enable me to travel widely and collect.'[44]

He started in the South; whether he had more trees felled in the name of science or haggled with the lumbermen is not recorded, but the collection of 500 tree trunk sections of different species were displayed at the Museum of Natural History in New York in 1893, along with Mary Robeson Sargent's exquisite botanical watercolours of each leaf, flower and fruit. The whole collection has since disappeared without trace.

The immediate outcome of Sargent's interest in the woods of America was that Olmsted and Sargent helped George Washington Vanderbilt spend some of his fortune on his Biltmore Estate at Asheville in North Carolina. Some 125,000 acres (50,000 ha.) (allowing for a vast chateau and 35 acres (15 ha.) of gardens, an arboretum and tree nursery) were reafforested or restored to agriculture, after soil erosion. Biltmore dealt in superlatives: 250 rooms in the chateau, 2,500 roses in the rose garden, 'a real working deer park, grandest symbol of European aristocracy', an immense model dairy farm, and 265 miles of trails in the forest. Olmsted's 'wild' landscaping still shelters the 'most complete collection of wild azaleas in the United States'. This was made by the estate superintendent, a Cornell-educated Canadian named Chauncy Beadle, who was recruited by Olmsted and stayed for 55 years. In the 1930s Beadle, a chauffeur and two doctors, calling themselves the 'azalea hunters' scoured the eastern mountains for all the vanishing species they could find. In 1940 the collection contained more than 3,000 plants in fourteen species with some natural hybrids and variations.[45]

Back at the Arnold Arboretum in 1890, Sargent was firmly established at his director's big desk, where he recalled Professor Asa Gray's observations on the similarities of the ecologies of eastern North America and eastern Asia. The political omens were good and with some sort of blessing from Washington, the Arnold adopted an extended mission, a horticultural twinning, that would reunite the plants of America with their Eastern cousins, something that had not been done since the birth of the earth. Sargent intended to send his own collectors to Japan and China, but decided that firstly, in the summer of 1892, he would go himself. He travelled west on the Canadian Pacific to Vancouver and took ship for Yokohama, then went north to Hokkaido. After making some courtesy calls and useful contacts he botanised in the forests where the torch azalea *Rhododendron kaempferi* is common, collected seeds of this, to him, almost mythical azalea and of magnolias (though not *Magnolia sargentiana*, which had to wait until Wilson collected it in 1908), of the white-blossomed Sargent crab, *Malus sargentii*, and *Prunus sargentii*, the stunning cherry which many say is the finest of all, with its single pink flowers and an autumn performance of orange and crimson tints.[46]

It may come as little surprise that this terse, imperturbable autocrat, who seemed to name everything for himself, closely resembled the Prince of Wales (who became Edward VII in 1901), except that Sargent's mien was one of hard work rather than soft pleasures. He was an impressive man, borne out by John Muir's recollection of climbing Grandfather Mountain in western North Carolina with him. Muir began:

> I couldn't hold in, and began to jump about and sing and glory in it all. Then I happened to look around and catch sight of Sargent, standing there as cool as a rock, with a half-amused look on his face at me, but never saying a word.
>
> 'Why don't you let yourself out at a sight like that?' I asked.
> 'I don't wear my heart upon my sleeve,' he retorted.
> 'Who cares where you wear your little heart, mon?' I cried. 'There you stand in the face of all Heaven, come down to earth, like a critic of the universe, as if to say, "Come, Nature, bring on the best you have, I'm from Boston!"'[47]

But of course Sargent did care – he and Olmsted and Muir were united in the cause of the redwoods of Calaveras county, and of the national parks Yosemite and Yellowstone.

The pride of Sargent's heart, his rhododendrons, bloomed at Holm Lea where springs and early summers were celebrated by massed flowers, with streams of admiring visitors. The collection was care-

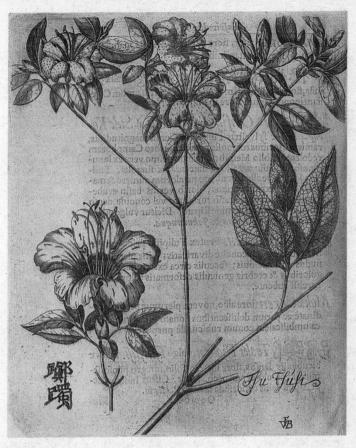

Rhododendron kaempferi, named for the German Engelbert Kaempfer (1651–1716) and illustrated in his *Amoenitates exoticae*, 1712, first published in English in 1727.

fully planted. The architectural writer, Mariana van Renssalaer, wrote admiringly, 'all those of defective form or with blossoms of unpleasing colour have been weeded out, so that no discordant note mars their blaze of purple, crimson, and white'.[48] Banks of 30-foot-high rhododendrons covered with flowers (which must have

Holm Lea, Charles Sprague Sargent's home in Brookline, an engraving of
the 1890s showing the rhododendrons as the chief feature of the large
and splendid garden.

been Lee's early plantings) stood next to the house; the enormous
house was almost covered in honeysuckles, and drifts of yellow
water iris fringed the distant lake, with more and more banks of
rhododendrons and azaleas. But Holm Lea's speciality was the awn-
ing that shaded the wide terrace around the house, sheltering the
massed flowers, tender azaleas, camellias and scented pelargoniums,
from the hottest sun, which made Holm Lea, at the celebratory
time of year, rather like living in a flower show tent. Brookline
neighbours admired each other's displays; Sargent's cousinly rivalry
was with Horatio Hollis Hunnewell at Wellesley, who had been
keeping up with his botanical relative. Hunnewell's diary is full of

similar entries for those late 1890s summers: 'June 8: The azalea garden is superb . . . The rhododendrons are not quite in full flower. Fine plants of "C. S. Sargent" and "Mrs Sargent" are just coming into flower; also "F. L. Ames", which I consider one of the very best perfectly hardy varieties that we have . . .'

And on 11 June:

> Rhododendrons, if possible, finer than ever! All agree there is no shrub to compare with them for grand effect. Those in the lattice tent are much admired – the foliage under the lattice shade being very dark green, equal to any in the English climate, owing to the partial shade they get under the lattice, which is very similar to what they have in the cloudy English climate. Had many visitors today: Mrs Nat Thayer and daughters . . . Mrs. F. L. Ames, Mrs. Montgomery Sears, Professor and Mrs. Sargent, Miss Jones . . .[49]

'Miss Jones' was Sargent's protégée who became America's most famous woman landscape architect and garden designer, Beatrix Jones Farrand (1872–1959). In her long career designing dozens of gardens, most notably those at Dumbarton Oaks in Washington DC, she was perhaps more even-handed about rhododendrons than her 'Chief' but she did prove how well they would grow as far north as her native Maine. At the end of her career many of her collection, of which some had come from the Arnold Arboretum (Beatrix hardly ever left empty-handed after a visit when her 'Chief' was alive), were taken to the Asticou Azalea Gardens in Northeast Harbor, where they flower still.[50]

Professor Sargent had his failings, but not as far as his precious rhododendrons and azaleas were concerned. Ernest 'Chinese' Wilson (1876–1930), warned that he was autocratic, found him the 'kindliest of autocrats' and after their first meeting when Wilson was en route to China for the first time in 1899, they became firm friends. Sargent had great faith in Wilson's systematic way of working in the field, of identifying likely flowers in the spring and returning to the same places for seeds later, and in his knowledge

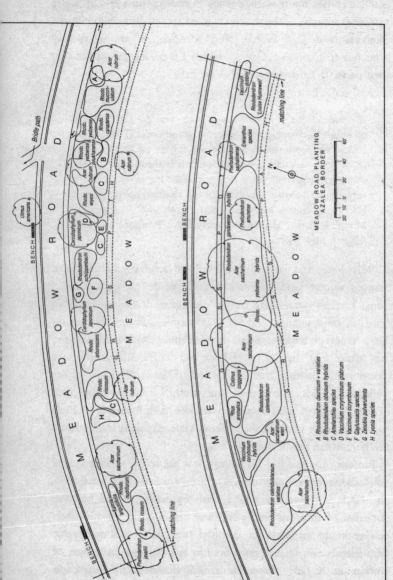

Beatrix Farrand (1872–1959), plan for the azalea border at the Arnold Arboretum, carried out in the late 1940s and published in *Arnoldia*, 15 April 1949.

Ernest 'Chinese' Wilson (1876–1930), on the left, and Charles Sprague Sargent (1841–1927) in front of *Prunus subhirtella*, the Higan cherry, at the Arnold Arboretum.

of which plants were botanically interesting. After a second Chinese trip shared with Veitch's Nursery, Sargent lured Wilson to work at the Arnold, and with his wife Helen and their daughter Muriel Primrose (born May 1906), he moved to Boston. There were two more Chinese trips (one, in February 1910, travelling overland via Siberia) and Wilson earned his fame for *Lilium regale*, the blue poppy, the paperbark maple and many rhododendrons. His triumphs though were to come in his trips to Japan, island hopping the Ryukyus that string like pearls through the East China Sea to Taiwan and across to Korea. He liked Korea, despite the evidence of large-scale deforestation, and thought that the pink and white azaleas on the Diamond Mountains (which are now in North Korea) exceeded anything he had seen in Sichuan or Japan. The pearly-pink flowered *Rhododendron schlippenbachii*, mixed with *Magnolia sieboldii*, dominating the undergrowth for miles and blooming to perfection, must have been a breathtaking sight, even for an experienced plant hunter. And, of course, there was more to come: his trip to Kurume on the southernmost Japanese island of Kyushu, where he had heard of the dwarf hybrid azaleas first raised in the early nineteenth century and kept a fine secret for a hundred years. He was welcomed by Mr Kijiro Akashi, who had already devoted 40 years of his life to his plants; he had some 250 different varieties and Wilson chose his famous 'Fifty' for introduction to America.[51]

When Charles Sargent died 'with his boots on' in March 1927 he had ensured his beloved rhododendrons their twentieth-century popularity and success.[52] He had shared Wilson's finds generously, he had introduced to the West Dr Emil Bretschneider (1833–1901), a former physician at the Russian legation in Peking (Beijing) whose *Botanicon sinicon*, notes on Chinese botany from native and western sources (1895–8), at last produced a 'hymn sheet' common to botanists of East and West. Dr Bretschneider and the Arnold's Dr Alfred Rehder (1863–1949) were to be stalwarts of rhododendron taxonomy. And Sargent had made rhododendrons fashionable in eastern America, so that his former pupil and discerning millionaire, Henry F. du Pont, made Winterthur in Delaware his woodland garden 'the equal of Bodnant or Exbury'[53] with its azalea woods flowering in creams and soft pinks.

Sargent, though no one mentions it, was as near a successor to old John Bartram – a President's Botanist? – as anyone of his day. Ernest Wilson succeeded him as director at the Arnold and the future was set fair; but the Wilsons, Ernest and Helen, were both killed in a car crash in 1930 after visiting their daughter, Muriel Primrose.

The rhododendrons' story must move elsewhere.

CHAPTER FOUR

What James, Harry and Clara Did

IT IS ONE OF THE QUIRKS of history that a man may look at a flower on a fine morning, let it be an April morning, and, so long as he notes down his chance encounter, his name will pass to posterity for the sake of this inauspicious moment. So it was on a spring morning in 1796 that a certain Captain Thomas Hardwicke, leading an armed mission to pay a friendly visit to the ruler of Garhwal at Srinagar, and given permission by the East India Company to botanise along the way, found a tall red rhododendron tree in flower while he was passing through Kumaon district, south-east of Dehra Dun. In truth it was hardly a 'find', for these red rhododendrons, called *bruans*, or *bras*, or *barahke-phool*, were one of the most common plants of northern India, seen by millions of eyes, the flowers and leaves traditionally tied into long ropes for temple decorations, the petals freshly gathered for chutneys and jellies and pressed for a soft cooling drink. It was known that the young leaves relieved headaches if laid on the brow, so this was a plant thoroughly absorbed into the domestic habits of the ancient villages from Uttar Pradesh to Kashmir. But Captain Hardwicke was a stranger, and he was British, so he had *discovered* the glorious *Rhododendron arboreum* and his name was to be blessed by botanists for evermore.

Of course, she should have been called the Indian rhododendron, but Linnaeus had already given the name *indica* to the quite different evergreen azalea, a small plant with large flowers, which had come to him from America but was known to have originated elsewhere. (Even so it was wrongly named, for the azalea came not from India but Japan.) So *Rhododendron arboreum*, the tree-like rose tree, she became, an elegant giant happily growing to 65 ft, and equally happily covering herself with gorgeous blood-red flowers. Soon her wonders multiplied, pink and white varieties were found, and her range broadened to the Nilgiri Hills in south India and to mountain groves in Nepal and Bhutan. *Rhododendron arboreum* inspired the British love for rhododendrons as souvenirs of the Raj.

Since the days of Marco Polo the only strangers to brave the high passes of the Himalayas had been Jesuit missionaries and Capuchin monks – that is until the British came to India. Some 30 years before Hardwicke had captured his rhododendrons, a Captain Kinloch leading a British 'mission' to Nepal had become the first Briton to set eyes on the greatest mountain range in the world. After that the missions, which loom so large in imperial histories, were regularly setting out from Dehra Dun or Darjeeling, heading northwards. The thin red lines of soldiers, muffled against the snow or the sun, crossed and recrossed the homelands of the rhododendrons – where they drift and flower for enormous distances along the ranges from Assam through Bhutan, Nepal and Kashmir and up through the valleys to the Tibetan Plateau – but invariably with other purposes than botanising.

The failure of the monsoon in 1769 and resulting famine in Bengal spurred the East India Company (who were largely blamed for the famine) to look northwards. Captain Kinloch tried Bhutan after Nepal, but ran into trouble with bandits and so Bhutan was always marked 'unexplored' on the map. Warren Hastings (1732–1818) sent two expeditions to Tibet, first his friend George Bogle in 1774, and then his cousin Samuel Turner; the lure was cashmere wool, walnuts, madder and musk. Bogle saw the precious stones and furs, silver-chased saddles, tea and tobacco of the tribute missions setting out for China, and came home with his head full of legends of the great ants who threw up sandhills of gold, and the River of Golden Sands, as the Yangtze was known.[1] Turner was really looking beyond Tibet to China and the possibility of establishing by degrees an immediate intercourse with that empire, as Hastings had instructed him. He was interested in the topography but not, apparently, in the flowers. However, one of Hastings' last acts before he resigned and went home to his own garden at Daylesford in Gloucestershire in 1785 was to sign an order setting up the Company Botanic Gardens, which were to concentrate upon economic botany; Bogle had reported in detail on the fertile fields and abundant crops of Assam, and tea, coffee, cotton, tobacco, spices and sago were to be developed commercially in northern India. In contrast to this domesticated vision, the mountain country of Tibet flaunted its medievalism. The warlike Gurkhas raided the Panchen Lama's monastery at Tashilhunpo (which had withstood the Mongols), taking the treasures of centuries. Emperor Qianlong sent his Manchu army over the passes in the winter of 1792, marches of greater endurance than Hannibal's crossing of the Alps, the Gurkhas were defeated, and the Tibetans cowed under the rule of a Chinese Representative, the Amban.[2] The British decided it was best to approach China by the front door after all, sending Lord Macartney's lavishly endowed embassy to Peking in 1793. Macartney's page was the botanically minded and precocious 11-year-old George Staunton, who had learned Chinese from the interpreters on the voyage from England. Staunton reported in detail on the imperial garden at Gengde, 'The Mountain Manor for Escaping the Summer Heat', and its lovely lake reflecting picturesque temples, bridges, thousands of trees and the misty mountains, but he did not mention the rhododendrons.[3]

Captain Hardwicke found his *arboreum* in flower, but had no chance to collect seeds in that spring of 1796. At Calcutta's Botanic Garden at Sibpur, the superintendent William Roxburgh (1751–1815), enormously knowledgeable on northern Indian plants of all kinds, took *arboreum* in his stride; Roxburgh was a modest, frail Scot, one of the first serious 'economic botanists' in our modern sense, concerned with the cycles of drought and famine and experimenting with the large-scale planting of Bengal teak for amelioration of the climate as well as profit. Roxburgh brought *arboreum* into the Botanic Garden, including it in his *Hortus bengalensis* of 1814,[4] but it was his friend and colleague Francis Buchanan-Hamilton (1762–1829)[5] who collected the seeds and sent them to England in 1809 or 1810. Buchanan-Hamilton also found the white flowered *arboreum* and the smaller scented-leaved *anthopogon*, known as *talis* in Punjabi and *talisfar* in Kashmiri (its leaves are used as a stimulant in ayurvedic medicine), which is common above 10,000 feet from Kashmir to Bhutan. He sent seeds of these to the Royal Botanic Garden in Edinburgh in 1820.

The blood-red *arboreum* flowered at Alexander Baring's garden, The Grange at Northington near Alresford in Hampshire, in 1825, an event as long-hoped-for as a royal birth. A marriage was arranged for the following year, May 1826, when at least one truss of the red blooms was carefully settled into a box of damp moss, for a journey through that soft Hampshire landscape of fields and woods, through spring green and may-blossomed lanes to East Stratton, Micheldever and Whitchurch, a journey of some twenty miles to Lord Carnarvon's Highclere Castle. There the flowers were unwrapped with solemn care, and – finest squirrel-hair brushes at the ready – *arboreum*'s pollen was 'painted' on to the stamens of a specially bred and flowering child of a mating of the American *catawbiense* and the Mediterranean *ponticum*. It was a marriage of East and West, of the Old and New World species, which the rhododendron enthusiasts (a newish breed in themselves) hoped would produce a race of hardy, late-flowering gorgeous blooms for the cool temperate gardens of England. Eighteen hundred seedlings were reared from the marriage, named 'Altaclerense' in honour of their birthplace, and some were distributed to other gardens and nurseries. Highclere and its head gardener James Gowen and 'Altaclerense' had set the rhododendron fashion. Everyone wanted them now. Large and established nurseries such as John Pearson of Chilwell, Nottingham,

Dickson's of Chester, John Veitch of Exeter and the celebrated Handsworth Nursery in Sheffield featured them in their catalogues, and clamoured for more. Especially for more of *arboreum*'s cousins from the East.

To return to the Calcutta Botanic Garden where the charms of sago and tea were rather upstaged by the rhododendrons: William Roxburgh had returned home in 1814, hoping to mend his health, but he died in Edinburgh the following year; his friend Buchanan-Hamilton had followed him as superintendent, but only for a year before he retired to Scotland and the life of a highland gentleman-scholar at Leny near Callander. The next superintendent was Nathaniel Wallich (1786–1854, a doctor, born in Copenhagen); Wallich went to Kathmandu in 1820 but was not allowed any further, so he persuaded some Indian pilgrims to collect seeds for him. As a result of this ruse he sent seeds of many of the great Himalayan species rhododendrons (the white flowered *arboreum*, *campbelliae* and *cinnamoneum* among them) to Edinburgh Botanics, but they could not be labelled, as he had no names for them. At least, from the pilgrims' report, he knew of their existence, but it seemed they were in forbidden territories.

It was now certain that fabulous rhododendrons grew in the mountains, but how to reach them? Nepal was forbidden, Tibet under Chinese rule. In 1837 a young doctor and botanist, William Griffith, joined Captain Robert Boileau Pemberton's mission to Bhutan. They were gone for over a year. They trekked across the little country, less than 200 miles wide, from Dewangiri in the south-east to the (then) capital Punakha in the west. Griffith enjoyed the 'beautiful paths through fine oakwoods', more rugged paths along ridges clothed with trees covered with pendulous mosses and lichens, copses of rhododendrons, oaks, chestnuts, maples, violets and primroses with always 'the scarlet tree' *Rhododendron arboreum* in flower everywhere. Above 8,000 feet he could view 'dry open ridges covered with rhododendrons'; occasionally a delicious view of open downs, small oakwoods, and a temple with a weeping cypress hanging over it, a remote lamasery in a land ruled by its monasteries or dzongs. The Pemberton mission was scathing about the 'Booteahs' – 'pernicious priests, strangers to the truth and greedy beggars' – and applied a very British judgement, scorning their lack of horticultural skills and their haphazard reliance on semi-wild figs, oranges and nuts and subsistence farming that had not changed in centuries. Pemberton added a grudging admission that they prided themselves as fighters, perhaps because some of the Bhutanese warriors had the audacity to capture two British field guns, sparking a diplomatic incident in which dreadful reprisals would follow if the guns were not returned. They were. In Punakha, the capital, William Griffith found the royal garden 'no such thing as a flower garden, scarcely an acre of oranges, pomegranates, mangos . . . Grown by an Assamese gardener' but he approved of their taste in wild flowers. Peach, almond and pear blossoms made the spring enchanting, and the rhododendrons, red and white, were favourites and used as offerings to their priests and guests – 'they depend on their jungles for flowers,' he concluded.[6] Griffith knew that he was seeing many differing rhododendrons but he had no means of naming them. (Recently, some 160 years later, a skilled and experienced Bhutanese botanist, Rebecca Pradhan, has studied her country, particularly the areas in the south that are now national parks and wildlife sanctuaries, lands crossed by the Pemberton mission, and found 46 of the Himalayan species growing in the wild. 'In fact,' she says, 'we have no other rhododendrons to study because we have so many growing in the wild.' In central southern Bhutan, in the Thrumsing National Park, a 'rhododendron garden' has been made by simply enclosing a woodland area in which 24 different species grow, and making paths through the woods.)[7]

In 1838 the Pemberton mission's final verdict on Bhutan was damning; there were 'more natives of Pandemonium than any place on Earth's surface'. This prompted Joseph Hooker's retort to his father: 'I would not go there for the world without 500 men in front of me and as many in the rear.'[8]

In Britain the evident glory of *arboreum* and rumours of the other Himalayan species were making the case for a collecting expedition: but who was to go, and to where? As it happened, the answer was supplied in a quiet Devon churchyard, at Broadclyst near Exeter, in November 1839, when they carried old John Veitch to his rest. John Veitch was 87, a fine specimen of the dour tenacity of Scots border gardeners. He had come south to work for Sir Thomas Acland at Killerton, set up his own nursery with his employer's help, and prospered. Old John had hung on to the strings of the Veitch Nursery until almost the last. He had officially handed over to his middle-aged son James (1792–1863) in 1837, but now James felt he was really in charge. He believed that the horticultural future was in pines and evergreens, and scouting for a likely collector he lighted upon two Cornish gardeners, William (1809–64) and Thomas Lobb (1817–94), sons of the gamekeeper at Carclew, home of one of the nursery's best customers, Sir Charles Lemon. The Lobbs had a salty tang to their Cornish blood, they knew that Sir Charles gave great rewards to sea captains who brought plants home for him, and so they were keen.

William the eldest went west in November 1840; news of David Douglas' (1799–1834) terrible death in Hawaii (he fell into a bull pit and was gored by a trapped bull) had reached London in 1835 and James Veitch felt that seeds of all the wonderful pines he had found should be collected as a matter of urgency. William Lobb eventually worked his way from California to Oregon, finding along the way the Californian native which had perhaps bloomed in Aztec botanic gardens, a deliciously scented, pink-trumpeted azalea, *Rhododendron occidentale*. When Veitch received *occidentale* in 1851 it was neither named nor appreciated – 'of little value' sniffed John Lindley (1799–1865) at the Royal Horticultural Society.[9] Was it the taint of a commercial collector or Himalayan tunnel vision? *Occidentale* had to wait a long time but eventually became the parent of a race of scented, late-flowering hybrids. (William Lobb settled in California and died there.)

James Veitch sent Thomas Lobb east in 1843, to the Malay Peninsula and Burma, and he returned in 1845 with a sensational plant. 'Certainly one of the finest things ever introduced into our gardens,' trumpeted Veitch.[10] This was the first tropical rhododendron, a vireya (named in honour of a French pharmacist, Julien Joseph Virey, coined by the botanist Karel Blume). That Thomas Lobb brought it home alive 'was a very considerable feat', marvels the present-day vireya expert George Argent. 'What care and attention must have been given to these plants over a journey of many weeks by sea in closed glass Wardian cases?'[11] The bright orange flower, named *Rhododendron javanicum*, extended the plant's range southwards; Thomas Lobb found many more of the scented, colourful tender species, including an epiphyte with frilled white, yellow-throated flowers named *veitchianum*. But because of worries about the tenderness of these beauties, he turned his attention northwards. Veitch had heard that there might be a chance of access to the Himalayas.

Sir William Hooker was determined that Kew must have the status of Imperial Botanic Garden; all those Scots medics working for the British East India Company and sending their finds to Edinburgh Botanics were beginning to be irksome, especially to a former Glasgow University man. Even more galling was the general antipathy in Edinburgh to Joseph Hooker's candidacy as Professor of Botany and Regius Keeper, whose 'testimonials from nearly all the professors in the universities of Europe', and the Home Secretary, were, it was felt, 'given as a compliment to the father rather than the merit of the son'.[12] Edinburgh chose one of its own, John Hutton Balfour (1808–84) in 1845, and he was to reign for more than thirty years.

So Joseph Hooker was out of a job; he was not particularly interested in rhododendrons, being more of a mosses and lichens man as a result of his trip to Antarctica and the southern seas; he was 30 and engaged to Frances Henslow, daughter of the Professor of Botany at Cambridge. With such a demanding father *and* prospective father-in-law this tall, studious and rather vague-looking young man needed a coup. Undoubtedly primed by Sir William, Hugh Falconer in charge at Calcutta Botanic Garden was supportive and Lord Auckland, First Lord of the Admiralty, sanctioned navy half-pay and a free trip in Lord Dalhousie's party leaving on HMS *Sidon* in November 1847. So Joseph was off to India; on the overland part of the journey to Suez he tried to overcome his lordship's stated indifference to botany by showing him a piece of gum arabic, but 'he chucked it out of the carriage window'.[13]

Hooker arrived in Darjeeling in mid-April and started assembling his party of Lepcha collectors and porters, skilled woodsmen who could put up a waterproof hut out of bamboo and banana leaves in less time than it took to get wet through. He also had time to attend to his sense of wonder:

> Much as I had heard and read of the magnificence and beauty of Himalayan scenery, my highest expectations have been surpassed. I arrived at Darjeeling on a rainy misty day, which did not allow me to see ten yards in any direction, much less to descry the Snowy Range (a sixty-mile crow's flight away) . . . Early next morning I caught my first view, and I literally held my breath in awe and admiration. Six or seven successive ranges of forest-clad mountains, as high as that whereon I stood (at 8,000 feet), intervened between me and a dazzling white pile of snow-clad mountains, among which the giant peak of Kinchin-junga rose two thousand feet above the lofty point from which I gazed.[14]

Also in Darjeeling Hooker fell in with a most remarkable man, who was to enable much of his success: Brian Houghton Hodgson (1800–94).

Hodgson was a maverick Briton who knew more about Nepal than any man alive, but was not allowed to go there. He had set up home in a stone bungalow, 'Bryanstone', on a mountain ridge outside Darjeeling, with a view that Hooker sketched over and over again, and eventually turned into a watercolour illustration for his *Himalayan Journals*. In it, a yak herder comes home through almost parkland-like trees with Kangchenjunga rising above the clouds, the prospect 'commanding confessedly the greatest known landscape of snowy mountains in the Himalaya and hence in the world'.[15] Amongst the trees, in the vast distances of the snows, was rhododendron country.

But first, Hodgson had a history. He was born in Cheshire in 1800 – his father was a banker who lost all his money. At sixteen, the usual age, he was sent to Haileybury, the East India Company's college, where he was a gold medal student, with the brightest of futures. In India he was soon sent to Kathmandu, but there was too little to do so he was returned to Calcutta as a deputy secretary in the Persian department, a place for high flyers. Calcutta proved impossible because he was struck down with recurrent fevers; the high mountain air suited him, so he returned to Kathmandu. He was there for over twenty years; no white women were allowed so he took a Kashmiri Muslim common law wife with whom he lived openly and devotedly, and had two children. As there was still plenty of free time he studied every aspect of Nepalese culture, making himself the outstanding British expert, and he became an accidental botanist as he studied and collected birds and animals, and trained local artists to paint them. Lord Auckland, Hooker's supportive ex-governor-general, had also used Hodgson's knowledge, but Auckland's successor Lord Ellenborough thought differently; as Hodgson could not work in the south he had gone home, but as he could not stomach England, he had come back to Darjeeling in the autumn of 1844. Esconced in his comfortable eyrie, with his books and collections, a lean and nervous figure, dressed in tattered jacket and trousers of heavy Tibetan wool, with pale hair and beard and large, sad eyes, Hodgson appeared as a prophet, in empathy with the gigantic mountain that was his constant companion. He flitted like his beloved birds – Hodgson's redstart, the Tibetan partridge, babblers, flycatchers, warblers, thrushes and finches, of which he took painstaking observations – and he liked shy animals, civet, mongoose, weasels and the lesser panda. It was this remarkable man who schooled Joseph Hooker, as every evening they sat over their 'geography' until Hooker felt that he acquired a better knowledge of where the flowers were than anyone else.[16]

In order to get higher up the mountains Hooker intended to try Sikkim, the tiny, ancient state (of 2,800 square miles) sandwiched between Bhutan and Nepal. Sikkim was not to become part of the British Empire until 1866, but it was hoped that the Rajah would be amenable. It was not so: 'The Gods and Divinities of my country are numerous and very watchful . . .' he intoned; 'I have consulted the lamas as to whether it is good and proper that the British gentleman should examine the trees and plants of my country. The result is that it will not be proper.'[17] So Hooker botanised happily where he was, among ferns, mosses and lichens, as well as orchids, magnolias and arums, and lo! waiting for him in the woods not too far from Darjeeling was his first rhododendron, none other than *grande*, with her great glossy leaves, silver-backed (which is why Hooker called her *argenteum*), and lemon yellow orbs of flowers, the first astounding Himalayan giant – though perhaps some of its magnificence was wasted on a man who delighted in lichens.

On the advice of Hodgson and Archibald Campbell, the political agent in Darjeeling, Hooker went to the Nepalese border, over the foothills of Kangchenjunga, and into what is now the Kangchenjunga Conservation Area. This is still sparsely populated and its difficult tracks are the same paths that Hooker tramped. Hodgson had wanted to come but was not well enough; Hooker still had his gifts of home-made potted meats to comfort his English appetite, and so in harsh weather and rather in gratitude for everything, especially the potted meats, he named *Rhododendron hodgsonii*: 'It is found alike at the bottom of the valleys, on the rocky spurs or slopes of the hills, in open places, or in the gloomy pine-groves, often forming an impenetrable thicket, not merely of twigs and foliage, but of thickset limbs and stout trunks, only to be severed with difficulty, on account of the toughness of the wood.'[18] Aspects of Brian Houghton Hodgson's life echo now in the affectionate words of Michael and Sue Thornley on their *hodgsonii* growing at Glenarn: 'raffish and gregarious, an extrovert with wide-open habit, displaying an extraordinary mauve trunk and well-manicured silvered foliage. But more than any other feature it is the flower that catches the eye, like an outrageous buttonhole. Each spring the small electric pink trusses, with golden dotted stigmas, startle the eye although their colour all too quickly fades to washed-out rose.'[19] Hooker noted *hodgsonii*'s usefulness, its wood carved into spoons and cups and yak saddle-frames, its leathery dark green leaves for packing yak butter and curds.

Hooker also immortalised Robert Wight (1796–1872), whose long service to India and botany was coming to an end. Wight, a surgeon with the Madras Medical Service, had started sending herbarium specimens of Indian flora to William Hooker when he was Professor of Botany at Glasgow in the 1820s. In 1831 he had taken home in his baggage '100,000 specimens, including 3–4,000 species in six cases weighing 2 tons!' Wight learned lithography on home leave and took a press to India, he employed Indian collectors and artists (he gave great credit to the latter, notably his chief artists Rungia and Govindoo, naming a genus of orchids after the latter), all in the cause of his volumes of Indian flora, which were gradually being published during the 1840s.[20] *Rhododendron wightii* is now something of a collector's item, with its flower heads of five bells, lemon yellow and spotted with crimson, and slim, brown-suede-backed leaves.

Hooker's haul of no less than 43 different species doubled those known to cultivation; his friends entered the rhododendron hall of fame: Brian Hodgson, Hugh Falconer, Major Madden, Mrs Campbell, Thomas Thomson and Lady Dalhousie (the supportive Lord Auckland's *aucklandii* gave place to Dr William Griffith of the Pemberton mission, though the *Botanical Magazine* plate 5065 politely refers to *Rhododendron griffithianum* as Lord Auckland's rhododendron, and this rather confusing politesse remains). In London these rhododendrons made a huge splash in the horticultural pond, especially when 30 of them appeared on a beauty parade in *Rhododendrons of Sikkim-Himalaya*, and in the judiciously sporadic appearances of the *Botanical Magazine* plates.[21]

The seeds that Hooker had sent or brought home were propagated at Kew with resounding success; the first generation seedling emigrants were sent out to friends and supporters and certain nurseries. Some familiar names leap from the lists; they went to the Aclands' Killerton and Sir Charles Lemon at Carclew, and the home of 'Altaclerense', Highclere Castle. Florence Nightingale at Embley Park in Hampshire was also enthusiastic. Some also went to Prince Albert at Osborne on the Isle of Wight and to Parson Parsons, a successor of Gilbert White at Selborne in Hampshire, both gardens being appropriately on chalk since rhododendrons grew on limestone crags in their native habitats (the horticultural fussiness that suggested that they would not was yet to come). The venerable Charles Darwin (1809–82) at Downe in Kent received twelve Sikkim seedlings;[22] they were planted beside the sandy walk where 'Charles paced every morning with clockwork regularity', sheltering Emma Darwin's wild flowers.[23]

Many of the other recipients are long forgotten, but some were famous nurseries: Veitch of course, the Handsworth Nursery in Sheffield (keen on rhododendrons since the earliest arrivals), and Standish and Noble on the Bagshot sands in Surrey, pioneers of that famous rhododendron-land. A hundred years later some of the Standish and Noble seedlings were to be inherited by James Russell at Sunningdale, a story to be continued. In all, 779 seedlings are listed as distributed throughout the 1850s and undoubtedly many were handed on, for the gardens that now claim them do not tally with the modest lists kept at Kew. A Hooker seedling was a valuable currency, and those that survived into maturity conferred a kind of honour on their gardens.

The Hooker rhododendrons – for once the son was more celebrated than the father – were a spectacular flourish in Sir William's campaign to establish Kew at the pinnacle of imperial botany. The largesse was distributed to Italy, Spain, France, Belgium, several German gardens with royal connections, to Belfast, Glasnevin Botanic Garden at Dublin, Edinburgh Botanics, to New Zealand, St Helena, Jamaica, Baltimore and to Professor Gray at Harvard.[24] Joseph Hooker's 'immortals' had made rhododendrons a worldwide commodity.

At Darjeeling, after Hooker's departure, the rhododendron squall must in retrospect have seemed a curious business to Brian Houghton Hodgson and the Campbells who resumed their real lives, much as the staff at Calcutta Botanic Garden returned to the serious business of food crops and economic botany. For most of the civilian British in the mid-nineteenth century life was not secure enough to venture into an interest in native plants and gardens, and struggling to make the tea and cinchona plantations successful was 'gardening' enough. Even further west at the leisured Simla, summer retreat of the viceregal court, efforts went into growing roses and sweet peas as the symbols of home, while the rhododendrons of 'wild' hedges and groves went unregarded, or regarded as weeds. English eyes were not to be lifted to the ancient garden traditions of Mogul India for another 50 years.

Henry John Elwes was at Darjeeling or in the Khasia Hills (now Meghalaya) several times in Hooker's footsteps; riding out from Darjeeling he found Nepalese immigrants clearing great stretches of the sal (Shorea robusta) forest, the home of the orchids and rhododendrons, but he also reported this vivid picture:

> for some miles along the ridge the forest was so dense that I had no view on either side, but at last the path came out on a steep, narrow ridge where Rhododendron hodgsonii was in flower. On the nectar of its purple-pink blossoms were feeding two of the most beautiful birds of the Himalaya, Myzornis pyrrhura, and a honey-sucker known as Aethopyga ignicauda . . . Both of them had their heads covered with pollen from the flowers.[25]

In 1886 in the Khasia Hills he found the hill station of Shillong had grown up since Hooker's day – and everywhere the bungalows were spreading. If there was an interesting botanist or gardener Elwes would find them out, and at Shillong he found 'one of the best kept and richest' gardens in India cultivated by a Hanoverian officer of the Forestry Department named Mann. Elwes was much taken with a fine red salvia and the balsams (impatiens) and begonias, so it was clearly not rhododendron time, but the garden contained 'numerous native and exotic trees, shrubs, orchids and herbaceous plants' that surely included them. He also passed several failed and neglected gardens. A few days later (he says it was September) he went up Shillong Peak to a patch of 'primeval forest' with wooded glens of oak, laurel, magnolia and wild cinnamon densely covered with orchids and a climbing yellow dicentra; on the edges of the wood were 'numerous trees of rhododendron and of *Daphne wallichii* whose sweet-scented flowers are now in perfection' with fringings of cardiocrinum lilies, tall blue delphinium, a red-berried pseudo-ginseng and rue, *Thalictrum javanicum*.[26] With such natural wonders perhaps garden-making seemed a little futile to anyone but a confirmed collector?

Fortunately this was not entirely the case and for at least two young travellers in these parts, who were neither professional foresters nor botanists, the enchantment of the Indian flora, and especially the rhododendrons, was completely captivating. James and Harry Mangles came from a family of servants of the Empire and they were to make Mangles a name of consequence in the rhododendron world. They need introducing.

James Mangles (1786–1867) had joined the navy at fourteen, fought his way around the world in frigates of the line and retired after commanding the sloop *Racoon*. He explored in the Middle East and then came home to live in one of the Regent's Park terraces, where he gardened in containers (boxes and vases) in a 'patio' plot 16 feet by 10 feet, as well as in a conservatory, a small greenhouse and on eight balconies. John Claudius Loudon was impressed, calling the captain's house 'unique of its kind, as exquisitely adorned with painted flowers within, as with real ones on the outside'. The captain had the Grand Junction Canal reservoir at the end of his garden, so he planted the bank of that too, supporting the plants in porcelain-fronted boxes. The flowery vista greeting him every morning from his bedroom window was 'the most cheering object' which he wanted other town-dwellers to share. (The captain's flowery vision is nicely perpetuated in the allotments that now occupy the site of the former reservoir basin.) To beat the London soot Captain Mangles had all the plants changed regularly by a Bayswater nurseryman, which he reckoned could be done for £70 a year; quite a sum. In 1839 he published his little book (now rarely found), *The Floral Calendar*, to encourage town gardeners. He was the first Mangles to fancy rhododendrons, having seen them at Highclere Castle, where he picked up tips on hybridising – though readers of *The Floral Calendar* were advised to remove the 'antlers' rather than the pollen-bearing anthers. He also thought they made good cover for wildfowl, and should be planted on Duck Island in St James's Park.[27]

Captain James had a more famous cousin, Ross Donnelly Mangles (1801–77), who joined the Bengal civil service and rose relentlessly through the ranks of magistrates and collectors of customs and revenues that peppered British India. On an extra-long home leave he courted and married Harriet Newcome in 1830 and they returned to India to advance together to dizzy heights for the untitled (though he was called 'Lord Mangles' behind his back), deputising for Lord Auckland. Ross Mangles came home in 1841, followed his father as MP for Guildford, was the last chairman of the East India Company and a member of the Council for India. (His son, Ross Mangles, won a VC at the time of the Mutiny.)

Ross Donnelly Mangles' sister (they were a family of twelve children) Ellen married on her sixteenth birthday and set off for the other side of the world. Ellen married Captain James Stirling, the indomitable leader of the Swan River Colony, who were promised

Arcadia but given sand, and the founder of Fremantle and Perth in Western Australia.

The Stirlings enlisted Captain James Mangles' encouragement for a fellow-settler, Georgiana Molloy; he sent seeds for her garden at Augusta on Flinders Bay, certainly the first garden in Western Australia. But kindly Captain James also asked for seeds and dried plants in return, sending Georgiana and her small daughters botanising in the karri forests and bush. Georgiana Molloy is now remembered as one of the very first to take an interest in native flora, coming 'to see life as a precious gift and an opportunity to revel in the extraordinary and unexpected beauty of God's creation without trying to conquer it'.[28]

Ross and Ellen's brother, Charles Edward Mangles (1795–1874), sometime captain of the armed East Indiaman *Marchioness of Ely*, married Harriet Newcome's sister Rose, became an MP and chairman of the London and South West Railway and settled at Poyle Park, Tongham, near Guildford. Charles Edward and Rose had ten children, including James, Harry and Clara.

James (1832–84) and Harry (1833–1908) were educated for India at Haileybury. James was a district magistrate in Bengal for seven years but his health was not up to the climate so after falling in love with Indian rhododendrons, in about 1856, he came home to study law. Somewhere along the way he had strayed to Kew Gardens, hoping to catch sight of some of Joseph Hooker's Sikkim seedlings, only to be shown around by Sir William, who gave James some pollen from a flowering *arboreum* in the Temperate House, and suggested he try hybridising. James' first 'hackneyed' (as he thought it) effort was to apply the pollen to the only rhododendron he had, a *ponticum*. James had caught the rhododendron bug and the outcome (propagated by Standish and Noble's Sunningdale nursery prior to 1860) was violet-white, spotted black, and named 'Mrs Mangles'. He had married Isabella Walker in 1858, and they settled into a house at Valewood, a place as lovely as it sounds, in a secluded valley near Haslemere on the Surrey/Sussex border.

In truth Valewood is lovely, though it must have felt isolated at times and was certainly damp. The sandy bulk of Blackdown hill dwarfs the house of rubble stone, which James and Isabella enlarged, raising the roof to three brick gables and adding a classical porch. It is on the west side of Blackdown, which encourages the rain, and the streams had been dammed into a large lake in front of the house, before continuing their gurgling way beside the track down the vale. There were oaks and birches, and James planted pines and evergreens; there was the farm halfway down the vale for milk and butter, and perhaps laundry and garden help, and the mill for flour at the end, where the track met the Haslemere road and the outside world. Valewood was the perfect place to grow rhododendrons; in fact, local historians think they were already there, planted as cover for game birds in the late eighteenth century.

Throughout the 1860s James, ostensibly a barrister with chambers in the Inner Temple, pursued his passion, visiting nurseries – it was no accident that the best nurseries were on the London road, and the Mangles' L&SWR, at Sunningdale and Bagshot, convenient for James (as for Lionel de Rothschild some 60 years afterwards) – taking home the finest species and best of the early hybrids to Valewood. His aim was to breed hardiness into the beautifully coloured and scented tender rhododendrons; little is known of what he actually did, for hybridising is ever a secret sport, but some clues can be gleaned from the articles he wrote, after he had been crossing and planting for twenty years. He began (in the *Gardeners' Chronicle*, 14 June 1879) with the view from his window, the crimson flowers of every hue, the purples and the whites that 'dazzled my eyes' along with 'a host of my own seedlings'. The plants that pleased his fastidious taste included Waterer's Knap Hill *catawbiense* hybrid 'Mrs R. S. Holford', salmon pink and named for the mistress of Westonbirt; 'Lady Eleanor Cathcart', a large shrub with large rose pink flowers splashed with dark maroon, which John Waterer at Bagshot sold for a guinea a plant, an enormous price in the early 1860s; 'Blandyanum' was rosy crimson, of complex parentage being *catawbiense* x 'Altaclerense', the Highclere child of three parents, *arboreum*, *ponticum* and *catawbiense*, that marriage of East and West. Others among James' hybrid collection are long forgotten – he had 'Barclayanum' a cross from Penjerrick near Falmouth, named for Barclay Fox, the son of the house who worked hard to make this famous garden but died in 1855, predeceasing his father by twenty years.

Something more can be learned of James Mangles through his famous friendship with the Tennysons. Alfred and Emily, in retreat from the storm of celebrity seekers that spoiled their summers at Farringford, became his neighbours over the hill of Blackdown in July 1869. They had probably met earlier, for the Tennysons had been scouting the area for several years before they bought Black Horse Copse, and the poet, famously accosting the architect James Knowles on Haslemere station with 'You had better build me a house', was not always the shy violet he pretended. Knowles (working for expenses only) had produced a poet laureate's house, Aldworth – huge, stony, with deep mansard roofs, railed balconies, gothic windows and fancy dormers – an ugly, palatial house which stood on the rather builder-blighted hillside, which was immediately covered with turf from Farringford. The Tennyson/Mangles relationship was that of a casual neighbourliness. On 4 September 1870 Tennyson and his son Hallam wandered over the hill to ask James about trees, admire the pelargoniums and request a crimson rhododendron. The following week James walked over with roses as his offering, for a friendly conversation over lunch. Sometimes things were more formal and James and Isabella would take the light carriage down their own lane to the Haslemere road, along the road for a short distance, then right and up the longer and steeper lane (now Tennyson's Lane) to where Aldworth sat, over 500 feet above sea level. Undoubtedly many pine and rhododendron seedlings went this way; the Tennysons were keen on planting their surroundings, and the following year the poet dropped in while he was passing in late March, especially hoping to see some rhododendrons in flower. He grumbled about the rabbits in his own garden, stayed to supper and gossiped about Lord Byron's doings, Princess Louise's wedding and Henry Thornton's Bill to allow a man to marry his deceased wife's sister, before reading aloud from *Maud*.

James, mindful of his neighbour's desire for privacy, took care never to be seen with a notebook; but when his visitors left he dug out a morocco-bound scrapbook that was already a hundred years old, turned it upside down and wrote his diary entries in the back. Perhaps he kept it hidden, for almost another hundred years passed before the scrapbook was found in the old laundry room at Valewood by James's great-granddaughter and her husband, Iris and Alec Norman; it was soaking wet and they dried it out page by page. The diary has recently been published[29] and with it a photograph of James; he had a benign face, thinning hair, soft eyes that might have been blue, a good moustache, modest sideburns, just a hint of a double chin, not a face of vigour but fitting his known character – a courteous, urbane gentleman with nervous energy and a sympathetic zeal.

Sadly his rhododendron notebooks did not survive in the old laundry or anywhere else: his *Gardeners' Chronicle* pieces were often brief, and only lasted through three years, but he warmed to his task. Shy at first when pressed by the editor – 'Pray, do tell us of your own hybridising' – he made mention of an *arboreum* 'touched' with pollen but little more. Later, in April 1881, he spoke out:

> It may almost seem, for instance, a profanation to think of refining the ineffable delicacy of *R. veitchianum*, or gilding the golden glory of *R. javanicum*, and yet I do not envy the cultivator who has no ambition to leave his own mark among his flowers, for the sake of science as well as for his own. But the truth is that Rhododendrons do not, as a rule, easily submit to hybridising. Hundreds of experiments have utterly failed with me, and, among others, I have not yet persuaded *R. dalhousiae* to bear seed under the influence of foreign pollen, but the other way the cross has been often effected.[30]

Mostly he reported on his trips to other rhododendron growers, especially to 'the Mecca of the Faithful' as he dubbed Edinburgh; he was ever praising the Botanics and Downie & Laird's nursery as well as his many friends. He made a pilgrimage to the site of Miss Walker's home at Drumsheugh, where George Gilbert Scott's St Mary's Cathedral was being built with a large legacy of Walker money, as had been her wish and her heart's desire. Mary Walker had died in 1870 and she was known for her 'Rhododendron Almanac', her collection that gave her flowers in every month of the year with the help of her cool conservatory: her Waterer hybrid *arboreum x caucasicum* 'Nobleanum' flowered from October to April, rosy-purple *dauricum* started off the year, followed by Hooker's lovely *ciliatum*, with her pale scented trumpets, and then the *arboreum* hybrids, rather hardier than the species. The 'pink and dappled bells' of *glaucophyllum* flowered in April, by which time the exotically flowered *formosum* and the vireya *javanicum* were filling the conservatory with colour and scent. In August the rockery sported the common Indian *anthopogon*, with its strongly aromatic leaves. Miss Walker was clearly much taken with Hooker's Himalayans, for she also had the fabulous *edgeworthii*, the tender *dalhousiae* and *maddenii*, the latter lasting till October. She had spiritedly refuted the idea that rhododendrons were only a flower of springtime.

After the 'mecca' of Edinburgh, James made it his business and pleasure to explore other parts of Britain's burgeoning rhododendron world; indeed, he pioneered this new society of gardeners and growers. He saw 'a feast for the eye' in the acres and acres of oranges, yellows and scarlets which scented the air of Anthony Waterer's azalea fields at Knap Hill at Woking, and at the Veitch King's Road nursery in Chelsea he appreciated the first vireyas: 'a neat compact batch of seedlings with good dark green and glossy foliage, and on one of them several trusses of expanding flowers such as I had never seen before. The colour was a particularly striking crimson.' James reported on the first rhododendron 'shows', which were actually commercial affairs – in July 1881 he informed his readers of a change of advertised plan – 'I propose to change the venue and interview Mr John Waterer in his tent in London'. Each summer Waterer set up a display tent on the London doorstep of thousands of well-heeled prospective customers, and this year the sumptuous gardens under canvas were laid out in Cadogan Square, a Sloane flower show. For the sober, narrowly printed columns of the *Gardeners' Chronicle*, he achieved a near-comic description of his meeting with the whole Waterer clan disguised as rhododendrons: the 'venerable John' and his 'venerable spouse' as late-flowering *arboreum* hybrids, both 'glowing with crimson health, Fred and Michael as chips off the old block, Kate with her hazel eye, and Helen and Barbara the loveliest of all . . .' He quoted Hooker's *Himalayan Journal*: 'In the Zemu Valley rhododendrons occupy the most prominent place, clothing the mountain slopes with a deep green mantle glowing with bells of brilliant colours.' James felt the Londoner 'may well be proud of his little Zemu Valley in Cadogan Place' and the efforts and hard work that had created it: 'Entering the tent one is dazzled at first by some of the rich red tints, which are saved, however, from seeming flaunting or gaudy by the masses of dark foliage . . . But crimson yields to pink, and pink melts away into creamy white in ever-changing cadence, and then a bold dash of purple supplies the needful shadow . . .'[31]

James Mangles' best hybrids were made in the early 1880s and he was never to see them flower; never in robust health he became suddenly ill and died on 24 August 1884. The following year Veitch named a *griffithianum* hybrid 'Manglesii' in his honour. The rhododendron world has always felt that James' pioneering knowledge died with him; they called him the 'high priest', as of a cult, for his fastidious taste and restraint, and for his private, almost secret, passion. After his brother's death Harry Mangles took charge of his rhododendron seedlings and young plants: some were given away, but many journeyed the few miles northwards to Elstead and up on to the heath above the Wey valley to Harry's garden.

Harry Mangles had stayed in India until 1872, when he bargained a coffee plantation in Coorg state for a plot of 'little worth', part of the Hampton estate at Seale, on the Surrey greensand between Guildford and Farnham. Harry built a house, Littleworth Cross, in the fashionable 'old English' style of sandstone, timbered gables, a lot of tile hanging and tall chimneys. He gardened on the sandy heathland, bare except for some pines, heathers and the inevitable *ponticum*, planted for game cover. The household at Littleworth was the bachelor Harry, his temperamental, 'hoity-toity' sister Rose (1835–1901) and Clara (1846–1931), second youngest of the ten brothers and sisters, and a keen botanist, who made at least one trip to the Mediterranean with another of her brothers.

The Littleworth household had well and truly caught the rhododendron bug. James' seedlings were carefully tended and Harry and Clara began hybridising on their own accounts. They had splendid facilities: a large sandstone-walled kitchen garden, several glasshouses and James' canvas shelters, which he had called his 'cathedral houses', as well as the pine-shaded woodland, now largely walled and sheltered. Several of the seedlings must have flowered for the first time in the spring of 1889, and one, a soft beigy-pink and large-flowered, was named for Harry's gardening friend and not-too-distant neighbour, Gertrude Jekyll (1843–1932). She came over in her pony cart on a May afternoon to see her name-flower and met a young architect, Edwin Lutyens (1869–1944), who remembered the day for ever afterwards. 'We met at a tea table, the silver kettle and the conversation reflecting rhododendrons. She was dressed in what I learnt later to be her Go-To-Meeting Frock, a bunch of cloaked propriety topped by a black felt hat, turned down in front and up behind, from which sprang alert black cock's tail feathers, curving and ever prancing forwards.'[32]

Ned Lutyens was just twenty years old, and Gertrude Jekyll was a plump and artistically distinguished spinster of 45. He was not truly a guest at all, merely a young architect come to design a new gardener's cottage for the kindly Harry. Apparently she did not speak to him directly all through the rhododendron chatter, which would have been double-dutch to him, but 'with one foot on the step of her pony cart and the reins in her hand' she invited him to Munstead, her home, the very next Saturday. What happened to the lady and her young architect – how they became the best of friends, how he built a house for her and she introduced him to many other clients, and they made over 100 gardens together and he became one of the most famous architect in the world – is another story.[33]

But the fate of Harry Mangles' garden hung on that meeting and what came from it. In the 1890s it was blooming to perfection and, rather in the manner of Waterer's tent, the Mangles family were the flowery population. One of James' *griffithianum* hybrids, whose cerise-crimson buds still break there, he had named for his wife 'Isabella Mangles'. Harry named a mauve-white hybrid 'James Mangles', but perhaps James had named the pink 'Alice Mangles' for his daughter before she married and became Alice Daffarn. Alice lived at Valewood and had three children: 'Maurice Daffarn' (a red), 'Daphne Daffarn' (rose-pink, crimson-spotted) and 'Dulcie Daffarn', who, alas! cannot be traced. 'Daphne Daffarn' still flowered in the Rhododendron Dell at Kew in the 1970s and she was also in Hillier's catalogue. The delicate *fortunei* child, white-flushed-mauve 'Rose Newcome', was for James and Harry's mother; Clara and Rose had their name-flowers, and so did their younger sister, pink 'Emily Mangles'. The baby of the family, 'Agnes Mangles', married Arthur Chapman, for whom Lutyens built the first of his famous string of Surrey houses at Crooksbury nearby; the Chapmans had two sons, Paul and Michael, who each had a rhododendron, and Michael married the beautiful pink 'Lilian', the supposed daughter of Ellen Terry and George Frederick Watts, whom Watts painted as *The Flower Girl*.

There are two legendary Littleworth plants: 'Beauty of Little-worth' is one of James' *griffithianum* seedlings tended by Clara and named and exhibited by Harry, winning an RHS First Class

Certificate in 1904. 'Beauty' becomes a shrub of great presence, covered with bluish-mauve buds, which open to large white flowers, speckled with dark red; she is thought one of the best of all hybrids to this day. 'Glory of Littleworth', with milky-cream scented azalea-like clusters of flowers is rarer, quite different, and usually credited to Harry's hybridising. 'Glory's' parents were a Japanese azalea and a Ghent hybrid of 'poison-honey' *luteum* and one of the American azaleas.

'Hoity-toity' Rose Mangles died in 1901 and kindly Harry in 1908; Clara carried on. She exhibited 'Glory' in 1911 to great acclaim; 'Glory' is technically an azaleodendron, a name coined in the 1890s but now little used.

In the spring of 1915 Clara, the mistress of Littleworth and now approaching her 70th birthday, received a visit from a sporting gentleman, whom she knew by name if not actual acquaintance. He was a dashing character, habitually dressed in a Norfolk jacket and breeches, tweedy socks and polished brown short boots; he had laughing eyes and a winning smile. He was John Guille Millais (1865–1931), who lived at Compton's Brow, just south of Horsham, and he was working on a book on rhododendrons. Johnny, as present Millais generations call him, was born in March 1865, the fourth son and seventh child of the painter John Everett Millais and his wife, Effie Gray; he was a child of Millais' success and wealth, and of the passion that accompanied this status, almost an addiction, to deer stalking, grouse shooting and salmon fishing in Scotland. Johnny Millais seemed to perpetuate the breeziness of the grouse moor; when he was eighteen his father had sketched him shooting at the Grays' Scottish home, Bowerswell, rather than making him pose unwillingly like his brothers and sisters for some dreary domestic scene. What could such a young man do but opt for a life of adventure? He became a 'professional naturalist'; known as 'Johnny with the long gun' he haunted the Highlands and Islands, learning all he could about birds and animals, thoroughly in the Bartram tradition. After a brief spell in the army, the Seaforth

Highlanders, he began travelling, to Iceland, Africa, Newfoundland and western America; at home, happily married, he wrote books on his travels, definitive volumes on ducks, mammals and game birds and his African adventures, *A Breath from the Veldt*. There was a more than fictional similarity to a John Buchan hero – Erskine Childers' *The Riddle of the Sands*, for Millais was 'sent' to the Lofoten Islands in 1915 to study not only bird life but 'the German spy system' and the following year he became British vice-consul in Hammerfest, presumably for the same reason.[34]

In his home spells Millais had started cultivating rhododendrons at Compton's Brow in about 1906, with encouragement from Edmund Loder at Leonardslee nearby, and like most gardeners he had looked around for a book. Finding only Hooker's *Rhododendrons of Sikkim-Himalaya*, inspiring but impractical, he decided to write one of his own; he was perhaps prompted by his illustrator for the ducks and game birds, Archibald Thorburn, who was also a keen gardener. Millais' *Rhododendrons* was published in 1917; though still impressively large and demi-folio (how could rhododendrons be subjected to less?) he included pioneering chapters on native habitats, on species and on hybrids, on the cultivation and 'a rhododendron for every month'. He had also visited and listed 'the best rhododendron gardens', which is presumably what brought him to Littleworth Cross.

Johnny Millais brought the thrill of the chase to the rhododendron world; he stalked Littleworth's treasures and persuaded Miss Mangles to dig out her memories. He 'found' a plant which had been there for – how many? thirty? – years, with flowers that were identical to the already famous 'Pink Pearl', the most popular hybrid which Waterer's of Bagshot had unveiled in 1896. 'Pink Pearl' was a *griffithianum* hybrid, and if this plant was one of James Mangles' *griffithianum* seedlings, did it mean he had reached the Holy Grail first? The Littleworth plant flowered slightly earlier but otherwise the two were identical. 'Pink Pearl' had become a star, however, and the Mangles plant, labelled 'Early Pink Pearl', stayed in her quiet glade alone.

John Guille Millais (1865–1931), artist, adventurer,
sportsman and prime mover of the
Rhododendron Society in 1915.

That was the thing about the Mangles. They were quiet gardeners, not people for a lot of show and fuss. Miss Clara, if the truth was ever known, was probably irked by this energetic man with dancing eyes, who was disarmingly attractive, and she must have sighed with relief when he had gone. She did not want any of her rhododendrons hijacked into the 'trade' – James, Harry and herself had bred them simply for the enjoyment of their flowers and for their challenge. Littleworth was virtually James' garden, all his best hybrids with later additions flowering through some 40 years and with a direct connection to Joseph Hooker's Sikkim-Himalayan treasures and Sir William's keen hand at hybridising. Let the enthusiastic Mr Millais head off to Cornwall, which he did, and find that when two or three are gathered together with a similar enthusiasm, as happened when he met P. D. Williams and Charles Eley at Lanarth, they will form a society; in this instance, the Rhododendron Society. Clara Mangles lived on at Littleworth into a grand old age, never lessening her love of her rhododendrons, but as with old ladies' gardens a certain natural neglect crept in. She died on 24 January 1931. And what was to happen to the garden then?

Luckily, in such a time of economic gloom, Littleworth Cross was sold to some people named Horsefall, who loved rhododendrons, who continued to tend their charges and exhibit during the next few years. But then came the war and the large, expansively Victorian house became home to a boys' school, and the boys must have had a marvellous time climbing trees and making camps in the rhododendrons, though it cannot have been much good for the plants. In 1946, in common with hundreds of thousands of other substantial houses with large gardens in their post-war degradation and neglect, Littleworth Cross was advertised for sale, in several lots so as to make it an attractive speculation. One of the speculators was frustrated to discover that his 'prime development site', the pine and rhododendron woodland, was useless, as by some restriction, perhaps in anticipation of the 1947 Town & Country Planning Act, the wood could not be felled. This news was heard by a Mrs Violet

Gordon, a widow 'of a certain age', who lived nearby; Mrs Gordon knew Littleworth Cross, she even knew where the best rhododendrons were, and she put in an offer for ten acres, which to her surprise was accepted, and she bought them in 1947. Her friends thought she was mad – what on earth did she want another garden for? She explained. 'it was not such a garden as one usually thinks of, it had no mown grass or borders of flowers, but just sandy tracks through pines' – oh, and some 'large clumps of seventy to eighty years old rhododendrons'. The eyebrows rose even higher, but Violet Gordon had her reasons; she was overjoyed with her purchase and amused that so many, including the sellers, wondered what she could do with this land of 'little worth'.[35]

Reel back almost sixty years, to that rhododendron tea party in the spring of 1889 when Gertrude Jekyll met Edwin Lutyens: any young architect might envy the number of 'jobs' that sprang from that meeting – the gardener's house and other smaller buildings for Harry Mangles, Crooksbury for Harry's brother-in-law and Munstead Wood for Miss Jekyll herself. Nor did it stop there, for endless introductions on all sides launched the young Lutyens on his country house career,[36] so it was quite natural that when the Mangles found some new young friends who needed an architect, they knew who to suggest. The friends were Gerard and Ida Streatfeild, who were living at Tilford and for whom Lutyens designed Fulbrook, a short walk across the heathland from Littleworth Cross. The Streatfeilds and their only child, Violet, moved into Fulbrook in 1902;[37] Lutyens had promised Ida Streatfeild 'a house you will love to live in' and they were very happy in the romantic, rambling house, full of small and pretty rooms. Gerard Streatfeild was a keen naturalist and gardener, and Violet (mostly) his willing slave in the planting of their new garden. She recalled: 'from early days at Fulbrook at certain times of the year it was a kind of pilgrimage to go to Littleworth on Sunday afternoons'. They walked across the common, looking for flint arrowheads or Roman pottery along the way, 'or drove in the pony cart to see the rhodies in bloom. It was a sort of ritual ... I was frightfully bored – especially as I always had to get out and walk for the fat pony's sake.' She remembered it being so dusty and hot, how she had a job to keep awake through all the boring rhododendron chatter but how Clara served such wonderful teas with early strawberries.[38]

Somehow the rhododendron bug had captured Violet, too, which was why, after more than 40 years, her marriage to Douglas Gordon, her four sons and being widowed when she was 45, and now being back at Fulbrook with a large garden of her own, she made this seemingly eccentric commitment to Harry Mangles' rhododendron wood. She faced a formidable task: brambles, gorse and seedling trees were strangling the best plants, her would-be helpers soon faded away, except for one, a Polish ex-soldier who worked faithfully for a year. On the thin Surrey sand any periods of drought were her nightmares as her precious charges hung their leaves in unanimous misery. The wood had no 'facilities', the decrepit watering system no source, and Harry's two large glasshouses were falling down and had to be demolished. However, she managed to save two tender plants clinging to the ruins, moving them to the surviving small lean-to greenhouse, well sheltered but unheated, where she ate her sandwich lunch with them, a daphne and a mimosa 'cocking a snook at the wintry weather outside'. She was knowledgeable enough to know that her refugees with their tubular bell-flowers, orange and primrose yellow, were Harry Mangles' *cinnabarinum x maddenii* seedlings; the same cross was made by J. C. Williams at Caerhays and the orange form became a famous hybrid 'Royal Flush', to Williams' credit.

Violet Gordon saved the Mangles' rhododendrons. She worked from those that were labelled and known, pruning and propagating by layering, and observing, most of all observing, keeping careful watch on their habits and flowerings, until she knew them as familiars: 'Alice Mangles', 'Rose Newcome', 'Beauty' and 'Glory'; also the now gigantic *wightii* by the east gate and 'Early Pink Pearl', which she thought either a James Mangles original hybrid or perhaps bought from the Lawson Company in Edinburgh. She exhibited her stars at Chelsea Flower Shows. She renewed their comfortable habitat beneath the pines, ruthlessly discarded casual seedlings, added pieris and eucryphias and ground-covering *Cornus canadensis*. She put her heart and soul into this extraordinary and selfless labour of conservation, in the way it should be done, gradually, painstakingly, making a virtue of her slim – virtually single-handed – resources for ten years in a post-war world where the idea of 'history' or 'restoration' had yet to be born.

In 1958 Violet Gordon's second son Adam (despite his demanding role as comptroller of the Queen Mother's household) and his wife Pamela and their two young sons were able to buy half of the old Littleworth Cross house, which they named Hethersett, and another ten acres of Harry's garden, with yet more beleaguered rhododendrons. Rescuing rhododendrons became a family pastime whenever time permitted, and when Violet died in 1968 her flowery memorial was in safe hands.[39] Since then it has become the most enchanting rhododendron garden that I know, and has been the prime inspiration for this book. From the first touch of spring until the last days of summer it is a truly enchanted woodland where paths of emerald green moss wind deceptively, and the flowers are never still but dance as if they were exotic butterflies; mauves, pinks and creams flutter at head height, luminous frothy orbs of lucky Hugh Falconer's *falconeri* or the hybrid 'Beauty of Littleworth' present themselves for close adoration, all amongst elegantly spiralling rusty-cinnamon stems which tango in the sunlight and shadows like couples on a dance floor.

This woodland of nineteenth-century hybrids has a patina, a delicate refinement, because it has been protected from any invasions of modern strident colourings or blowzily oversized flowers. It may have been stopped in time but it is certainly not dead, nor even *passé*, and emphasises the longevity of rhododendrons; after more than a hundred years most of them are genetically in their prime, and the scars of physical damage from storm and drought are alleviated by constant gardening. If Joseph Hooker had liked his rhododendrons rather more, this woodland would be his Sikkim-Himalayan dreamscape, the wild taken one stage further by breeding hybrids of *griffithianum*, *thomsonii* and the others, giving them authenticity as plants rather than people. And without the tortuous ravines and leeches.

The Gordons have made hybrids of their own – as James Mangles said, it was hard to resist – and one of the loveliest is the cloudy-pink 'Fulbrook'. Pamela Gordon dismisses any mystique in the process, and having picked out the prospective parents she explains:

> if you are trying to make a hybrid from two flower trumpets, or florets and they are not exactly the same size use the smaller as the female. So, taking the larger floret remove the petals and leave the stamens; then remove the petals and the stamens from the smaller floret leaving the stigma revealed. Then brush the sticky stigma with the stamens from the larger floret. Cover with a polythene bag for a day or two and hope for the best! Don't leave the bag on too long, but make sure to mark the hoped-for seed head, which should fill out in about six months or so.[40]

This, from a practical gardener and successful hybridiser, is worth remembering as we head off into the world of twentieth-century hybrids.

The fellowship of nineteenth-century hybrids extends to other gardens: a magnificent large bush of the powder-mauve 'Colonel Rogers' flowers at Hethersett, a *falconeri x niveum* which Johnny Millais named for the owner of Riverhill at Sevenoaks, where he found it. (It is apparently a natural hybrid.) 'J. G. Millais' himself is an early red with fabulous parentage, the *thomsonii* child of red 'Ascot Brilliant x Pink Pearl'; Waterer's gave him a plant in 1914 and he was thrilled with it when it flowered the following year. Waterer's also produced the mauve 'Mrs J. G. Millais'. The Himalayan species were also used at Tremough in Cornwall, where the gardener Richard Gill created 'Beauty of Tremough' from *grif-*

LEFT *Rhododendron williamsianum* by Emily Sartain (1903–90) for the illuminated autograph of King George VI, Royal Patron of the Royal Horticultural Society 1936.

BELOW Queen Elizabeth the Queen Mother photographed at Royal Lodge, Windsor, by Cecil Beaton (1904–80), 1970.

Sir Lawrence Alma-Tadema (1836–1912) *Unconscious Rivals*, oil on panel, 1893.

OPPOSITE Albert Moore (1841–93) *Azaleas*, oil on canvas, exhibited at the Royal Academy 1868.

Marianne North (1830–90), foliage and flowers of *Rhododendron grande*: the artist painted many rhododendrons, which had a special affinity with her flamboyant style.

ABOVE Flowers of Papua New Guinea drawn by N.E.G. Cruttwell and I. Lowe for Papua New Guinea stamps issued 25 June 1989.

LEFT *Rhododendron brookeanum* (orange) and *Rhododendron apiense* (yellow) in the vireya house at the Royal Botanic Garden, Edinburgh.

Marion Dorn (1896–1964) surrounded by some of her fabric designs including a 'tablecloth' of rhododendron leaves, photograph by Horst, 1947.

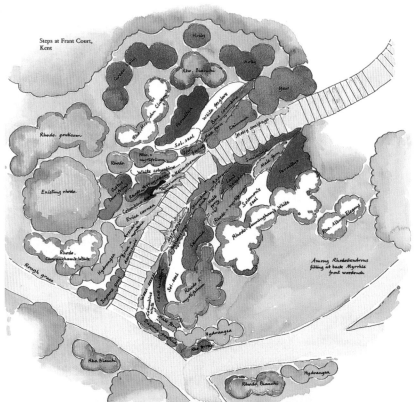

Steps at Frant Court, Kent

Titley & Marr's 'Rhododendrons' fabric, originally designed by William Pearman in July 1860 and printed by Stead McAlpin in Carlisle for Daniel Walters & Company, London.

fithianum x arboreum. John Luscombe at Coombe Royal in south Devon, a contemporary and sparring partner of James Mangles, had the first flowers of *thomsonii* and *fortunei* and in the late 1870s he had produced 'Luscombei', a floppy, rosy-flowered giant of great fame and controversy.

The most famous contemporaries of the Mangles hybrids flower at Leonardslee, the Loder family garden on the Wealden sandstone just south of Horsham, where Johnny Millais learned to love rhododendrons. Sir Edmund Loder (1849–1920) inherited the 240-acre (100 ha.) 'lea' or valley from his father-in-law in 1889 and he planted trees and shrubs rapidly, on the grand scale, and introduced a menagerie of antelope, kangaroos, wallabies, deer, beavers and 'bush turkeys' and other wildlife to fill his rather empty valley. 'Rhododendrons and exotic conifers were his greatest enthusiasms,' writes his great-grandson Robin Loder;[41] he certainly had *fortunei* and probably as many Hooker species as he could get hold of, but they could not have been settled in until the later 1890s, so he was really rather late in the game. Sir Edmund reared 'Loderi' in the early 1900s, from a *fortunei* of his own and the pollen from a *griffithianum* belonging to his neighbour F. D. Godman of South Lodge, a friend of Millais and the Mangles (and also, incidentally, a Himalayan traveller with Henry John Elwes and a client of Edwin Lutyens). Sir Edmund had to make the cross twice because he wanted more *griffithianum* characteristics than *fortunei* in the seedlings, which he selected carefully, and which flowered in 1907. He immediately gave them names, and then William Watson of Kew came to visit, saw and admired and named them 'Loderi'.[42] This magnificent scented flower head, of generously blushing trumpets, with foot-long, delicately-pointed *fortunei* leaves, usually covering a substantial shrub, is unmistakably one of the great aristocrats of the rhododendron world. 'Loderi King George', named for George V, is pink in bud, becoming pure white as it flowers and differing in throat markings. Other seedlings have different names and are usually referred to as clones – though Lionel de Rothschild used 'grex' as the collective noun for seedlings of the same parents – which often have variations only seen by expert eyes. The 'Loderi' puzzle does not quite end there. The supreme, if I am not running out of superlatives, is 'Loder's White', which intrigued Johnny Millais, who hunted down this story: either before or immediately after James Mangles' death some of his hybrid *griffithianum* seedlings were sent to F. D. Godman at South Lodge where they flowered in his greenhouse. One was so good that Godman gave it to Sir Edmund Loder for grafting and many plants were raised and sent to Cornwall to see if they were hardy outdoors there; they were, and as they had come from Sir Edmund they were named 'Loder's White'. So 'Loder's White' may have been 'Mangles' White' after all? Well, not quite, for Millais had also seen Thomas Luscombe at Coombe Royal, who claimed that he had sent Mangles seedlings that were also included with those sent to Godman. There it rests in uncertainty. 'Loder's White', notable for its purity of whiteness, a super-white long before emulsion paint, earns that overworked phrase which I have tried hard to avoid so far: 'the best hybrid ever raised'. The best advice is to go to Leonardslee; this grand garden has an overwhelming sense of home for rhododendrons in the steep valley sides amongst dicksonias, maples and redwoods, and the scent of the massed yellow azaleas hangs in the air long after they are faded. Leonardslee has not stood still, and if it has embraced too many modern hybrids with rather too much enthusiasm for my taste, the enormous pleasure of hunting the 'Loderi' in May, without interruption from antelope or kangaroo, is not to be missed.

'By the time Sir Edmund Loder died in 1920,' writes W. J. Bean, 'a new era in rhododendron history had opened.'[43] Before I venture into this new era, there is just a short postscript to the souvenirs of the Raj.

Bean meant that the botanical and horticultural spotlight was once again turned on China and the finds of Ernest Wilson, George Forrest and Frank Kingdon Ward; the Indian rhododendrons and those along the Himalayan slopes were left to a new race of people, the mountaineers. It all started with Arthur Bulley of Bees' Seeds who had a particular penchant for primulas and hoped there were more to be found in Sikkim. He employed Edinburgh-trained Roland Cooper to go in 1913, and to Bhutan the following year, but Cooper's primulas were upstaged by Forrest's from Yunnan. Cooper found plenty of rhododendrons but no new ones, and it seemed Hooker had done his job thoroughly. Cooper was the first to send seeds home in bottles of 30 per cent carbon dioxide, and a few years later Kingdon Ward followed suit, using 'Sparklets' fizzy drink cartridges.[44] Cooper, having failed his medical for war service, returned to Bhutan in 1915 and discovered *Rhododendron rhabdotum*, an epiphyte like *dalhousiae*, but with large white crimson-banded trumpets.

Undaunted, Bulley found a new ruse; he offered to support the 1921 Everest reconnaissance expedition, if the mountaineers would go plant hunting. He gave £100 and, pleased with this new source of funds, the expedition leader Colonel Howard-Bury agreed. The doctor, A. F. R. Wollaston, was appointed the 'naturalist' and the mountaineers duly pottered about on the high screes, higher than any plant collector had reached, finding gentians, saxifrages and primulas. *Primula wollastonii* immortalised and enchanted Dr Wollaston: 'it carried from 4 to 6 bells, each as big as a lady's thimble, of deep azure blue and lined inside with frosted silver'.[45] It was agreed that the 1922 expedition, a serious assault, would also botanise and 'Hints for Collectors' leaflets were issued. But the climbers were caught in an avalanche that killed seven of the expedition's porters and plant collecting was forgotten. George Mallory was on the 1922 expedition and may have been the keenest botanist; throughout the First World War his letters to his wife, Ruth Thackeray Turner, were often filled with instructions for planting seeds in their garden in Godalming, and asking for seeds so that he could have flowers where he was billeted, though they were always moved on too quickly. He seemed to think constantly of his garden, and of his 'desire to lie among flowers'.[46]

The deaths of Mallory and Sandy Irvine on the 1924 attempt discouraged British efforts for nine years. A superstitious pall gathered about the high peaks, enhanced by sitings of a mystery beast, the 'Abominable Snowman', seen feeding on rhododendrons, 'stooping and occasionally uprooting' dwarf plants, by Greek climbers on the slopes of Kangchenjunga in 1925. In 1937 John Hunt was in eastern Nepal, at 19,000 feet, when he found tracks of enormous human-like feet. After the 1939–45 war when expeditions resumed, Eric Shipton's 1951 reconnaissance party also found strange tracks. 'Abominable Snowman' or Yeti fever rose: were the rhododendron forests the home of this mythical beast? Was this the servant of the displeased Mother Goddess of the Earth, the mighty Chomolungma?

'On the dividing ridges we entered the lovely rhododendron belt, gnarled trees whose blossoms graduated with increasing height from scarlet to pink and, above 10,000 feet, to white and yellow. The forests were besprinkled with white magnolia flowers, scented, fallen from the trees. Mauve primulas bedecked the path and Himalayan bird life was a constant source of wonder . . .'

The voice, despite the unmilitary 'besprinkling' and 'bedecking', is that of Colonel John Hunt, leading his small army to the Khumbu glacier on the 1953 expedition. The birds included sunbirds, verditer flycatchers, redheaded and greenbacked tits and scarlet minivets; there were more rhododendrons, and 'a magenta-coloured azalea was also in scanty bloom on bushes among the boulders' at their 'delectable' holiday spot two hours' down from base camp (at 17,900 ft). Azaleas, with Tibetan tailless rats, snow pigeons, redstarts, a wren, and 'an enormous lammergeyer drifting listlessly, these were the last signs of life in what would be, from then on, a dead and icy world'.[47]

The news that Edmund Hillary and Sherpa Tenzing Norgay had climbed Everest broke in a London celebrating the coronation of the young Queen Elizabeth II: one of the Royal Horticultural Society's Wisley gardens' hybrid rhododendrons was immediately named 'Tenzing'. In the rhododendrons' homeland things were seen rather differently; the elderly acting Abbot of Thyangboche monastery, who had greeted Hunt's party on their way up and fêted them on their descent, simply but graciously refused to believe that they had reached the top of the sacred Chomolungma. He congratulated them on nearly doing so. Afterwards it emerged that on the summit Tenzing had scratched out a little hole in the snow, and in this he placed some small offerings of food – some biscuits, a piece of chocolate, and a few sweets as a gift to the Mother Goddess. Hillary placed the little cross that Hunt had given him.

After the conquest of Everest the anthropologist Charles Stonor led a prolonged expedition to search for the Yeti (on which he built up a substantial dossier), which meant enduring the winter amongst the rocks and glaciers, and therefore revelling in the coming of the hesitant spring in March. Stonor, who admitted to being a gardener, was intoxicated by the flowers in the Bhote valley, the masses of mauve daphne much used for paper-making, and through the field glasses he could see the leafless birch woods on the opposite ridges, lit with crimson and scarlet flowers: 'Agog to see the rhodos at close quarters, I hared up the opposite bank, through a stretch of birch wood, and came out suddenly into an open yak pasture, fringed round with the most gorgeous display of colour imaginable.' These flowers were a ruby-scarlet species, and *falconeri*: 'so smothered in blossom that one wondered how and why it does not flower itself to death each year'.

> Temptation was too strong; the Yeti was pushed into the background, the day's march cut short, and camp pitched without more ado in the midst of this feast of colour. Perhaps it is partly because there is such all-pervading, sombre severity throughout the winter months that the pageant of the rhododendrons comes as the special glory of the Himalayas. But no planned display in a park or garden, however lavishly arranged, could begin to hold a candle to these sheets of colour.[48]

CHAPTER FIVE

Power Flowers

'I GO DRESSED nearly as I did in Scotland,' Joseph Hooker had written to his mother on 24 May 1849 from Sikkim, 'with the addition of an umbrella to keep off the sun as much as the rain ... I always wear long worsted stockings & my trousers tucked up to the knees, on account of the leeches which get all over one's person, & of which I have sometimes taken off a hundred a day ...'[1]

The odd thing about the rhododendron culture is that, as Nature invariably provides some insect irresistibly attracted to the human ankle, whether in Darjeeling or Devon, the dress was the same. Heroes – mostly men, I regret to say, though I will find a woman wherever I can – in Harris tweed with heavy brogues and hairy socks carried through the rhododendron revolution of the early twentieth century and invented 'the plantsman's garden' – where habitat was all and no effete notions of design entered the gates – in the process. Rhododendrons, camellias, magnolias and their kinds took over when the shooting season ended and they vacated the diary before the grouse moors beckoned in August. They were plants that needed space, country gentlemen's plants, and though in the 1850s Hooker's seedlings had been widely distributed to all parts of Britain they had fared best in the moist airs of the Celtic fringes in the west. In fact, as in all gardening, the intensity of microclimates was to play the most important part in any successful rhododendron garden, but that was a refinement yet to come. It was a combination of circumstances rather than the intrinsic beauty of rhododendrons that found them a new heartland, though love blossomed before long.

When Johnny Millais had scouted out his Sussex neighbours and left Miss Mangles in peace in her Surrey woodland, he went to Cornwall. History relates that he arrived at Percival Dacres Williams' Lanarth at St Keverne, south of the Helford River, on a May day in 1916, and by way of welcome Williams quipped: 'We are the Rhododendron Society and Charles Eley is the Honorary Secretary.'[2] Certainly three rhododendron fanciers were gathered together, but was it the first Charles Eley heard of his 'appointment'? Williams (1865–1935), one of an extensive Cornish mining dynasty, had inherited Lanarth in 1891 and his green-fingered skills had turned his three-acre meadow and eight-acre windy hilltop wood into a plantsman's delight, the home of the lacecap hydrangea 'Lanarth White', a cyclamen-purple *Magnolia campbellii* 'Lanarth' and that most striking horizontally branched and creamy-flowered viburnum which also bears the name. Williams had raised almost all his plants from seed, including seeds collected by George Forrest, but his Cornish fame rested on his development of daffodil and narcissus varieties and being co-founder of the Cornish Daffodil and Spring Flower Society, set up in 1897 to encourage commercial flower production, a Cornish success. Something of 'P. D.'s' fame and personality comes from a letter to Eley from one William Arkwright of Thorn at Wembury, near Plymouth: 'a great event has happened at Thorn for P. D. has come seen and conquered us here . . . so delightful, tactful and so genuinely interested in the smallest details and such fun'.[3]

Charles Eley (1872–1960), no mean plantsman himself, the author of *Twentieth Century Gardening* published by *Country Life* in 1923, lived at East Bergholt in Suffolk, in the heart of what we call 'Constable Country'; his garden at East Bergholt Place is now in the care of his great grandson Rupert Eley and his wife Sara who run 'The Place for Plants'.

Charles Eley did become the first honorary secretary of the Rhododendron Society, which dates its founding from that meeting with Johnny Millais and P. D. Williams. They immediately appointed Williams' cousin, John Charles Williams (1861–1939) of Caerhays on the coast at Veryan Bay, between Portloe and Dodman Point, to be chairman. The Williamses, with the Foxes and Boscawens, owned most of Cornwall's good, and about to be great, gardens between them, and with a lot of intermarrying and endless exchanging of plants, the rhododendrons were to be woven into Cornish life, a subject worthy of a social history in itself.[4] The first Williams to come to Cornwall had migrated from Wales in the mid-seventeenth century and successfully bought land and houses, tapping into a seam of mining fortunes which lasted for generations; most of these Williams gardens have a place in Cornish gardening history and as a dynasty they have kept a remarkable hold on their houses to this day. Burncoose at Gwennap, south-east of Redruth has 30 acres (12 ha.) of woodland garden and a nursery, open to visitors; Scorrier, on the north-east side of Redruth, where William Lobb once worked as a gardener, was honoured by Richard Gill with his *griffithianum x arboreum* hybrid 'Scorrier Pink', and they have Tregullow nearby with its rhododendron-filled valley, as well as Lanarth and Caerhays. Caerhays is a crenellated and castellated fantasy built by John Nash in 1805–7 and bought by J. C. Williams' grandfather, Michael Williams II, in 1854; impatient of pleasing himself, because his mother would not move out, 'J. C.' bought the beautiful though neglected Werrington Park near Launceston in 1882, for shooting and gardening. When Caerhays became his alone in about 1890 he continued to send his overflow plants to Werrington, where many of Forrest's rhododendrons remain in the Terrace Gardens, grown to great size.[5]

'J. C.' was top of the Williams tree, with his castle and 60 acres (25 ha.) ripe for planting, and with somewhere near the magical figure of 40 inches of rainfall a year. He is an enigmatic figure who never sought the limelight. He kept a garden notebook from 1897 until 1934, scrupulously recording his plantings and hybrids, and he is most remembered for his *williamsii* camellias, though his rhododendrons – *cinnabarinum x maddenii* 'Royal Flush', lavender-blue 'Blue Tit', 'Yellow Hammer', and the *discolor x griffithianum* 'Angelo', which he called 'Cornish Loder' – have all been much admired. His great service to rhododendrons was that he financed George Forrest's third expedition for three years in 1912–15 and then persuaded Rhododendron Society members into syndicates to support both Forrest and Kingdon-Ward.

These four, Eley, Millais and the two Williamses, decided who should share their society; each member was required to contribute notes on their garden's progress and these were circulated in an annual volume, the first issued in 1916. In from the start was Tresco on the Scilly Isles, E. J. P. Magor's (1874–1941) Lamellen at St Tudy in north Cornwall, and George Johnstone (1882–1960), who had begun replanting at Trewithen, north-east of Truro, with 100 *arboreum* hybrids in 1905. At Tresco a lot of Hooker's species and some of their hybrids had been planted in 1894 and 1914, including the pink and fragrant 'Countess of Haddington', a *dalhousiae x ciliatum* hybrid that still survives in the Duckery Dell. Another founding member, Sir George Holford at Westonbirt, was so keen at cross-breeding his new rhododendrons that he had 'secret' nurseries around the arboretum; the former superintendent, Tony Russell, reveals: 'Sir George's Glade, close to Savill Glade, is on the site of a secret nursery and here today one can find straight lines of rhododendrons surviving as they were grown in nursery beds 100 years ago', though many of them 'defy identification' even in such a well-regulated collection, which passed from Holford family ownership directly to the Forestry Commission.[6] Westonbirt does still have *Rhododendron fictolacteum*, with creamy, crimson-spotted bells, much prized by society members in the early days, and photographed by Forrest in Yunnan in great banks of flowers growing to four times a man's height. A fine *fictolacteum* grew in the garden of another founding member, Eustace Wilding of Wexham Park near Slough.

The Sussex contingent included Sir Edmund Loder's Leonardslee, his brother Gerald Loder's (1861–1936) Wakehurst Place and the Stephenson Clarkes' Borde Hill, all still famous rhododendron gardens. Dame Alice Godman, widow, of South Lodge, Horsham, and Clara Mangles, spinster, of Littleworth were not forgotten for their valuable collections, but it was clear that, though money was never mentioned, the new candidates needed more of it than those two elderly ladies might muster. Henry McLaren, the 2nd Lord Aberconway's (1879–1953) Bodnant in North Wales and Sir John Ramsden's Muncaster Castle at Ravenglass in Cumbria, Sir Herbert Maxwell's Monreith and the Earl of Stair's Lochinch, both in Dumfries and Galloway, and Rowallane and Kilmacurragh in Ireland were all founding members, and are all still great gardens.

It was not a dynamic society and recruiting members was a gradual, gentlemanly progress of letters and visits, inevitably saddened by the effects of the Great War. Sir Edmund Loder's son Robin was killed in 1917 and his son Giles was only six when Sir Edmund died in 1920, but Giles grew up to be equally passionate about rhododendrons. J. C. Williams lost two sons in the war and Johnny Millais' eldest son was killed in 1918. Colonel Rogers of Riverhill at Sevenoaks, for whom Millais named that lovely hybrid, saw seven years' army service and could not really believe he was fortunate enough to get back to his beloved garden; the Earl of Stair was a prisoner of war, and must have felt the same about Lochinch, recalling that Hooker had visited his great-grandfather and recommended *arboreum*, of which 70 acres had been planted, a sight that 'baffles description' every April. A younger woman member signing herself Kathleen Cuthbert in 1920 was a war widow, and about to marry Lord Rayleigh; she wrote from Beaufront Castle in Northumberland of the 'old brakes of "Nobleanum"', that 1820 hybrid, which had flowered on 6 January, three weeks earlier than usual.

Ernest Wilson thought J. C. Williams 'the first amateur to appreciate the horticultural value of the Rhododendrons of western

China' and that Caerhays had 'the best collection of these new introductions'. Wilson named *Rhododendron williamsianum* for 'J. C.', which was appreciated since it is both distinct and rare. It grows as a well-shaped rounded evergreen bush with intricate branchings and small oval leaves with single or perhaps paired open pink bells. Wilson had found *williamsianum* on the cliffs of Mount Wa Shan in western Sichuan and six plants came to Caerhays via the Arnold Arboretum. Julian Williams recalls that they came with a plea from Wilson that great care should be taken with them 'as he had only found [it] in one place, which had been an extremely difficult site to reach. He doubted whether he would ever be able to return to the place, and if he ever did, it was extremely likely that the plant would have been destroyed by fire or some other disaster.'[7] The Caerhays plants were carefully tended, they grew to be six feet high and survived until the 1970s; by that time Chinese botanists had found *williamsianum* growing on Emeishan (formerly Mount Omei). The species has been a popular parent of modern British, German and American hybrids.

Under 'J. C.'s' chairmanship, the Rhododendron Society gently expanded to include 'professionals' from Kew, Glasnevin and Edinburgh Botanics, at director level, that is, and also Wilson and Forrest, as kind of honorary members, since neither had a rhododendron garden. They could have seen little of Ernest Wilson, who was now committed to America and the Arnold, and if the truth be told was giving way as supreme collector to the younger, more vigorous George Forrest. Wilson had always entered China by the front door, working his way across to Sichuan, western Hupeh and Yunnan where he had found 60 species of rhododendron, as well as his davidias, meconopsis and lilies, before turning his attentions to Japan and the islands and his magical haul of Kurume azaleas, maples and blossom trees. Wilson and Forrest were very different. Wilson was studious, he was being groomed as director of the Arnold, which carried a Harvard professorship, and he wrote well, describing his adventures in *A Naturalist in Western China* (1913) and most famously *The Smoke that Thunders*, the first part of his *Plant Hunting* (1927), and several other books. He was a brilliantly artistic photographer; his collection is at the Arnold Arboretum and has never been fully appreciated – as a photographer he was in Joseph Rock's (1884–1962) shadow and the world of photography seems so loath to acknowledge anyone who was not actually a professional. Forrest, on the other hand, was a practical if rather pedestrian photographer, his field notes were 'adequate' and he wrote only a few articles and letters to his patrons, notably J. C. Williams and Sir Isaac Bayley Balfour at Edinburgh Botanics. The Botanics claimed him and saw the Balfour–Forrest relationship as 'a happy train of circumstances which led on the one hand to the master being furnished with botanical material by his old pupil, and on the other ensured for the latter that brilliant exposition of his discoveries which, though no more than their importance merited, can have fallen to the lot of few explorers'.[8] Forrest went into China by the back door, to Rangoon and up through Burma to the open border to Tengyueh, from where he could reach the impossible alpine regions of the Sino-Tibetan border. These, in his own words, 'form the basins and watersheds of the Salween, Mekong, and Yangtze ... there, somewhere about 98–101 deg. E longitude and 25–31 deg. N latitude, the genus reaches its optimum'.[9] He was, and needed to be, a tough field botanist but also he understood rhododendrons better than any man alive, then or since.

So this embryonic Rhododendron Society of worldly wise and wealthy men presided over the floral revolution of the twentieth century: Wilson's bounty, then Forrest's haul from seven trips of no less than 309 new species and 5,375 numbered gatherings. Forrest returned from his fourth trip in March 1920 and gave them a slide show on 16 November in the Linnaean Rooms at Burlington House, London. One imagines a sporting club kind of affair with evening dress and cigars, and the guest of honour fidgeting uncomfortably in a suit, rather than his habitual khaki. He spoke well, recalling the French missionary collectors that had first identified so many

Rhododendron fictolacteum flowering in mixed forest in
Yunnan, photographed by George Forrest.

of the plants he was able to collect, and then he had some very
particular things to say. He opened with: 'nearly all Rhododendrons
under natural conditions are social plants, a fact which, were we
to acknowledge it in our treatment of them, would tend to a greater
success in their cultivation'. He had seen them gathering together,
six to eight differing species at a view, the smaller seeking the shade,
the more tender seeking the shelter of the larger plants in a complex
mosaic.

Then there was the limestone question, a Forrest hobby-horse:
'a host of species,' he said, 'have their roots fixed in the crevices of
limestone cliffs and boulders or in a limy rubble'. He had already

written to J. C. Williams in 1913: 'The Rhododendron authorities talk of the impossibility of growing rhododendrons on limestone. I wish I had them here just now to see *Rhododendron chartophyllum* and its form *praecox* miles (no exaggeration!) of bloom, and every plant on pure limestone, many growing on the bare rock.' His evidence was in the slide of this scene; he talked of rhododendrons taking 'communal form', that is adapting their height or spread to suit immediate conditions.

Fire, and how after a fire they 'spring into growth again', was another point he hammered home:

> the cause of the fire is immaterial. The forest was probably set alight intentionally to obtain dry timber, the tribes people have most weird and improvident methods. What I wish to point out is the marvellous hardiness of the Rhododendrons to withstand such a fire when the heavier timber succumbed, and also the remarkably symmetrical growth of each of the species since the time of the fire . . . I don't think I have witnessed such a fine sight as the mass of bloom borne by each individual plant, the size and purity of those blooms, and the extremely artificial aspect of the whole scene caused by the regular spacing . . . The whole scene gave one the impression as of having been laid out by an expert landscape gardener, as indeed it had by nature! . . . One thing is certain . . . these Rhododendrons agree wonderfully well with a set-back. I examined many of the plants, and without exception, they had been burned right down to the ground surface. Why not try the same with *Rhododendron fortunei* at home?

Were there general mumblings or outright guffaws? Forrest recanted, 'I do not suggest you burning down your timber, but to have the plants cut back to a few inches every three years or so.'

Forrest must have kept going for about two hours, showing dozens of slides, which were, of course, black and white glass plate slides, and he added the colours.

'As the Tali Range is approached *R. Scottianum* and *R. michrophyton* become the dominant species . . . this shows you *R. Scottianum*.

The flowers are very open, and their tips will be almost pure white, and occasionally flushed pink on the outside, and with a yellowish-green blotch at the base and always fragrant.'

'*R. Crassum* is a cliff plant . . . the flowers are almost pure white, with flush-pink on the outside and very fragrant.'

'This is *R. Vernicosum*, a shrub of the pine forests, with pale rose self-coloured flowers, about 10 to 12 feet in height, one of the finest species on the Eastern and Western flank of the Lichiang Range.'

'*R. Beesianum*, also with large blooms, which are fleshy and crimson-rose in colour.' (Beesianum was named for his first patron, Arthur Bulley's Bees' Seeds.)

They barked questions at him; he called the questioner 'sir'; it became gladiatorial, and they tried to catch him out.

He showed *R. chartophyllum*, sometimes with white flowers with crimson spottings, sometimes purplish with green spottings, growing in scrub.

'What nature is the scrub?'

'Very often oak-scrub. The whole of the [Lichiang] range is covered with prickly evergreen oak.'

'Do you know which evergreen oak? There must be several species.'

'Yes. *Quercus semicarpifolia and Quercus spinosa . . .*'

And between the hard facts he slipped in the delicacies: 'Mountain sides splashed with colour like a giant palette . . . Gorgeous beyond description . . . *Griersonianum* with 'large rose scarlet blooms, almost vermilion in some lights; one of the finest bits of colour I have ever seen'. '*Clementinae*, dedicated to my wife . . . One of the finest species we collected . . . 6 to 9 feet, with heavy leathery dark green foliage and very large flowers which are creamy-white with crimson markings'. '*R. sanguineum*, brilliant scarlet-crimson . . . this photograph was taken during a frightful storm; we had waited for four days and I was afraid to wait longer, you can see how the blooms are dashed over with the rain.' And similarly, 'This is a single truss of *R. praestans*. Most of these shrubs grow in places that are difficult to photograph. They are surrounded on all sides by plants of their own kind in Rhododendron forests, all growing on very steep slopes.'

This was, it is astounding to realise from our end of the media age, the first actual sight of the kingdom of the rose tree, an empire of entangled forms and flowers of such complexity that even Forrest had only touched its surface. Like all slide lecturers he seemed to run out of time, and sped up the pictures towards the end, the improbable Latin names slipping lithely from his lips. No one was going to question them, all were mesmerised by the changing images, the sheer impossibility of knowing or growing a tiny fraction of what they were seeing. One wonders if they stumbled to polite applause or gave him a standing ovation.[10]

In 1922 Ernest Wilson submitted a fascinating 'note' on the species that grew in northern Asia, from the Altai mountains through the Aleutians to Alaska; he added the rhododendrons of Hupeh province and Taiwan in the succeeding years. In 1924 Anthony Waterer died, aged 73; 'this should not pass without record,' noted Gerald Loder. Waterer was 'rough in manner, kind of heart, a keen businessman but incapable of a mean or ungenerous act', who loved racing and Surrey County Cricket Club. This was the society's first obituary.

In 1925 the first show was announced to be held in the Horticultural Hall in Vincent Square on 27 April 1926. There were no less than 48 classes of a complexity to curdle the imagination: 12 species, a single truss of each, 12 hybrids likewise, a single truss of *falconeri*, *wightii*, *grande*, *arboreum*, *niveum* etc., etc., classes for sprays of smaller Himalayan species, for Forrest's favourites, sprays of deciduous hybrids, for evergreen ditto, for six plants in pots, as well as trade and display exhibits. When the day came the visitors flocked in; rather sweetly they gave the prizes to the ladies. Triumphant overall, with most points in most classes, was Lady Aberconway of Bodnant; Mrs Tremayne of Heligan won with her single heads of *falconeri* and *wightii*, and Mrs Bolitho and Mrs Williams, George

George Forrest's caravan resting in the shade, giving an idea of the scale of
his collection enterprise.

Forrest and two (unknown) companions on a day's hunting.

Johnstone, J. B. Stevenson, Gerald Loder, E. J. P. Magor and Lionel de Rothschild all won prizes. The trade award went to Richard Gill of Tremough; it was his final triumph for in 1927 Henry McLaren paid tribute to 'the late Richard Gill', who had started as gardener at Tremough and leased the old walled garden for his amazingly successful hybridising. So many marvellous plants, many named for Cornish gardens: 'Scorrier Pink' has already been mentioned, but Gill also produced 'Trebah Gem', 'Glory of Penjerrick', 'Beauty of Tremough', 'Gill's Crimson' and many more.

The year 1927 was the last one of J. C. Williams' chairmanship; the following year the society was reborn as the Rhododendron Association under the leadership of Lionel de Rothschild. There were to be subscriptions, one guinea a year, 10s 6d for working gardeners, and aims 'to encourage, improve and extend the study and cultivation of rhododendrons by means of publications, the holding of shows etc.'. The 1928 volume was almost entirely a list of hybrids and species approved and recommended for gardens. The intention clearly was to attract a broader range of members; no longer just a company of friends, an almost secret society, the rhododendron lovers had come of age.

But there were rites of passage: first the death of Ernest 'Chinese' Wilson and his wife in that motor accident at Worcester, Massachusetts, on 15 October 1930; the following year both Johnny Millais and Clara Mangles died, and then in January 1932 the news came of George Forrest's heart attack at Tengyueh on the eve of his return home from his last expedition. Forrest's obituary by William Wright Smith, Regius Keeper at the Botanics, was desperately heroic: 'Fate deals her mortal blow oftentimes at most inopportune and unexpected moments . . .' and 'Nothing befits a man so much as his passing . . .' He quoted R. L. Stevenson: 'Home is the sailor, home from sea, And the hunter home from the hill . . .', and from Callimachus: 'They told me, Heracleitus, they told me you were dead . . .' The pages of the *Rhododendron Notes* published in 1932 seem marked with tears.

*   *   *

The old way of recruiting had been a little secretive, rather like the testing out of a restaurant for a Michelin star. In the spring of 1921 when Charles Eley had reported to P. D. Williams at Lanarth on his visit to Exbury in Hampshire, Williams had replied 'that man's energy is amazing and his garden will I expect eclipse "JC's"'.[11] The man in question was Lionel de Rothschild, who was accepted as a member, and now the eclipsing moment had come.

On a fine April morning of soft sunlight the ancient New Forest is well settled into springtime; the gravelly road to Beaulieu sets out southwards across a blasted heath known as Denny Lodge Walk, a rolling open forest of duns and browns emblazoned with gorsegold. Beaulieu, *Bellus locus*, chosen by Cistercians, with their unerring noses for the most beautiful places, is wooded, sheltered and serene, grey walls rising from still water. The road leaves Beaulieu, turning right to follow the Beaulieu River until it seems England will run out, then over a hill, not a great hill but the last hill, it drops through a time-trap into the England of a century ago. The hostile heath and monkish ghosts are forgotten; here is a garden kingdom, with all the reassuring domesticity of cottages, stables and potting sheds, trimmed in light navy blue (undoubtedly Rothschild blue) and cream paint, and with glimpses of rhododendrons flowering among the trees.

Lionel de Rothschild (1882–1942) was a young man who knew what he wanted. He was born on 25 January 1882 and brought up partly at Ascott near Wing in Buckinghamshire and partly at Gunnersbury Park in west London, both places with fabulous gardens of a rather High Victorian kind. His father Leopold owned the 1904 Derby winner, St Amant, but Lionel grew up disliking horses and anything to do with them; cars and fast boats were more his line. He swept through Harrow and Trinity College Cambridge (where he kept his motorised tricycle tethered to a lamp post outside his lodgings in Jesus Lane) and into his family bank, N. M. Rothschild & Sons at New Court in the City of London; so that was that, the business side of life set fair. But he did take his gardening passion and keenness for hybridising from his father, who was famous for his prize-winning waterlilies, with 50 varieties on the pond at Gunnersbury 'and fantastic tender blue ones in special heated tanks'.[12]

When Lionel was 30 he married Marie-Louise Beer, a great-great-niece of the composer Meyerbeer, whom he met in Paris ('Mariloo' is delightfully frilled, cream, a 'Dr Stocker' x *lacteum* hybrid rhododendron). They bought a country house, Inchmery, on the Solent shore, because of Lionel's friendship with Lord Montagu of Beaulieu, famously the holder of driving licence Number 1 in Britain, another speed merchant. Together they had actually broken the world water speed record on the Solent at 28.8 knots in 1906, and the crackle of high-powered exhausts from cars, boats and planes must often have rent the air and set the locals covering their ears in those Edwardian summers in this 'peaceful' corner of Hampshire. When Lionel wanted to take up motor racing the family put their collective foot down; his son Edmund was born in 1916, there was the uncertainty of the war, his father Leopold died in 1917 and Lionel became, at 35, the head of Rothschilds' merchant bankers.[13]

But how on earth did he come to substitute rhododendron breeding for this fast life? Lionel's second cousin, Miriam, a distinguished naturalist-gardener herself, asserts that a love of gardening has been in the family for generations, as she tells the story in *The Rothschild Gardens* (1996), and 'must surely be the expression of an inherited gene'. 'Individual Rothschilds,' she admits, 'proved more faithful to gardening than to banking.'[14] Lionel was certainly brought up to lavish gardening; ordering at Gunnersbury was by the hundreds and dozens and 2,500 for something small like lily of the valley. At Ascott, where he had his own garden when he was five, there were 1,200 fruit trees in pots 'rotated in greenhouses to give the maximum variety and longest fruiting season' and a bed of 600 roses was nothing unusual.[15] But why rhododendrons? Was it the drab banking world that made him love colour so? One of his French relatives had been moderately successful with hybrids and rhododendrons had a place in most Rothschild gardens; between 1889 and 1913 the family had won 374 awards at Royal Horticultural Society shows for 'hippeastrums, blue waterlilies, orchids, pelargoniums, lobelia ... white crinum, moss roses, alpine strawberries, figs, melons, apples, pears and nectarines, grapes' – and rhododendrons.[16] Perhaps for him the rhododendron was a modern plant of the early twentieth century, impressive, challenging? The Rothschilds lived very much in their own world; with cousins all over Europe and houses all over southern England they had little need of anyone else. But it has to be said that as Jews, even rich Jews, they were not welcomed in all corners of English society. The hunting fraternity was an example, something usually obscured because to avoid a snub they simply started their own hunt, the Rothschild Staghounds in the Vale of Aylesbury. Did Lionel de Rothschild really find his empathy with rhododendrons because of their common history of exodus and migration, because he, like them, was an exotic being in a world of grey compromise?

Really, of course, it was that they grew supremely well on New Forest sandy gravels, with an added breath of sea air. At the end of the war his bachelor uncle Alfred died, leaving him enough money to buy the Exbury estate, some 2,600 acres (1100 ha.) of farms, a hamlet and the neglected house, which had been built by the Mitford family about a hundred years earlier. He took Mariloo to see it. 'Come,' he said, 'let us explore ... I want to find the two cupressus (sempervirens) mentioned in Lord Redesdale's memoirs.' Each armed with a billhook they hacked their way through the overgrowth and found the trees and their labels, saying that they had been grown from the seeds of a wreath that had fallen off the Duke of Wellington's funeral car in 1852.[17] Exbury was enchanted from the start.

They moved into a restored and enlarged Exbury House in May 1922. A locally found workforce of 150 was already clearing the undergrowth from woods of pines, oaks, planes and beech, making paths and drives; a trenching team dug the Home Wood two spits deep, adding peat but no manure or fertiliser. There were two acres of greenhouses, including a 100-foot-long rhododendron house and a tropical house for the vireyas. Sixty gardeners and 15 greenhousemen moved in, the hamlet of Exbury was enlarged for the married staff, and the rest were housed in a model, modern 'bothy'. The worst thing about Exbury was that it was terrifyingly dry in summer and so two miles of piping were laid to carry water from the bore-hole supply.

Miriam Rothschild says that no member of her family actually worked, physically worked, in their own garden until about 1940, presumably driven then by the absence of so many gardeners in the services. At Exbury from the start Lionel de Rothschild did his own hybridising, the delicate passing of pollen; he probably expected his gardeners to sow seeds and care for the seedlings, but he supervised the placing of every plant in his woodland walks, having them moved around several times till he was suited, and he certainly pruned and prinked at things he did not like. His grandson Lionel writes of him being meticulous in his gardening, no detail too small for his attention, and of his garden tours planned to take advantage of the effects of the light on certain rhododendrons.

He had started hybridising at Gunnersbury before his marriage and continued at Inchmery; he told against himself the story of his visit to Caerhays when J. C. Williams asked him rather fiercely, 'And what crosses have you been making?' When told, Williams replied 'Burn the lot.' Williams referred him to the Mendelian theories of genetic transmission, and pointed to some plants growing nearby, saying that seeds of any of those, taken at random, would be better than those Lionel had been using, for they were primary crosses. Unabashed, he did collect some seeds and the offspring grew successfully at Exbury.[18] But on another occasion J. C. Williams generously allowed him to dig up a *sinogrande* and take it home in the boot of his car.

Lionel de Rothschild's energy and enthusiasm amazed everyone: having juggled with the finances of Europe for five days, at five o'clock sharp on a Friday afternoon this short, never slim but very svelte man would leap into his waiting Rolls and speed down the A30, perhaps stopping at Bagshot if there was something precious in the way of a plant to be picked up at Waterer's, and on to Southampton and Exbury. On arrival he handed out fat cigars to his gardener and foreman and off they went on a tour of inspection, reviewing what had been done, or not done, and minute instructions were handed out for the next week's work. In spring, marriage weekends were arranged at flowering time, when a message would come down from New Court for head gardener Arthur Bedford ('Arthur Bedford' is a lavender-flowered hybrid, 'tall, fairly compact, vigorous') to have a dozen blooms cut and ready for mating with a growing plant. His weekend guests were urged to make crosses as took their fancy; each was 'provided with a sable-haired brush for transferring pollen, paper bags to cover the fertilized seed pods to prevent further pollination, labels bearing his (or her) name and a pencil to record the parents'. The seedlings were sent on later. One of his aims was, like Miss Walker of Drumsheugh, to have rhododendrons every month of the year, to walk out on a frosty February morning and find the pink bells of *moupinense* and the white-fringed flowers of Hooker's *ciliatum*. Forrest's *stewartium* gave its first British flowering at Exbury in the very early spring of 1930, and Mr McCabe's yellow giant, named for the deputy commissioner of the Naga Hills, *macabeanum*, is another early rising favourite. To have every tree that would grow in southern England was an almost incidental Exbury campaign; the rhododendrons had the company of magnolias, dogwoods, eucryphias, gleditschias, griselinias, swamp cypress, liquidambars and maples (these last some thought to be ideal for rhododendrons, others thought they might be toxic to them) as well as the New Forest oaks and pines. There were carpets of daffodils, hyacinths, hostas, cyclamen and primulas as well. In the Exbury rhododendron house Hooker's delicate and scented *dalhousiae, maddenii, lindleyi, edgeworthii* – the names are becoming mantra-like – and the exotic, also epiphytic *nuttallii*, 'the most magnificent of rhododendrons', were a collection more precious than any picture gallery's.

Lionel de Rothschild bought both species and hybrids avidly but wisely, with an uncanny sense for the beautiful and interesting. In 1934 he wrote to Mr Koichiro Wada, a nurseyman at Numazushi in southern Japan, hoping to acquire a new rhododendron he had heard of. This was a small shrub with curled slim and pointed leaves that had a woolly, suede-like indumentum, white at first then tawny brown, and deep rose-pink buds that burst into enormous clusters of pale pink fading to white flowers. This plant had been described by a Japanese botanist, Professor Nakai, as having been found on Yakushima, an island of rain forest, permanently shrouded in mist, in the East China Sea some 120 miles from mainland Japan. Mr Wada sent two very small plants of *Rhododendron yakushimanum* to Exbury where they were tended and thrived, but slowly, so slowly that nothing in particular happened for almost fifteen years, and it was to be left to other eyes and hands to introduce the popular 'yaks' to the gardening world.

In his all too brief gardening time between the wars Lionel de Rothschild made over one thousand rhododendron crosses and had 462 new hybrids named to his credit. His 'blue period', based on his good plants of *Rhododendron augustinii*, bred the lovely amethyst 'Eleanore' and lavender-blue 'Electra', both still flowering gorgeously in the Exbury Aprils. Like J. C. Williams he pursued pure yellow, producing the famous 'Hawk' from the ivory 'Lady Bessborough' x *wardii*, having already reared her ladyship from a *campylocarpum variety* x *discolor*. He made the 'Hawk' crossing twice, the second time producing the clear primrose-yellow 'Crest'. He was equally successful at clear reds, disliking any touch of blue that spoke of the dreaded magenta: 'Karko' is a *griersonianum* x 'Red Admiral', the latter bred by J. C. Williams, 'Kiev' is deep blood red and 'Kilimanjaro' currant red with chocolate spots. But, as is easily the case with rhododendrons, any pretence to a favourite colour flies off on the breeze in front of a particular beauty which is probably none of those colours. Lionel's favourite was 'Naomi', named for his youngest daughter. He had bought a seedling from Richard Gill that was a *griffithianum* x *fortunei* x *thomsonii* child and named it 'Aurora'; he crossed 'Aurora' again with *fortunei* and 'Naomi' was born, honey-scented, large open flowers of mother-of-pearl quality, delicate pink undertoned with yellow. And not only 'Naomi' but her siblings – or grex, the name given to seedlings of the same parents that are slightly variable but equally good.

Lionel de Rothschild was never to see many of his now most famous flowers; he died in London in January 1942, aged 60. Exbury marched on to war, taken over by the Admiralty as a 'stone frigate' HMS *Mastodon*. In *Requiem for a Wren* the novelist Nevil Shute describes what Wrens Janet Prentice and May Spikins found when they arrived there in the spring of 1943:

> All afternoon the two girls wandered up and down woodland paths between thickets of rhododendrons in bloom, each with a label, with water piped underneath each woodland path … They found streams and pools, with ferns and water lilies carefully preserved and tended. They found a rock garden half as large as Trafalgar Square … cedars and smooth, grassy lawns. They found long ranges of greenhouses … They learned with awe that the staff of gardeners had been reduced from fifty to a mere eighteen old men … They found the Beaulieu River … and the sea, with the seagulls drifting by upon the tide.[19]

Just over another year later a young American naval officer, invalided to a desk job after his part in the D-Day landings, also arrived at Exbury. He was something of a gardener, a keen plantsman, but he had never in America or anywhere seen such a wonderland of flowers. It made him determined that when the war was over he would try to make his future in Britain, making gardens. His name was Lanning Roper (1912–83); he eventually succeeded in his aim and became one of the nicest gardening gurus of the next 40 years.[20]

Undoubtedly rhododendrons were caught up in a craze amongst men who would not have gardened with lesser and more effeminate flowers. They were for men who had everything. It was partly the sensuality of the many-throated flowers in their ice-cream colourings – though that was also the allure of orchids – but much more the wrestling with the rhododendrons' required habitats. It was controlling the rockwork and rivulet courses, creating a mountain kingdom, given the cue by Sir Frank Crisp's (1843–1919) infamous 'Matterhorn' rockery at Friar Park, Henley-on-Thames, the greatest of its day. Sir Frank had acres of 'alpine landscape' handmade by the expert firm Backhouse of York, a rock-edged lake, waterfalls and a network of caves beneath, as well as the miniature 'Matterhorn' fashioned into its quirky shape and with a wrought-iron model chamois added for good effect.[21] In May 1905 *The Garden* illustrated Hooker's enchanting *Rhododendron ciliatum* nestling comfortably in the Friar Park rocks, and the ultimate achievement was in persuading these denizens of the high Himalayas to feel at home. The rhododendrons gave purpose to the engineering challenge, as at Cragside, the eyrie of armaments manufacturer Lord Armstrong (1810–1900), 'the Great Gunmaker', in Northumberland. The Armstrongs, William and Margaret, had already filled Jesmond Dene with rhododendrons when they lived in Newcastle, and then spent the last 30 years of the nineteenth century working on Cragside, quite simply buying a boulder-strewn mountainside and building a picturesque mansion halfway up. Lord Armstrong added 'the most extensive and ingenious hydraulic system ever found on a country estate, one that pumped water, turned spits, powered a sawmill, farm machinery and a dairy, made silage and eventually ran a dynamo providing electric light'.[22] In and around the engineering, which also included a beautiful single span steel footbridge across the Debdon burn, the paths and drives were laid amongst the rocks, which were manhandled into steps and 'rockeries', planted with ferns, heathers and hybrid rhododendrons and many varieties of pines. For the last century the picture has been of a Ruritanian castle floating amongst spring flowers.

Rhododendrons were rather snidely called 'stockbroker' flowers in the 1960s, but their true fanatics were a cut above city dealers. John Marsden-Smedley (1867–1959), who made woollen underwear at Lea near Matlock in Derbyshire, reached retirement age before he decided, in 1935, on the inspiration of Exbury and Bodnant, to make his rhododendron garden. This was extra to his already large garden, higher up the millstone grit outcrop, in an ancient quarry full of huge boulders, which his stonemasons manhandled into steps and terraces. Lea Gardens are high, almost 700 feet above sea level, above the valley of the Derwent, a place of thick morning mists and plentiful rainfall, perfect for rhododendrons.[23] Far up in the north-east of Scotland, at Blackhills near Elgin, an ex-tea planter, Thomas North Christie, was confidently planting rhododendrons, *grande* and *falconeri* and their kind, in his woodland of pines and larches.[24] To the west of Blackhills, at Cawdor Castle, the Thane of Cawdor (1900–70) was planting his haul from his trip with Frank Kingdon Ward.[25] In the far west, in the balmy, humid airs of the Cowal peninsula of Argyll, Harry George Younger handed over his woodland with rhododendrons to Edinburgh Botanics in 1929, and it has become the Benmore Botanic Garden, famous for the Himalayan and Chinese species. To the south, passing John Holms at Larachmhor and the Gibson brothers at Glenarn along the way, in the Rhinns of Galloway Kenneth and Douglas McDouall were constructing the peat terraces that would give home to masses of dwarf rhododendrons and other exotic plants at Logan, now also part of Edinburgh Botanic Garden.

In the south, Henry Broughton (1900–73), the younger son of Urban Hanlon Broughton, and his American heiress wife Cara Rogers, who together gave Runnymede to the nation, were making their own 50 acres (20 ha.) of rhododendron woods at Bakeham House, Englefield Green, during the 1930s, with the help of Eric Savill and John Barr Stevenson. Stevenson (1882–1950), a director of the contractors Holland, Hannen & Cubitt, began his garden at Tower Court, Ascot, on the western fringe of Windsor Great Park, in 1918. During the 1920s he acquired both a beautiful and energetic wife,

Roza, and a concern that the collectors were sending so many rhodo-dendron species that everyone was getting 'muddled'. 'My husband,' wrote Roza Stevenson later, 'became convinced that much could be learned by grouping them in our gardens by series. Gradually, as his vision became reality, he evolved the plan for a book embody-ing these same principles. Thus out of our collection of living species, meticulously grown under name and collector's number and arranged by series and sub-series, the important record entitled *The Species of Rhododendron* took shape and it finally appeared in 1930 as edited by my husband.'[26] The Stevensons worked hard shift-ing their plants around to conform to the taxonomic series and the Tower Court collection became famous as 'the book in being'. Both Jack and Roza Stevenson are important figures in twentieth-century rhododendron gardening, and they will return in my story.

The family who had everything, the royal family, had developed their affections for rhododendrons gradually, mirroring the more modest tastes of their subjects for 150 years or so, before indulging in a flamboyant passion. When Frederick, Prince of Wales, was 'killed by gardening'[27] in March 1751, dying as a result of a chill that developed after he had been out in the rain supervising his new garden at Kew, rhododendrons were very new migrants. His widow, Augusta of Saxe-Gotha, only in her early thirties, after nine children and an impossible husband, gratefully resigned herself to her passion for gardening, ably assisted, after a decent interval, by her magnificently handsome 'garden adviser', John Stuart (for whom *Stewartia* was named), the 3rd Earl of Bute (1713–92). Bute procured all the novelties available, including the treasures of his deceased uncle, the Duke of Argyll at Whitton, who certainly had Bartram's American rhododendrons. Baskets of rare plants and packets of seeds apparently poured into Kew for Princess Augusta, who would hardly be remembered but for her gardening. The trea-sures were so many that if the flowering *maximum* was honoured with one appreciative glance on a fine morning in May, at sometime in the 1760s, it would have blushed with pride.

We easily forget the primary business of queens and princesses, but after Augusta's daughter-in-law, Charlotte of Mecklenburg-Strelitz (*Strelitzia reginae*), had been through fifteen pregnancies in 21 years, she too retired to botany and gardening. Queen Charlotte, her biographer Olwen Hedley emphasises, cultivated serenity and taught her many daughters that 'Content is wealth, the riches of the Mind, And happy he who can this treasure find.'[28]

In 1762 Charlotte's loving husband, George III, had given her the Queen's House, which we know as Buckingham Palace, and the arrival of strelitzia from the Cape of Good Hope in 1773 had coincided with her move into the White House at Kew; she had been interested in both gardens. But in her 'retirement' she sought peace, and on 4 May 1790 she wrote to her new Master of the Horse, the 'gardening' Lord Harcourt, that 'I have been so fortunate as to obtain from Mrs Darell the Garden & House at Frogmore'. This was Great Frogmore (the queen already owned Little Frogmore or Amelia Lodge),[29] more than 30 acres (12 ha.) of well-treed seclusion down the hill from Windsor Castle, in what is now the Home Park. At Frogmore Queen Charlotte joined the latest gardening fashion, substituting a serpentine lake and Gothic follies for the enclosed gardens and formal canal. She was advised by a former equerry, now her vice-chamberlain, Major William Price, the brother of Uvedale Price, the great advocate of the Picturesque. Trees and shrubs were planted by the thousand, and included rhododendrons sent over from Kew; they quickly became an 'umbrageous thicket' through which paths wound to the lake's edge, the mock ruin, the Temple of Solitude: – 'it all constitutes a truly picturesque ornament ... The surrounding scenery is judiciously contrived to assimilate with the character of the place, the view of every distant object being excluded by trees and underwood.'[30] Queen Charlotte and her daughters spent their days at Frogmore, in the garden and the botanical library; the Queen commissioned the botanical artist Mary Moser to decorate one of the rooms with garlands of flowers and Princess Elizabeth painted other rooms in the *chinoiserie* and

Etruscan styles. In the evenings they returned to Windsor Castle, to the increasingly mad frolics of George III.

The rhododendrons and evergreens took so well at Frogmore that they dictated its sequestered style. It became the home of Queen Victoria's mother, the Duchess of Kent, who was, in 1861, buried in the Temple of Solitude which became her mausoleum. When Prince Albert died in the December of that year (his death partly attributed to a chill from walking in a wet, cold garden at Trinity College, Cambridge, with his erring son) the devastated Queen turned his every utterance into law; thus guided she decreed that she and Albert, too, wished to be buried at Frogmore, where the new Royal Mausoleum eventually received his remains in 1868. Queen Victoria visited regularly, finding solace in 'this dear lovely garden' as she called it; through the 40 years of her widowhood little was changed, and perhaps the rhododendrons and evergreens at Frogmore did most to suggest the funereal glooms that became the abiding image of Victorian shrubberies.

At Kew, where William Hooker became director of the new Royal Botanic Gardens in 1841, the following year saw a scheme by William Andrews Nesfield for shaped beds filled with a low, red-stemmed juniper and *Rhododendron ferrugineum*, the rusty-leaved, crimson-flowered alpenrose; these beds, on the terrace in front of Decimus Burton's Palm House, edged with clipped box and 'quaint and formal' evergreens, must have made a sight worth seeing.[31] The remains of Princess Augusta's rhododendrons were soon joined by Joseph Hooker's gorgeous company from the Sikkim-Himalayas, planted out during the 1850s and 1860s into the Rhododendron Dell, formerly Capability Brown's Hollow Walk. (*Rhododendrons of Sikkim-Himalaya* was dedicated to Princess Mary of Cambridge, Queen Victoria's unloved second cousin, and mother of May of Teck, the future Queen Mary.) Some of Hooker's seedlings were also sent to Prince Albert for his new garden at Osborne House on the Isle of Wight, where they joined his extensive plantings of azaleas, magnolias, camellias and lilacs, all laid out under his personal supervision in the happiest of poor Albert's projects.

Queen Victoria's son, Edward VII, took rhododendrons in quite a different direction, planting them all over his Sandringham estate as cover for the pheasants and other game birds. The walks and rides of the Sandringham woods and the roads around the estate are still wreathed in *ponticum* flowers every spring.[32]

But all these royal connections are as aperitifs to the tale of two rhododendron-mad brothers. Where to begin? In the background of Joshua Reynolds' portrait of William Augustus, Duke of Cumberland, there is an eyecatcher, a small fort on a hill overlooking the duke's new laid-out landscape of Virginia Water. The duke, second son of George II, was appointed ranger of Windsor Great Park in 1746 and he had brought some of his troops south after the dreadful Battle of Culloden to employ them as landscape gardeners. The little fort, a triangular Gothick belvedere on closer inspection, designed by Henry Flitcroft (1697–1769), had no particular use except as a picnic house for royal ladies, but it was well looked after and bided its time. In 1811 when the Prince of Wales became regent, Windsor Castle was crowded with mad King George III and his keepers, his mother and his sisters (when they were not escaped to Frogmore), so the prince made his home at Royal Lodge in the centre of the Great Park, to be near the court, but not too near. Thus the prince 'discovered' Virginia Water and transformed it into his fantasy landscape, with a gilded and painted *chinoiserie* fishing pavilion and the classical ruins of a temple hauled from Leptis Magna, the ancient Libyan seaport, and erected by the Royal Engineers as a romantic ruin with rocks and waterfalls. The fat Prince Regent was obsessed with privacy for his frolics, so the surroundings of Virginia Water were thickly planted with pines and evergreens, rhododendrons and laurels. In 1828, the little belvedere became a fort, given battlements by the George IV's (as he was by then) fantasy-master Sir Jeffry Wyatville (1766–1840), and the battlements lined with 31 brass cannon, which fired a salute on royal birthdays. Then the royal cavalcade moved on to other favourite places and no one thought much about the little fort for a hundred years, though it continued the salutes and was occupied by a resident bombardier, for many years Master Gunner Robert Turner, the oldest soldier in the British Army.[33]

The two brothers were Edward, always called David, and Albert, 'Bertie', the eldest sons of George V and Queen Mary; they grew up to be inseparable, and yet were so different – David, the daring, dancing, golden, popular Prince of Wales and Bertie, mousy, stammering, 'with slower wits and more phlegmatic nature', following in his wake and cloying in his adoration. 'There is a dreadful blank in my life,' Bertie mourned in 1922, 'directly you leave on one of your tours.'[34] It was a space wisely filled when he became engaged to the lively and enchanting Elizabeth Bowes Lyon a few months afterwards. David, because being Prince of Wales meant that he was different from all other people, became more daring, riding recklessly to hounds, racing in point to points, learning to fly (from his personal airfield on Smith's Lawn in the Great Park), chasing impossible women. He seemed to thrive 'on the improvised and unexpected' and wilt 'when trapped into a formal ritual'.[35] His was a war 'of cuts and snatches' directed at his humourless father and shy mother, who found Bertie so much easier to deal with (and to love?), and at the courtiers who hedged about them all. David moved out of Buckingham Palace to York House, St James's, 'an invented residence' in the rabbit warren of the old palace, and then, in 1929, he asked if he could have Fort Belvedere. What could he possibly want with 'that queer old place,' asked the King, 'those damm weekends I suppose'. But, says his biographer Philip Ziegler of the 35-year-old Prince, 'it was more than that, it was a home, the first home he had ever had' and it was to become 'the house he always said he loved more than any other material thing'.[36] Helped by his current belle, Freda Dudley Ward, the prince ordered the restoration and redecoration of his fort and had a swimming pool and tennis court made; the gardening he kept for himself and, adds Ziegler, 'it was the garden and surrounding grounds that gave him greatest joy.'[37] The Prince Regent's rhododendrons and laurels had grown into a jungle, and now this Prince of Wales' every spare hour was devoted to 'plunging into the undergrowth' in an orgy of rhododendron slashing, cutting vistas and clearing paths; the footmen would bring out his lunch, an apple and a cup of tea, locating him by whistles, and His Royal Highness would leave it until the very last minute to emerge and go indoors to wash and dress for a duty. He made his visitors do their bit, he flew the Duchy of Cornwall flag from his 'little independent fort pipping its nose at Windsor Castle' and he played the bagpipes, another passion, to his heart's content. His friends began to feel that the prince's 'redeeming charms were having a hard battle with these eccentricities'.[38]

After the slashing, came the planting. The prince had many gardening friends, among them Philip Sassoon, who was making his own lavish gardens at Trent Park and Port Lympne, and he talked rhododendrons with his hosts in the hunting shires. He also met Eric Savill (1895–1980), a young veteran of the First World War, badly wounded in 1916 on the Somme, and now a partner in his family firm, Alfred Savill & Sons, the London land agents and surveyors. Savill was frequently at Windsor, staying with Owen Morshead, who had been appointed librarian at Windsor Castle in 1926; they had arrived in Cambridge together in 1913 and became firm friends. By the whispers through the ether and the way these things were done, possibly the prince's influence, Savill was appointed deputy surveyor of the 15,000 (6,000 ha.) acres of Windsor parks and woods in 1931, and he helped the prince choose both species and hybrids for his rhododendron collection at the Fort. The prince became quickly known for his real rhododendron passion, shared by many in the Windsor 'circle', that ring of houses and gardens that fringes the Great Park, including Jack Stevenson at Tower Court, Ascot, Henry Broughton at Bakeham House in Englefield Green and Tom Lowinsky at Tittenhurst Park, Sunninghill (whose collection was sold at the time the prince was gardening).

In 1934 the prince visited Lionel de Rothschild at Exbury, and it is most unlikely that he came away empty-handed; he became patron of the Rhododendron Association that year and remained so as King Edward VIII.

And what of Bertie and his Elizabeth, the Duke and Duchess of York? She had grown up to be a keen gardener, surrounded by her gardening Bowes Lyon relatives, and with her encouragement the duke was soon tackling the overgrown regency rhododendrons in the garden at Royal Lodge, which became the Yorks' country home. For the duke gardening became his chief relaxation when he gave up hunting and sold his horses as one of the royal economies made in response to the depression years of the early thirties. He kept some of his hunting friends, including the Americans, Ronald and Nancy Tree, who had entertained him at Kelmarsh Hall in Northamptonshire's Pytchley country, 'the most inviting hunting box in England'. Royal rhododendron gossip encouraged Nancy Tree to plant a hedge of pink and white hybrids at Kelmarsh, and in return it must have been Ronald Tree who introduced the duke to the landscape architect Geoffrey Jellicoe (1900–96), working for him at the Trees' new home Ditchley Park, Oxfordshire, and at Kelmarsh, and who was commissioned to 'improve' the garden at Royal Lodge in early 1936. At Royal Lodge he gave the two-storeyed Gothick villa a presence in its garden by building a terrace, which offered a viewing platform for the garden, as well as a place to take tea in the sunshine. The duke's new-found passion for rhododendrons planted the garden with sweeps of species and hybrids and most especially the salmons, pinks, creams and yellows of Ghent and Knap Hill hybrid azaleas, a range of soft and lovely colours which became synonymous with the duchess' taste in clothes, as she moved through her roles as Queen Elizabeth and as Queen Mother.

The Duke of York cultivated his gardening friends, too, and after a visit to the Countess of Stair at Lochinch in May 1935, he took more than usual care with his message of thanks:

As to my visit, I am overjoyed Eclecteum (to be chosen out) and Aberrans (wandering) Cyclium (round) so many Erastum (lovely) and Arizelum (notable) gardens in so short a time, has left me Charitostreptum (gracefully bent) with a Recurvum (bent back), and somewhat Lasipodum (woolly footed). I must say I am filled Coelonerum (with impressed nerves) at all the Agetum (wondrous) & Aperantum (limitless) beauties of the gardens Cyclium (round) Lochinch . . .[39]

There is something more than sad in these two brothers, once inseparable, and with their twin rhododendron passions, now pacing their separate roads as the crisis loomed; the woman that the Prince of Wales loved, Wallis, was taking her place as mistress at Fort Belvedere. King George V died in January 1936 and the irredeemable processes made David into King Edward VIII. An unhappy story is told of his new-found powers: when that spring he went to inspect the gardens at Windsor Castle he was conducted around the peach house, and told of the promised bumper crop to come, the pride of the head gardener; he made no comment but at the end of his tour gave instructions for the peach blossoms to all be cut and sent to Mrs Simpson and her friends.[40] As the summer of 1936, the year of three kings, gave way to autumn, the Fort and Royal Lodge faced each other across the rhododendrons and fate pursued its course: the rumours, whispers, gossip and arguments, the terrible confessions and secrecies, heartbreaking 'interviews' between the king and his mother, the king and his brother – the Duke of York unable to say it to his brother's face but writing afterwards that 'he longed for me to be happy, adding that he of all people should be able to understand my feelings; he was sure that whatever I decided would be in the best interests of the country and the Empire'.[41] In the end, as all the world knows, the king decided that he could not carry his burden without the support of the woman he loved, and as Wallis Simpson was completely unacceptable to the British government or people, let alone the royal family, the king gave up his throne. It is said that when as

Duke and Duchess of Windsor they were settled in Paris the duke missed Fort Belvedere and his rhododendrons most of all, that he was deeply hurt that he was never to be allowed to return there, and that the thought of it all 'mouldering' broke his heart.

Throughout these troublesome times Eric Savill had been pursuing his idea of making a garden in the Great Park; he had chosen a boggy piece of rhododendron, laurel and bracken-ridden waste on the eastern boundary at Englefield Green, south of the Cumberland Gate, and set about having it cleared. Clearing and digging steered the water into two ponds with a stream connecting them; one of the earliest plantings was of a lorryload of primulas, discarded from spring bedding in St James's Park and destined for the bonfire, but valuable to the new garden, which had royal approval but very little in the way of resources. One of the gardeners procured a basket of 'kingcups', Caltha palustris, in return for rabbits. Gradually wild and semi-wild plants arrived, sometimes of their own accord – primroses and bluebells, narcissus, water iris – and neighbouring gardeners sent in willows, ferns, forsythia, and some small rhododendrons and azaleas. Seedlings thrived in the moist loamy soil of the new garden and a nursery was established. Then the war came; King George VI and Queen Elizabeth and their daughters found their brief moments of peace and relaxation in their garden at Royal Lodge; the king, making an official visit to HMS Mastodon at Exbury, managed to lose his aides and enjoy the woods for a brief while. In the park Eric Savill's plans had a low priority amidst the privations of wartime, but his new garden went on growing and was not forgotten.

In 1946 there had to be adjustments and many changes. The Savill Garden, as the King named it in 1951, was almost overgrown and needed clearing and gardening, planting with rarer plants in line with Sir Eric's ambition that it should show as many differing kinds of gardening and the largest variety of plants possible. The Savill Garden has always had some lovely rhododendrons but they were really only a stepping stone in this story. The King and Queen wished to develop another area of the park, some 400 acres (160 ha.) of woodland south of Smith's Lawn, a superb site for a rhododendron garden to cheer the nation in the drab post-war world and give a home to many marvellous plants that were going begging in the aftermath of broken lives and lost fortunes. The prospects cheered the garden makers themselves: 'a curving wooded valley sloping gently down to Virginia Water, this main valley being intersected by another, thus forming an enormous inverted Y with curving arms, the sides, high and steep in places, contrasting with the centre of the valley, which is open and gently declining to the water'.[42] There were magnificently spreading oaks and beeches, with birches, Scots pine and sweet chestnuts, perfect rhododendron companions.

And so the Valley Garden gave a home to flowery refugees. The best rhododendrons were rescued from Fort Belvedere (which had been empty and was ousted as a royal residence in 1955 and let on a 99-year lease) and Eustace Wilding's collection from Wexham Place near Slough, purchased by the pill company Aspro for executive housing at the end of the war, also came. Using his courtier's charm Sir Eric Savill, who had been told about the threat to the Wilding garden by a neighbouring gardener, Mrs Clark, played up the king's undoubted pleasure at acquiring the magnolias, maples and fothergillas, as well as the rhododendrons and azaleas for his imaginative new project. The directors of Aspro, who probably had not the first clue as to what these wonders were, were, of course, honoured that the king should take them away. And so for two winter seasons the lorries shuffled from Windsor to Slough and back again, and the shade of Eustace Wilding must have been pleased. Clearly Hope Findlay and the gardening staff at the Savill and Valley gardens became experts in plant moving, but their biggest challenge was to yet to come.

Jack Stevenson at Tower Court had been a huge supporter of the Savill and Valley schemes from the start; he suggested that the green oval dell known as the Punch Bowl, set slightly apart from the main valley, was the perfect place for displaying Kurume azaleas, and he offered his own collection of the 'Wilson Fifty' as stock plants. Cuttings were duly taken to the Savill nursery where they proved as 'easy as geraniums', the best growing from July cuttings placed in a cold frame. In 1948 the 2-year-old plants were ready to go out into the cleared sandy soil, with leaf mould and peat added, awaiting them in the Punch Bowl. Within another two years thousands had been planted, in bold sweeps of 50 to 200 plants of a single variety and colour. It is one of the astounding sights of the English spring; from April to throughout May, this bowl of colours merges from apple-blossom pink into deeper pinks, mauves, whites and creams into rich deep reds, carmines and orange-scarlet flowers, seen through the tracery of larch and silver firs.

Though Jack Stevenson could never have seen the full glory of his Kurume children in flower in the Punch Bowl, at least when he died in 1950 it was with the consolation that they had a home. For his widow, Roza, the great problem was the Tower Court species collection, which was too crowded and which she could not manage to maintain. With a heavy heart she decided to sell, hoping to find a single owner; when the king heard this news he immediately sent Sir Eric Savill to open negotiations. The price was £11,000, an enormous sum, which the Treasury refused to pay, but the story has always been that the king personally persuaded the chancellor of the exchequer, Hugh Gaitskell, to do so; perhaps it helped that the chancellor's predecessor and colleague was Hugh Dalton, the son of the king's old tutor.

At Tower Court the plants were crowded into about two acres; their new home was 30 acres (12 ha.) on the slopes of Breakheart Hill, west of the Valley Garden, where the site was cleared of all but the best high-canopy oaks, pines and birches. The task was enormous; pessimism being the nature of gardeners many said it could not be done. The new site was too exposed, the plants were too big to be moved; but Sir Eric Savill consulted the collectors, including Frank Kingdon Ward and Joseph Rock, and he read up about George Forrest. He realized that cold would not bother these denizens of the Himalayas, and work started in the autumn of 1951. The agonies of the process are best described in detail by Lanning Roper:

A team of six went over early each morning to Tower Court. Two men tied up the branches close to the central stem to prevent damage and so that they would take up less room on the trailer, while the others started trenching operations. First the extent of the root area had to be determined, and it was not unusual to find that roots had spread out to a radius of eight to ten feet from the trunk. In such cases the roots were lifted and separated from the soil, later being wrapped about the root ball. Generally, however, a trench was dug at a distance from the plant to include the major root system and to the depth of it so that the ball could be lifted free. Thanks to the characteristically shallow-rooted nature of rhododendrons, a depth of two to three feet was usually adequate, although the diameter of the ball might be as much as six to eight feet. Meanwhile a ramp with a gentle incline had been dug to the base of the root ball on the side from which the plant was to be lifted on to the waiting trailer. Next, excess soil was pricked off meticulously with a fork from the root ball until the root ends were exposed. The root ball was then tipped over on its side until the stem was in a nearly horizontal position, and at the same time burlap was slipped around the ball to hold it firm. Then a hand-cart with caterpillar treads was pushed in close so that the plant, when lowered back to a vertical position, was firmly seated on the platform, with its root ball securely covered with burlap to prevent too rapid evaporation of moisture and the attendant drying out of the root hairs. The hand-cart was now pulled (not an easy operation in wet weather or on dry sandy soil even with the aid of planks) to the trailer, on to which the plant, still on its cart, was to be loaded.

The journey to Windsor was an exacting one. Although the shortest route by way of Blacknest Gate was only about eight miles, it was often necessary to take a much longer route because of the old iron footbridge over the Sunningdale–Ascot road, which precluded the passage of any very tall plants. (Ironically, now that the collection has been moved, the bridge has been demolished.) The largest plant in bulk was probably the type plant of *R. falconeri*, which weighed about one and a half tons with a spread of over eighteen feet and a height of about fourteen feet. There were even taller plants, such a *R. houlstonii* and *R. hodgsonii*, as well as giant *fictolacteum*, *diaprepes*, *planetum* and *sutchuenense*. In the Arboreum Series the largest plant was *R. floribundum* 'Borde Hill', measuring fourteen feet by twelve feet.

In the case of the plant of *R. falconeri*, it took over two hours to cover the distance from Tower Court to Breakheart Hill, and at several points it was necessary to turn back because the road was too narrow or there was no clearance under wires. In fact, it was often necessary to lift up the telegraph wires so that the plant could slide beneath them. It was important to stick to the middle of the road where clearance was greatest, thus forcing other vehicles to crowd on to the verges. There was no police escort such as one sees for lorries and trailers carrying huge boilers or propellers, and there were times when it would have been a great help. In any event, the journey was always safely made with no serious casualties. Each night when the gang returned to Windsor they brought with them the plants lifted that day. These were stacked in the general area where they were to be planted, the root balls being covered with leaves. About every two weeks there was what came to be known as a 'setting out day'. Sir Eric and Mr Findlay would direct the placing of each plant and decide what other trees and shrubs should be used for interplanting.[43]

After all this labour the royal rhododendron gardens, a unique gift to the people of Britain and visitors who would come from all over the world, entered upon their public life. The Valley Gardens are open every day of the year.

As for the royal brothers, their schism continued in their gardens. Geoffrey Jellicoe's brief partnership with Russell Page (1906–85), who had contributed to the design and planting of Royal Lodge, did not survive the war. Jellicoe designed the hedged and enclosed flower gardens for Sandringham in 1947. Page continued his career, finding clients mostly in France and America. He worked for the

Duke of Windsor at his Paris house and his country retreat: Page did some lovely things; at the mill at Gif 'we replaced a very steep grass bank, facing north and sloping sharply down to the shaded mill-race, with a series of narrow terraces ... held up by low dry walls. In the wall-face we planted London Pride and *Campanula portenschlagiana* and in the beds themselves clumps of white and pale pink Kurume azaleas ... set out in informal drifts.' A feathery dwarf syringa and spirea 'Anthony Waterer' were added. In the Paris garden Page needed a great deal of ingenuity, recalling that 'the Duke happened to dislike all evergreens'.[44] His once beloved rhododendrons had gone the way of his throne.

CHAPTER SIX

'Pink Pearl' Queen of the
Bagshot Sands

THE NURSERY TRADE has narrow histories; nurserymen were silent and secretive by nature, spending long hours at their potting benches, rising at dawn to stoke the greenhouse boilers, wary of strangers who might steal their stock. They married 'in the trade' and their wives and children worked in the business, and so taciturn dynasties were bred. To a nurseryman the past was about as much use as a tray of desiccated seedlings. They cared not for records or reminiscences; the future stock was all. They emerged in Tudor times, when London was a city of gardens, as seedsmen and growers tucked into the alleys around St Paul's. Their prosperity fed on three things: the influx of difficult foreign plants, plenty of customers and plentiful labour, and as they prospered they needed more space and so they shifted from city to suburbs – in the late eighteenth century those first rhododendron migrants were grown in Hackney, Islington and Chelsea – and then into the rural margins. But nursery people were never country people, they were townees cut adrift, and they became more secretive than ever. Only one tenacious spirit, the late Dr John Harvey, has plucked their names from deeds and wills in muniment rooms up and down the land and put them into *Early Nurserymen* (1974), a book of pale, small print packed on to thick pages (in my copy at least), staccato gobbets of names and dates, as though the nurserymen, and a few women, are standing up to be counted, but saying little more.[1]

Dr Harvey did not like to enter the nineteenth century (he was a medievalist by nature) and that was to be the great century for nurseries. An even greater influx of new plants, a rising middle class and plentiful labour plus fast rail transport enabled local firms to become national: James Backhouse of York sent his gardeners to Cambridge to landscape Newnham College garden, he supplied country estates and traded with other nurseries all over the country, and still served local customers at home. Backhouse was more customer friendly than most nurserymen, which is why he is so well known. It is hard, after 50 years of garden centres that are all 'up front' with little behind, to remember that nurseries were just the opposite; they were all behind. Mere customers were never allowed beyond the front office into the rabbit warrens of potting sheds and cold frames, let alone into the fields of closely guarded treasures.

Rhododendrons changed all this; indeed, I would go so far as to say that if there had been no rhododendrons there would have been no garden centres, not that that should be held against them. Certainly without rhododendrons there would have been no nurseryland on the Bagshot sands, not even the famous name of Waterer's.

Rhododendrons are, after all, not easy to hide: 'As the nursery is approached from Woking Station,' wrote the Gardeners' Chronicle reporter in June 1899, 'a foretaste of the feast of colour is obtained from the high road, whence glimpses can be caught, low in the distance, of great stretches of Rhododendrons in bloom – a scene not only very beautiful, but peculiarly striking, set, as it is, amidst the meadows and hedgerows of pastoral Surrey. When the nursery is reached there is seen stretching away through it a straight avenue, close on a mile in length, bordered for the most part by towering masses' of scarlet, mauve and pink blossoms.[2]

The Waterers had been in Woking since Tudor times, but the

first nurseryman, Michael (1745–1827), appeared in 1796, inheriting some land from his aunt on the western edge of Woking, at a place called Knap Hill, which enabled him to set up on his own, taking his son Michael (1770–1842) to share in 'the art and mystery of a nurseryman' in 1809.[3] This art and mystery, in part, meant hybridising, *maximum x catawbiense*, the two Americans, producing some pink and rose shades of flowers. Michael II became mad about rhododendrons, and he had the magic touch. He took his flowering plants into Chelsea and rented a temporary site in the King's Road each May to tempt villa dwellers and fill his order books; that done, he took his family and staff off in a horse-drawn charabanc to Ascot Races, their only holiday of the year.

In 1829 he was able to buy a second nursery, from the widow of John Taylor of Bagshot, for £1,665. This was about 30 acres (12 ha.) on the edge of the village of Bagshot, some five miles northwards from Knap Hill, on the opposite side of Bisley and Westend commons. The commons, covered with oak and birch, gorse and broom, were part of the spread of sandy wastes across northern Surrey, tertiary sands carpeting the London clay. These 'Bagshot Sands', early-warming, free-draining acidic soils, with peat and loam in patches, resting on the water-retentive clay, were, Michael Waterer had discovered, perfect for the development of root systems, especially for the American evergreens. Most of these sandy wastes, useless for agriculture, were (and still are) the training grounds of the British Army; Knap Hill was next door to the Bisley ranges, royal reviews were taken on Chobham Common, and the sandy soldiery land spread from Camberley and Sandhurst into Berkshire, and down the London to Basingstoke and Winchester road to Farnborough and Aldershot. This ecological marriage of the soldiers of the Raj in their villas at home, their memories of Indian rhododendrons and Waterer's ability to supply these plants for their gardens and clubhouses, spawned the whole romantic ethos of what William Robinson (1838–1935) called 'the Surrey style' – a world that looked backwards to Harry Mangles at Littleworth and forwards to embrace

Betjeman's adored Joan Hunter Dunn, 'Furnish'd and burnish'd by Aldershot sun':

> By roads 'not adopted', by woodlanded ways,
> She drove to the club in the late summer haze.
> Into nine-o-clock Camberley, heavy with bells
> And mushroomy, pine-woody, evergreen smells.[4]

Both nurseries flourished for Michael Waterer, but only briefly, for he was struck down in a cholera outbreak in 1842; he had no children so he bequeathed the Bagshot nursery to his brother John (1784–1868) and the Knap Hill nursery to his youngest brother Hosea I (1793–1853); after a while the two nurseries went their separate ways.

At Knap Hill Hosea I had expanded to 103 acres and 50 staff by the 1851 census; his specialities were late-flowering hardy hybrids, and standards: '10 and 12 feet high, with clean stems 5 feet in length and 6 inches in diameter, bearing heads 30 feet round and loaded with flowers'.[5] These, presumably grafted on *ponticum* and liable to revert, were for villa gardens where space was at a premium, and they remained popular for 100 years. Hosea I died in 1853, leaving Knap Hill to his nephews Anthony Waterer I (1822–96) and Robert Godfrey (*c.* 1812–74), who started developing the Knap Hill deciduous azaleas during the 1860s and expanded the nursery still further. In fact, Anthony I built a 'special relationship' between Knap Hill and America, which began with plants sent to Andrew Jackson Downing for landscape schemes in Washington, at the Capitol, the White House and the Smithsonian Institute. Downing died in a steamboat accident in 1852, and his executor Henry Winthrop Sargent, Charles Sargent's cousin, raised money from Congress to pay Waterer's outstanding bills. This encouraged a Sargent–Waterer friendship, something of a boom in American customers, and Anthony I bred the hardy 'Ironclad' *catawbiense* children for the New England market, and the Sargent family in particular. Anthony's son, Hosea II (1852–1926), went to work in

RHODODENDRONS ON THEIR OWN ROOTS

The finest named hardy kinds can now be supplied. These are much to be preferred to grafted plants, which are in many instances most unsatisfactory to the purchaser.

ANTHONY WATERER,
KNAP HILL NURSERY, WOKING, SURREY.

A frequently featured advertisement by Waterer's of Knap Hill Nursery in the *Gardeners' Chronicle* in the 1890s.

Philadelphia, where Waterer's display at the Centennial Exposition of 1876 caused such a sensation that the 'spark of interest in rhododendrons in the USA was fanned into flames'.[6]

It was Anthony's son, Anthony II (1850–1924), who discovered, when he took over Knap Hill in 1896, that his father had made some wonderful 'improvements' on the old 1830s azaleas, the '*Hybridae belgicae*' raised by the baker Paul Mortier of Ghent, which he had kept solely for his own pleasure. The Knap Hill strain came from adding some Chinese blood to the Pontic *luteum* x American azalea parentage of the Ghents. P. D. Williams described the 'remarkable' colours of Anthony I's secret store: 'the crimson deep and solid, the scarlets brilliant as a new hunting coat, the yellows attaining the colour of rich Guernsey butter, the oranges bright with crimson filaments to the anthers, and of course there were beautiful pinks and whites'.[7] These, the most famous flowers to come from Knap Hill nursery, were not to enter the public realm until the 1930s, and then via other hands: after Anthony II's death in 1924, Hosea II came home from America to run the nursery, but he died in 1926, and his sons, who were American citizens, put the 130-year-old nursery up for sale.

At Bagshot, on that famous site south of the old A30 as it rolls up Bagshot Hill, John Waterer I now called his nursery the American

Pennell & Sons, advertisement from *The Garden*,
28 October 1905.

Nursery; he grew all the American plants but especially rhododendrons, advertising *ponticum* 'usually acknowledged the best Evergreen' for 'under-cover', being disliked by hares and rabbits, from 10s 6d to one guinea per hundred.[8] He was 'a pillar of the community', at home in The Cedars, unmissable at the foot of Bagshot Hill for the elegant Lebanon cedars outside (and one is still there), and when he died in 1868 he had increased the nursery to over 200 acres (80 ha.) and was worth about £180,00. Unfortunately the kindly John I, in dividing his legacy between his children, divided the nursery: needless to say things did not work out and before long one brother was suing another and another brother's widow and the upshot was that John II (1826–93) had to raise a substantial mortgage to gain control of the nursery, and his father's riches had virtually disappeared overnight. Fate, however, was not unkind, for it was John II, whose family James Mangles had met in their rhododendron guises in that show tent in London in 1881, who raised 'Pink Pearl'.

The story of her birth has been told many times, with, as is the way with rhododendrons, many variables. John II certainly did not keep records of his crosses, nor did he study genetics; he worked entirely on his Waterer instinct for a good plant. His son Gomer Waterer (1867–1945) did write down, 'My father raised this plant and I always understood him to say it was a seedling from "George Hardy" x Broughtonii';[9] the latter was a first-generation cross, *arboreum x maximum*, possibly raised at Knap Hill by Hosea I and named for his friend Frank Broughton. W. J. Bean, in *Trees and Shrubs Hardy in the British Isles* (8th edn, 1976), says that 'Cynthia' was this parent, and she was a large 'lady', up to 25 feet, profusely pink but magenta tainted, raised by Charles Noble and called by him 'Lord Palmerston'. 'George Hardy' was one of James Mangles' *griffithianum* hybrids (*griffithianum x catawbiense*), which had found its way to Bagshot and been marketed by Waterer's. The story goes that John II had spotted this seedling flowering and it looked so good that he visited every day, but said nothing. One morning it had disappeared and, being a taciturn nurseryman, he still said nothing, but on his rounds a day or two later, passing some of the nurserymen's cottages, he saw his plant occupying pride of place in a front garden. It was usual for the men to take plants for their gardens, and this man clearly had a good eye – he should have been promoted – but 'Pink Pearl' was returned to the nursery and cosseted into fame. John II did not live to see this stardom, however.

It was masterminded by his son Gomer, who had a real flair for showmanship; he unveiled her to the RHS in 1896, she was 'launched' with an Award of Merit in 1897, given a First Class Certificate in 1900 and was a best-seller by 1902.[10]

The virtues of 'Pink Pearl' are that she is completely hardy, she flowers while young and will not mind the full sun of an open garden; she has deep pink buds, which open to enormous flowers, with as many as nineteen softer pink flutes on a flower head, held on a ruff of long green leaves. The flowers grow paler as they grow older and are almost white when they fall. They have a pearlised tinge certainly, but the stroke of genius, presumably Gomer Waterer's, was to enhance this into her name. Pearly opalescence is a marketing favourite with romantic connections – diving through warm green waters, the tiny seed pearls in a child's necklace or an old lady's treasured ring, the pearls that tumble from the shoulders of the Virgin Queen, the booty of pirates brave, 'pearls before swine' or the blue-green metallic sheen of a 1960s Sunbeam car – all speaking of intimate treasures that make the glowing aptness of the name 'Pink Pearl' a major factor in this flower's success.

The world was quick to claim her, even though some were disappointed she did not inherit the *griffithianum* scent, and others were frankly rude – 'the barmaid at the hunt ball!'[11] sniffed one woodland gardener who would not admit her. But Queen Alexandra praised her and most people followed suit. *The Garden* for 7 January 1905 sported a muzzy but impressive photograph of her blooming in South Africa, 'the largest plant in the world, six feet wide, five feet through,' claimed H. M. Arderne of The Hill, Claremont, Cape Town. 'Rhododendrons will never grow in South Africa,' Cecil Rhodes had scoffed when it was suggested he should plant his glen at Groote Schuur 'with that most beautiful of English shrubs'. Mr Arderne, whose own 'Pink Pearl' had been imported in her debut year of 1897 and clearly liked the slopes of Table Mountain, had proudly convinced Rhodes otherwise and sent 1,500 rhododendrons to Groote Schuur.[12] Some weeks after Mr Arderne, Charles Linger, head gardener at Heyscroft, West Didsbury in Cheshire, claimed a plant bought in 1898 to be five and a half feet high by four and half feet wide with 30 flower buds, as against the ten shown in the South African photograph. Come May and the editor of *The Garden* was inundated with rhododendron letters. F. J. Thorne, gardener to Major Joicey at Sunningdale Park, put pen to paper in praise of his 'Pink Pearl', seven years old, completely frost-hardy despite nasty rumours to the contrary and showing over 70 flowers; the photograph would follow. Instead, the editor went to see for himself, reporting on 3 June that Sunningdale Park was 'pink with blooms' and 'Pink Pearl' was unequalled for colour and size of flowers. The following week in 'hot sunbaked Weybridge' it was more rhododendrons, and six miles further on at the embryonic Wisley the azaleas were gorgeous and a plant of 'Gauntlettii' was in flower, large and pink, and the best compliment that could be paid was that it looked like 'Pink Pearl'. It was not until 1 July that *The Garden* found space to mention that summer's London displays: Knap Hill's was 'a grand display' in Rotten Row in Hyde Park, with dozens of hybrids including the famous white 'Sappho' with her maroon blotchings, the rich salmon 'Mrs R. S. Holford', showy 'Kate Waterer' and the New England 'Ironclads' for 'H. H. Hunnewell', dark rich crimson, and 'Mrs Arthur Hunnewell', pink with primrose centre and 'very pleasing'. The Bagshot display was in the Royal Botanic Society's garden in Regent's Park, beds and borders forming 'a charming garden' in which 'Pink Pearl' was prominently present.

'Pink Pearl' was more than the most popular hybrid, sold in her thousands through the twentieth century until she inevitably became a cliché for blowzy bad taste, the floral equivalent of 'candy floss', those huge pink balls of spun sugar sold at the seaside and fairgrounds in the 1950s. 'Pink Pearl' was a turning point in the story of rhododendrons in cultivation. In the stages of this history she marks the third; at first, it was enough merely to own a rhododendron, then it became the thing to hybridise them, both stages the provinces of enthusiasts. The birth of a commercially successful hybrid, not bred for the members of the Rhododendron Society or their fellows with woods full of species and their own hybrids, but for the gardening public, was significant. 'Pink Pearl' marks the entry into the third stage: gardening with rhododendrons. She was not alone among popular hybrids and was the spur to many more. She shifted the perspective on collecting, and though the faraway adventures of Reginald Farrer and Frank Kingdon Ward still attracted plenty of readers, their books for gardeners – Farrer's *My Rock Garden* (1907) and *The English Rock Garden* (1919), and Kingdon Ward's *Rhododendrons for Everyman* (1927) – were most popular.

Gardening with rhododendrons. How was this to be done? It is as well to begin at the fountainheads, with William Robinson and Gertrude Jekyll. Robinson was a great fan, and he planted them abundantly beside his entrance court at Gravetye Manor, where they still flower. He was very particular that the plants should have space to be appreciated, and were not lumped into a 'serried formal mass'; Robinson always favoured judicious rather than mob planting, which separated the gardeners from the landscapers, but was also a point of view on the side of the medium and smaller garden, quite difficult to sustain in his day when horticulture was dominated by the head gardeners of great estates. In rhododendron terms Robinson's anathema was Lady Marion Alford's plantings of a long avenue and walks solid with pinkish hybrids at Ashridge in Hertfordshire, where they too still flower.

In *The English Flower Garden* he gives a long list of French, German and British hybrids, over 200, which the Victorian gardener could choose from. The critical factor was colour, and Robinson's colour rules were adopted by Gertrude Jekyll, applying a feminine good sense because 'it was impossible to buy everything that was on offer'. Colour harmony, and choosing with great care, visiting the nurseries and buying only those that 'were beautiful in themselves' in threes and fives of one kind and some singles, and planting them well without overcrowding, these were her rules.[13] At Munstead Wood, along her 'Green Wood Walk' she grouped crimson

Rhododendron nobleanum, an early hybrid, illustrated in
William Robinson's *The English Flower Garden*, 1893 edition.

inclining to scarlet or blood with dark claret and true pink; she
favoured crimson 'John Waterer', rosy-scarlet 'Alexander Adie',
deep scarlet 'James Marshall Brooks' and the pure pink 'Bianchi'.
'Bianchi' was allowed near the rose and salmon pinks, of which
there were not many save the famous 'Lady Eleanor Cathcart' and
'Mrs R. S. Holford'. Set quite apart were the 'rose colours inclining
to amaranth' – another word for magenta – then the magenta-
crimsons, crimson-purples, leading to the 'cool clear purples of the
ponticum class, dark and light, grouped with whites'. Lilac 'Everestianum' was good with the whites; Miss Jekyll liked Waterer's
'Sappho' but did not have room for it, and she, being loyal to what
she called 'good old plants', thought that good *ponticum* seedlings
chosen from the nursery were often the most effective. Restraint

was all; at Munstead she only allowed the first and second and last groupings, the crimsons through to pink, pink to salmon pink and the purples, lilac and whites. Of whites she had an 'old kind' called 'multum-maculatum', which she thought one of the earliest hybrids, with the longest, narrowest and darkest green leaves of any she knew and loose, narrow-petalled flowers, milk-white, the lower petals spotted with scarlet, beautiful as cut flowers; though now out of favour, she felt the need 'to champion this delicate class of beauty simply because everyone else glorifies the "great bouncing beauties"'. She had planted her rhododendrons in about 1890, amongst some birch seedlings; in ten years she had the desired effect of the silver stems rising from the green and shining clumps, and she planted white *Lilium candidum* at the rhododendrons' feet for a summer effect. The exquisite but modest lilies were another instance of the loyalty and restraint that ruled her gardening, for she had begun her garden in the 1880s with the inspiration of G. F. Wilson's (d. 1902) pioneering work on his patch of Wisley Common, where he had introduced rhododendrons as shelter for his lilies, the flashier *Lilium giganteum* (*cardiocrinum*). At Wisley the lilies and rhododendrons had done so well, *Country Life* noted in September 1897, that newer hybrids had been added, so this was how rhododendrons came to one of their most famous homes, the RHS garden at Wisley, and how the iconic mix with *cardiocrinums*, a dream of many rhododendron gardeners, was born.

Jekyll's championing of the cool, clear purple *ponticums* is reassuring; in another context she warned of the word 'crimson' in catalogues – 'one cannot know whether it stands for a rich blood colour or for malignant magenta' – which is why she used the purple-flowered amaranth 'as a definition and as a warning'.[14] Why was magenta so malign? Her acute eye for colour was offended by the aniline dyes developed in her youth. In the 1850s the young William Henry Perkin (1838–1907) had almost accidentally, whilst trying to make synthetic quinine, produced a black substance from oxidated aniline, which he dissolved in methylated spirits to give a purple, Perkin's Purple. In

Rhododendron indicum at Coolhurst in Sussex, illustrated in William Robinson's *The English Flower Garden*, 1893 edition.

defiance of many established dyers the Perkin family had developed and marketed their 'mauve' dye, which became fashionable. *Punch* complained that London was afflicted with 'mauve measles', and a columnist in *All the Year Round* (proprietor Charles Dickens) observed: 'purple hands wave from open carriages – purple hands shake each other at street doors – purple hands threaten each other from opposite sides of the street' and purple gowns and parasols were everywhere 'like so many migrating birds of purple Paradise'.[15] Jekyll had lived through these 'mauve decades', and to her the name of Perkin's Purple was too close to that of the insecticide London Purple for comfort. Besides, the whole noxious process of extracting aniline dyes flouted Ruskin's and Morris's views on the sacredness of colours. After aniline purple, a French chemist mixed aniline with tin chloride and achieved the deep red-purple he called *fuchsine*, after fuchsia, and a variation on fuchsine produced *roseine*, named for marketing purposes after the Battle of Magenta, where the French Army defeated the Austrians in June 1859.[16] This unstoppable trail of unsavoury chemical colours, unethical and unnatural in the eyes of the environmental lobby of that day, the Arts and Crafts Movement, thus tainted the mauve and purple *ponticums* and their hybrids by colour association. It was a taint that lasted until conservationists found other reasons to hate them.

Gertrude Jekyll planned lovely and subtle effects for her garden clients using her modest selection of favourites. As a devout disciple of John Ruskin she used *ferrugineum*, the alpenrose, a great deal, as 'punctuation' with variegated euonymus and *Hebe buxifolia* in a border of magnolias and choisyas, or planted with white columbines, verbascums and foxgloves, or with daphne and rosemary. At Frant Court near Tunbridge Wells (see page 7 of second picture section) she planted a flight of steps on a bank of existing clumps of *ponticum* and 'Cunningham's White', her planting described by Richard Bisgrove in *The Gardens of Gertrude Jekyll* (1992):

> On the inner side of the curve the planting is simple and restrained, with large groups of *Rhododendron* 'Cunningham's

White', pernettya and *R. x myrtifolium* (now *kotschyi*) forming the backbone. These support the curve, and their decreasing height accentuates the slope of the ground. Skimmia, *Daphne pontica* and *Rhododendron ferrugineum* form a lower middle ground of solid evergreens, while long groups of Solomon's seal, male fern, hellebores, columbines and smilacina are used as brushstrokes of woodland freshness to leaven the evergreen frame. Pale, frothy mysirhis is used as a filler among the slow-growing rhododendrons, with woodrush to the front, the grassy tufts of the latter repeated in the dark green foliage of *Iris foetidissima* nearer the path.

On the outer curve, many of the same plants are used but the drifts are shorter and they curve away from the path, drawing the eye into the planting. With existing rhododendrons already providing some height, the background is of *Rhododendron* 'Cunningham's White' and other hardy hybrids, with *R. ponticum* and hollies, taller plants than on the opposite bank, to enclose the more decorative planting in a bowl of dark green. Skimmia and pernettya, *Rhododendron x myrtifolium* and *Daphne pontica* echo the planting across the path, with the lower *R. ferrugineum*, dark rounded bushes of *Cistus laurifolius* and deciduous hydrangeas to vary the scheme. Within this matrix of rounded, mainly evergreen shrubs, thin strands of lighter planting are interwoven – columbines in blue, deep purple and white, Solomon's seal and male ferns, as on the other side of the path, but also helianthemum, heathers, teucrium and *Arenaria montana* on this sunnier slope.

. . . the Frant Court plan is noticeable for the very obvious way in which the plants edging the path – meconopsis, glossy asarum and smilacina on one side, saxifrage, teucrium and arenaria on the other – are clearly intended to flow on to the steps, occasionally right across them, unifying the planting on either side and making the steps an integral part of the planting plan.[17]

At Bowerbank, 'a relatively small rectangular garden in Wimbledon', the drive was separated from the road by *ponticum* and lilac and white hybrids, hollies and *Mahonia aquifolium*; 'the subtle interplay of long rhododendron leaves in rounded masses and the more upright growth of holly, each leaf spined and curving to reflect light from its black-green surface, is continued in the paler, leaden hue of the mahonia'. This unremarkable mixture (probably long felled as a rubbishy jungle) emphasises the hugely positive role of the gardener in the Jekyllian universe: 'with generous feeding and regular pruning to maintain [the mahonia's] handsome appearance, it would lap elegantly around the base of rhododendrons and holly, sending the occasional taller shoot up to display its soft yellow flowers against the darker background of the other shrubs'.[18] Pale 'mahonia' yellow was a delicious foil to the *ponticum* purples.

She did also plan one rather radical long border, fifteen feet deep, with pairs and threes of each of the rosy-scarlet 'Alexander Adie', crimson 'H. W. Sargent', deep rose with a crimson flare 'Mrs John Waterer', blush 'Marie Stuart', creamy chocolate-blotched 'Lady Annette de Trafford', pale rose, black-spotted 'Marchioness of Lansdowne', backed with pale yellow tree lupins and tall Michaelmas daisies, with pieris, gaultheria, pink and white columbines and smaller asters and daisies in the front.[19]

In contrast to Jekyll's freedom to range from the smallest wildflowers to the largest exotic shrubs in any given planting scheme, the nurseries were bound by the rules of good business to plant what they sold. Hence the 'contractor's border' was born, identifiable at a glance for camellia 'Donation', *Magnolia stellata*, 'Pink Pearl', cut-leaved maples in purple and gold, perhaps a cistus or three, kalmias, and a swathe of Kurume azaleas along the front. Of course, if you have paid a fortune for a top nursery to plant your border it has to have a signature, but the 'signatures' were too often boring and blowzy. 'If you must have a border do not let it look like the Burlington Arcade in "Tie Season"!' was the way Mr Victor Norman Gauntlett put it to his swish clientele (a king or two, a dozen dukes, foreign royalty, quite a few marchionesses, nearly sixty earls and four and a half columns of lords and ladies), which he listed in his handbook-sized catalogue, one inch thick, 400 pages of maples, bamboos, tree peonies, magnolias and iris as well as rhododendrons. Gauntlett's fashionably named Japanese Nurseries at Chiddingfold were just down the road from Miss Jekyll and she must have driven her pony cart there (though as a mere Miss she does not get listed); until the mid-1960s it was a very important nursery, planting some of the best Surrey and Sussex gardens. Gauntlett was confident that rhododendrons and azaleas could be grown in any good loamy soil; his recipe was to take the top spit off a pasture, chop it with manure and rotted leaves, and give a six-inch mulch of leaves in autumn and manure as a winter top dressing every third year. It was not difficult. Gauntlett looked after his clients, choosing the best varieties and hybrids for them. About 75 rhododendrons were approved with an added 30 'specials'.[20]

The garden of Ramster, just south of Chiddingfold on the A283, is a Gauntlett garden, made for Sir Harry Wacchter. In 1922 Ramster became the home of Lady Norman, sister of the 2nd Lord Aberconway, and she had hundreds of rhododendrons brought from Bodnant during the 1920s and 1930s.[21] It also seems feasible that Gauntlett's nurseries contributed to Dr Wilfred Fox's Winkworth Arboretum, a little to the north at Hascombe. Dr Fox (1875–1962), founder of the Roads' Beautifying Association in 1928, bought 95 acres containing this greensand valley in 1938 and spent the rest of his life filling it with colourful exotics. Deciduous azaleas (probably from Knap Hill), sorbus, maples, magnolias and evergreen azaleas – these, massed by a flight of steps at the head of the larger lake, were his favourites.

In 1914 Waterer's at Bagshot had amalgamated with Bernard Crisp's Wargrave Plant Farm. Crisp was the son of Sir Frank Crisp at Friar Park, the alpinist and alpine gardener, and so rock garden construction and plants for moraines became part of the Waterer repertory, with roses, water plants, fruit trees and bulbs, as well as the 60 acres (24 ha.) of rhododendrons at Bagshot. This move was both the inspiration and the means to the rockery garden revolution of the 1920s. Though George Forrest had brought back so many high-altitude species, his *lapponicums* and his own stalwart, creeping *forrestii*, it was to be Reginald Farrer and Frank Kingdon Ward who brought the enthusiasts for miniature gardening the plants beyond their wildest dreams. E. H. M. Cox (1893–1977), who travelled with Farrer on his last trip in 1919 to Hpimaw in Upper Burma, wrote on his return, while his memories were fresh, of *Rhododendron calostrotum* which 'covers the open moorland with a carpet of grey green foliage from which rise large round blossoms, almost platter shaped, of a rich magenta rose, by no means a bad colour, on pedicels an inch or two in height – flowers so large and in such numbers that we marvelled at such a small plant carrying such a wealth of bloom'.[22] Such dwarfs were abundant, three or four different species growing together, fighting for possession of every nook and cranny, others so tightly packed in flat-topped thickets 'that it was quite possible to walk along the top without falling through'.[23] These plants, small with opportunistically large flowers, tough denizens of bleak highlands, survivors of razor-sharp winds and periodic droughts and fires, were strange beasts, clearly quite different from *sinogrande* and her kind. It took a special person to appreciate them; not for the first time the flowers reflect the man, and indeed the whole rock gardening phenomenon seems to evolve around the figure of Reginald Farrer: 'a malevolent gnome, with a wish to be fascinating but an ill-restrained bitterness of tongue'.[24]

Farrer (1880–1920) had a boyhood interest in collecting flowers at his family's home at Ingleborough, high in the fells on the Yorkshire and Lancashire borders, and his interest was turned into a passion on holidays in the Alps. This rather inadequate, solitary though clever young man found himself at Balliol College, Oxford, in the late 1890s in a particularly brilliant company, including Raymond Asquith and the cousins Bron and Aubrey Herbert. They were all in their ways nature fanatics, outdoorsmen, headstrong and adventurous, and Reginald, 'ugly, pygmy-bodied', whom they teased for his odd voice, 'singularly unattractive, high and harsh', simply could not keep up with them.[25] Worse, he conceived an obsessive and almost lifelong passion for the elusive and romantic persona of Aubrey Herbert (the man 'who was' John Buchan's *Greenmantle*,

and was twice offered the crown of Albania) and either observed
Aubrey's progress jealously from afar or followed him halfway across
the world. When Aubrey was in Tokyo in 1902, Reginald turned
up on a plant hunting expedition; a few shiftless years later, Aubrey
en route to Australia 'found' Reginald was a passenger on RMS
Ophir as well. He had become a Buddhist and was going to Ceylon
to study religion and flowers. In between times Reginald found life
at home only tolerable when he was absorbed in his rock garden. He
published *My Rock Garden* (1907) and opened his Craven Nursery in
Yorkshire. His astringent prose appealed to many amongst a garden
ing fraternity that was overwhelmingly male; he set out the challenge
of the infinite variables of making a rock garden, of soil, climate,
aspect and construction. (Farrer castigated popular misconstruc-
tions as the 'Almond Pudding', 'Dog's Grave' and the 'Devil's Lap-
ful') and 'then, when we have allowed for all these, remains the
great stumping fact, that out of one seed or pod no two plants (any
more than 2 babies in a family) have precisely the same constitutions
or the same idiosyncrasies'.[26] He was happiest amongst his alpine
miniatures, his primulas, saxifrages, iris, gentians and meconopsis
– a 'stocky figure clad in khaki shorts and shirt, tieless and collarless,
a faded topee on his head, old boots, and stockings that gradually
slipped down and clung about his ankles as the day wore on,'[27] as
Euan Cox remembered him – and he became their champion.

When the war came he was unfit for service but became a desk
boffin; his friends Raymond Asquith and Bron Herbert were both
killed, and Aubrey Herbert, having bluffed his way into the army
despite his extremely poor sight, just survived. Reginald penned
books on his travels and bad novels and resorted to his plants in
his indulgent and biblical catalogue, *The English Rock Garden* (1920);
he felt Robinson's *English Flower Garden*, marching steadily into
dozens of editions, had long been 'crying out' for its rockery equivalent, and the rock gardener had for too long been bludgeoned into
buying 'he knows not what'. The two volumes are packed with
plants with unpronounceable names that make rhododendron seem

simplicity itself for, as Reginald Farrer asserted, it was 'perfectly absurd to pretend that there can be a common English name for a species neither English nor common',[28] and gave rock gardening a legitimacy. For the author, who had fallen out with his family and could not afford to live anywhere else in England, it was back to plant hunting: 'I am really doing the thing that suits me best in the world,' he wrote to Aubrey Herbert in 1919 from Upper Burma, 'unless you want a lodge-keeper?' (Aubrey and Mary Herbert were settled at Pixton in Somerset). 'I do not see that I can do better than make plant collecting my business in life, and be only too thankful for the miraculous mercy that turns one's greatest pleasure in living into a possible livelihood.'[29] He proposed to be in Burma another year and head home via Peking in 1921, but he did not make it. He died in Burma in November 1920.

On page 221 of volume 2 of The English Rock Garden Farrer reached the rhododendrons, which really asked for a whole book, he wrote, rather than the page that followed. Was it the book from Upper Burma and China that he did not have time to write? This seems likely, for his chosen dozen are all old stagers, including Ruskin's alpenrose; 'the colour seems squalling and mysteriously vulgar', but the white ferrugineum was all right, as were the medicinal chrysanthum, prostrate with large yellow trumpets but of 'sullen mimpish temper', the upstanding favourite, racemosum – 'fluffy flowers in pink wands' all the way up the stems, the aromatic little Indian anthopogon, the most unrhododendron-like camtschaticum (named for the Russian outpost of Kamchatka on the Beringian coast where Peter Simon Pallas found it in the 1770s) with nodding purple poppy-like head and saxifrage-like leaf clusters, and Hooker's ciliatum with 'noble creamy-rosy trumpets'. Finally, 'the rock garden rejoices' in the neat bushes hidden by early lilac-pink flowers of praecox. Farrer's rhododendrons were all confirmed familiars (many, e.g. racemosum, ciliatum, praecox, still are) and he knew full well that so many more of the alpine varieties were to be found on the Burmese–Chinese borderland.

After the unhappy Farrer it was up to the thoroughly professional Frank Kingdon Ward to bring the rock gardener the bounty of the hills, to scale the heights of the eastern Himalayas to 11,000 feet and the alpine regions, reaching the 'seas of sulphur, carmine and rose-pink', where 'rivers of purple *lapponicum* flow into lakes of brick-red, lemon and snow-white *anthopogon*; strains of cherry-brandy *glaucum*, clumps of merry little pouting *campylogynums*, pink and plum purple, are plastered like swallows' nests against the grey cliffs, and pools of canary yellow *trichocladum* glow from the brown grass slopes. Along the snow-fed streams the twin flowers of a royal purple *saluenense* nod in rising spate!'[30] The wordy Mr Ward, his prose so suited to his flowers, was the son of Henry Marshall Ward, the Professor of Botany at Cambridge, and partly brought up at Englefield Green (where his father taught at the Royal Indian Engineering College), where he was inspired by talks with returning forestry officers to travel eastwards. His Cambridge course was cut short because his father died in 1906 and he went off to be a schoolteacher in Shanghai, soon falling in with an American plant and animal collecting expedition in his holidays, which gave him the taste for more exploring. Connections at home, his mother and Isaac Bayley Balfour at the Edinburgh 'headquarters', secured Arthur K. Bulley's patronage for Kingdon Ward's first expedition in 1911. Bulley had 'lost' George Forrest to J. C. Williams, and Forrest warned the newcomer off his territories, which was the making of Kingdon Ward's future as he had to go further and higher, up on to the Mekong–Salween divide, into the tortuous high valleys of Tibet and most famously to the Tsangpo River. He made almost annual forays from 1911 to 1939, with a break for 1914–18 war service with the Indian Army.[31]

Kingdon Ward made his mark at home with his book on his first expeditions. *The Land of the Blue Poppy* (1913) put his name into history as the collector of the iconic *Meconopsis baileyi*, named for Colonel Frederick M. Bailey, veteran of Tibetan exploration, who played a mentoring role for Kingdon Ward much as Brian

Houghton Hodgson had for Joseph Hooker. Rhododendrons always seemed to figure prominently in Kingdon Ward's view of his hunting grounds but they shine supremely from his famous 1924 expedition to the Tsangpo River in south-eastern Tibet, a venture evocatively described in his 1926 book *Riddle of the Tsangpo Gorges*. At something over 13,000 feet on the mist-drenched Doshong La he found the rough carpets and hanging drifts of glowing colours of what he called 'a Rhododendron Fairyland' of dwarf species and their variations – *forrestii*, *calostrotum*, *neriiflorum*, *campylocarpum*, his own yellow-belled *wardii* and so many others – almost beyond counting. He wrote of 'ruffled seas' of foliage, of 'a pink foam of blossom', of bands of sulphur and pink striping a sheltered slope, of the intense burning scarlet flowers with jet-black honey-glands of 'Coals of Fire' (*Rhododendron cerasinum*), of brilliant banana-coloured hassocks, fiery curtains hanging from every rock and the 'pools of incandescent lava' of 'Carmelita', one of many *forrestii* natural hybrids.[32]

Undoubtedly the influence of Farrer and Kingdon Ward inspired the alpine flower lobby (hoards of holiday hill-walkers and amateur mountaineers) to bring about the great popularity of rock gardens in the later 1920s and throughout the 1930s. Acreages of tastefully arranged rocks, with pools, waterfalls, a Japanese lantern or two and perfect plants were the display garden stars of the Chelsea Flower Shows through these years, winning gold medals for the specialists, George C. Whitelegg of Chislehurst, the Mawson family's Lakeland Nurseries, Clarence Elliott of Six Hills Nursery, Stevenage, Hertfordshire, and B. H. B. Symons-Jeune, whose *Natural Rock Gardening* was published by *Country Life* in 1932. The rock gardeners were acquisitive of plants and rocks and the arguments were heated and severe: 'Some say use the local stone,' wrote George C. Whitelegg in the *Studio Gardens and Gardening* of 1932,

> but if this is an ugly stone, why use it? Is it not permissible
> to improve (on geology) to take the beautiful product of
> one county to another? ... I personally prefer the beautiful

restful-coloured limestone from Cheddar, that wonderful bit of Somerset which no rock-garden designer can ever equal. Another ... a wonderful laminated limestone, is that which is found in North Yorkshire and in Westmorland. These two stones without doubt give the best effect because they are natural outcropping surface stones, weathered by generations of wind, snow and ice.

Just like the Doshong La. But, of course, these rock gardens were the most contrived of gardens, with lorryloads of stone carted from one end of the country to the other, whole gardens purchased from the shows and re-erected and, regardless of the limestones, pockets of acid or alkaline, loamy or gritty soils placed as the gardener willed. Rock gardens were also infinitely flexible and they caught the imagination of the gardening nation, a new constituency of suburban gardeners. Hardly a crescent or cul-de-sac of thirties semis anywhere was without a rockery set out to amuse the passers-by, especially on the larger corner sites. The 1932 *Gardens and Gardening* illustrated one in Leytonstone on a 190 x 50 feet plot, the long thin London garden, with low rock slopes blooming with alyssum, aubretias, iberis and alpine phlox, a miniature well, and dwarf rhododendrons, berberis, brooms as well as the inevitable prostrate cotoneaster.

The rhododendrons from the wildest corners of the Himalayas were thus tamed into suburban gardens, which brought them to the widest public and prepared the way for their tremendous post-war popularity. Once the hybridisers and the nurseries had done their work it was possible to have a dwarf rhododendron in flower for most months of the year. Immediately after the war, when the garden world became obsessed with labour saving or low maintenance, every species and hybrid from ankle to knee height found itself drafted into lists of ground coverers (that abominable term that decrees the good earth as shameful as a naked Victorian table leg and to be covered at all costs). Too often the exquisite violet-purple *impeditum* and her lovely company found themselves in the society of sheets of dusty, tangled ericas, near relations, in 'the heather garden' – the worst kind of low-maintenance planting, much better left out on the moors. At the opposite extreme were the ultra-sophisticated plantings by Russell Page, who believed that there was a 'right' rhododendron for almost every setting. An out-door room with white marble paving, a grass oval and ivy-covered trellised walls should be planted with greens and white – philad-elphus, deutzia, *Hydrangea paniculata*, viburnums and Waterer's lovely white 'Sappho' with box bushes, a few white narcissus and, for later, white nicotiana.[33] For the Paris Floralies he used thousands of potted plants, in free-flowing beds of colours and textures, in a 'European' version of one of Roberto Burle Marx's (1909–94) tropical abstract fantasies. Orange and yellow Exbury azaleas with Japanese maples, ferns, orange and golden lilies, yellow, orange and red polyanthus were set beneath birch trees; an orange, yellow and cream scheme linked to the white 'Sappho' again, with white hydrangeas, *Lilium longiflorum*, white columbines above a carpet of hostas, daisies and primulas merging into mauve, blue and white primulas, blue and white cinerarias, blue hydrangeas and huge bushes of blatantly magenta rhododendrons; pink and white Kurume azaleas flowered with white and pink *Primula malacoides* under a large Japanese cherry; milky-blue *augustinii* with the hybrid 'Blue Tit', white deutzia, the white azalea 'Palestrina' merged with a 'field' of the double tulip 'Peach Blossom', *Dicentra spectabilis* and clumps of white, pink and deep red astilbes; the finale was Exbury's 'Naomi' – 'in the full glory of shell pink bud and paler pink flower' – and camellia 'Eddy', and at their feet white, shell-pink and salmon-coloured cyclamen, then greens and whites, box, glox-inias, maidenhair ferns, lilies of the valley and bamboos with a creamy-flowered *Rhododendron johnstoneanum*, linked back to the beginning, the birch trees and orange azaleas.[34]

Russell Page's eye for the versatility of rhododendrons in this Parisian extravaganza reflects their European ubiquity in the between-the-wars decades. They were easily as popular as roses and tulips in Germany, France, Belgium and Holland, and each country had a thriving rhododendron culture, with Belgium, having given the deciduous Ghent hybrid azaleas in their many lovely guises to the world, and Holland leading the exporters. In Germany a strong home market had developed throughout the nineteenth century in response to the hundreds of cold-hardy hybrids from the Seidel family nursery in Dresden, which produced a whole alphabet of crisp names from Abel and Achilles to Willi and Zwerg up until the death of T. J. Rudolf Seidel in 1918.[35] The dazzlingly white 'Helene Schniffner' was a rare Seidel survivor into the later twentieth century. There were also spectacularly Germanic Wilhelma hybrids by Johann Baptist Muller, which were speckled, every petal sprinkled daintily all over in carmine or brown, and mostly named for the Württemberg royal family; 'Königen Olga von Württemberg' was mauve-white with carmine speckles crowding to the centres of the flowers, giving her dramatically dark eyes. Otto Schulz, who ran the nursery that supplied flowers to the artists of the Royal Porcelain Factory in Berlin, had made *griffithianum* hybrids, tinged with a glamour from this association. Schulz's seedlings were bought by the Dutch nurseryman, C. B. van Nes of Boskoop, but as many turned out to be rather tender he sent them to the English market, exhibiting regularly in London. 'Queen Wilhelmina', named for the much loved Queen of Holland, clear rosy scarlet with hardly any markings (perhaps the specklings had become too much?) and 'Princess Juliana' for her daughter, pale rose and equally unspeckled – both became widely known as Schulz/van Nes plants. Van Nes has been influential on British rhododendrons: 'C. B. van Nes' himself, a crimson-scarlet, and the scarlet, gloxinia-like 'Britannia' are two of the hybrids he bred on from the Schulz collection, which have in turn sired others.

'Pink Pearl' moved freely in this early Common Market; she was sold by the German nurseries, used for hybridising by another famous Dutch name, L. J. Endtz of Boskoop, and she was planted in French gardens. Along with her contemporaries she may yet be

SPECKLED RHODODENDRON.

The spotted Wilhelma hybrid introduced in the nineteenth
century by the Seidel Nursery of Dresden.

hunted down in some old French gardens. In Guillaume Mallet's
Parc des Moutiers, at Varengeville near Dieppe, banks of old hybrids
flower in the woodlands leading down to the sea inlet and Port des
Moutiers.[36] Nearby Le Vasterival, the Princess Sturdza's famous
garden has a collection of hybrids. Do they also lurk amongst the
cedars and sequoias in the park at Ferrières, given by the Rothschilds
to the University of Paris? They do still grow in the background to
the waterlilies and the blue bridge at Monet's Giverny. But the fact
remains that there were so many hybrids around in the thirties, the
progeny of almost fifty years of playing about with 'Everestianum',
griffithianum, old 'John Waterer' and the other favourite marriages
that were tried over and over again under differing circumstances
in the hope of a fabulous 'pearl' emerging from the thousands of
cast-off shells, that most are now just names in old nursery lists. A
vanished race of beauties, which succumbed to the frost or the sun,
a bitter wind or a burrowing mole, and for whatever reason are

lost. All we are left with are a precious few with poignant names: 'Souvenir de Dr S. Endtz', a rosy child of 'Pink Pearl' raised by Endtz, and long-dead members of famous nursery families, for example, the pale pink frilled 'Corry Koster'. Saddest of all, even if these plants from the past do still flower where they have been left in peace, we have no idea what they are or where they came from.

Across the channel the hybrids flowed from Exbury and Bodnant as well as the nurseries. Lionel de Rothschild's very personal enthusiasm for hands-on hybridising differed from the more paternalist regime at Bodnant, where the Aberconways were garden makers in the grand manner. A for Aberconway brings the 2nd and 3rd barons to the head of most lists of British gardeners, and as they were both presidents of the Royal Horticultural Society for a good chunk of the twentieth century between them, many would say that that is their rightful place. Bodnant is stupendously spectacular, the view from the topmost of the five gigantic Italianate terraces is of Snowdonia, a not un-Himalayan view that could well be filled entirely with rhododendron woods (and perhaps explains why *ponticum* has made rather too much of itself in the Snowdonia National Park). Rhododendrons stream through the Dell and along the rocky banks of the River Hiraethlyn. Bodnant is lavishly planted, it has a rose terrace, a lily terrace, a collection of magnolias, maples, wisterias, every kind of shrub and a famous laburnum tunnel, but as this is a book about rhododendrons all those others are left blithely by. Laura McLaren and her son, the 2nd Lord Aberconway, were the inspiration for the rhododendron hybridising and they were lucky enough to find that their (apparently reluctant) head gardener Frederick C. Puddle (*c.* 1877–1952) turned into a magician. Whereas Exbury specialised in pinks and yellows, Bodnant went for reds, breeding red with red to intensify the colour, especially with the dwarf *forrestii* varieties which were rather shy at flowering. The free-flowering and hardy 'Elizabeth' (*forrestii* x *griersonianum*), which immediately became a favourite scarlet, and orangey-scarlet Bodnant 'Fabia' (*dichroanthum* x *griersonianum*), a slightly larger bush, both made their debuts in the early thirties. 'F. C. Puddle' himself (*griersonianum x neriiflorum*) and his 'siblings' (or grex) were all equally good garden reds and a bounty for the smaller garden (rather as head gardener Puddle himself, succeeded by his son Charles in 1947, and eventually his son Martin in 1982, were to be good for Bodnant).[37]

At Knap Hill in 1931 Rothschild money contributed to rescue the nursery as an independent company, with Frank Knight (d. 1985) as manager; Knight, something of a man about the rhododendron world (he had come from Kew and was to go on to Notcutts at Woodbridge and then be director of Wisley) was also a hybridiser with original ideas. He reared second generation hybrids (i.e. with hybrids as parents): the pure white and scented 'Nimbus', frilled and purple-flushed white flowering 'Constant Nymph' and 'Sapphire', almost the elusive blue as her name implies, and a child of *impeditum* and a sprig of J. C. Williams' 'Blue Tit' given to Knight as a buttonhole at a Rhododendron Association show.[38] As the Second World War was starting Knight was ferrying Knap Hill plants to Colonel Harry Clive's garden in an old north Staffordshire quarry near Market Drayton. Knight planted the Knap Hill deciduous hybrid azaleas (many of them named for birds, 'Whitethroat', 'Redstart', 'Golden Oriole') that still flower there in their deliciously melding creams, yellows, salmons and scarlets along with many other species and hybrids of that world before the war.[39]

It may sound an odd expression of an age but in the thirties Britain was the rhododendron capital of the world. The happy immigrant species had settled into their Cornish coves and Surrey hills, their Western Isles and eastern dells successfully, their pedigrees were recorded at Edinburgh Botanics, and now their progeny were spreading to many of the gardens in a gardening land, and they were the subjects of constant debate, annotation and admiration by a growing company of rhododendronologists, though it must be added that the taxonomists were never interested in the hybrids, which (they would say) had multiplied into an uncontrollable mob.

The rhododendron nurseries were gaining ground, playing ever larger and more splendiferous roles in the flower shows; they were no longer obscure nurserymen, but the familiar and famous names of the twentieth-century gardening world such as Cheal's of Crawley, Wallace of Tunbridge Wells, Hilliers of Winchester, Cuthbert, Reuthe, Stewart and Slocock, as well as Waterer. It was a decade when a successful nursery had to be all things to all gardeners. They made and planted gardens for the well-heeled, and were usually seedsmen, hybridisers, propagators and florists as well. They sent their staff to continental or American nurseries for training, and advertised and exported to America, Canada, Australia and New Zealand and South Africa, to all the dominions of the British Empire beyond the seas, and so literally had worldwide reputations. Indeed, the reputations were almost accidental, as all gardening magazines and the influential *Country Life* originated in London and English gardens, and were read avidly (for there was little home-grown literature) throughout the English-speaking and gardening world.

Waterer's had kept their American connections and exported thousand upon thousand of rhododendrons over the years. Gomer Waterer ('Gomer Waterer' is a mauvish-pink splashed with beige hybrid of the early twentieth century, and he was named for the 'Comte de Gomer', himself a hybrid rhododendron) had worked furiously at this and become a transatlantic commuter. He had crossed on the *Lusitania* on the trip before her last, but those sailing with a huge order for camellias and rhododendrons for William Robertson Coe's 'Planting Fields' at Oyster Bay on Long Island were not so lucky, sunk by a German submarine torpedo. The camellias and rhododendrons were replaceable and a second batch was duly sent and formed the basis of the 'Planting Fields' gardens, now a public arboretum, where many of the Waterer plants must survive. Most of Waterer's obvious customers were in the northeast, where the Sargent and Hunnewell connection and the Arnold Arboretum had forged a desire for rhododendrons. Waterer's imports, often channelled through an American nursery, inspired a small but resolute band of enthusiasts who, as Donald Waterer has already been quoted as saying, 'fanned the flames' of a rhododendron craze, which persists to this day. The first home-raised hybrids in this part of the country came from Charles O. Dexter (1862–1943) at Sandwich, Massachusetts; Dexter was given a doom-laden medical diagnosis at the age of 59, in 1921, so he took to doing something he enjoyed, hybridising and raising some 10,000 rhododendron seedlings a year, and he lived for another 22 years. Few records of his work survive and he, like many growers, was too busy with his plants to stop and write things down, but some 125 of his named cultivars still grow in what is now the Heritage Plantation of Sandwich, flowering from Memorial Day in late May through to the middle of June.

Naturally enough tremendous work was done to 'improve' (enlarge the flowers, add colours, scent and hardiness) the American native azaleas. 'Pink Pearl' and other Waterer hybrids were used by Bobbink and Atkins of East Rutherford, New Jersey, in the breeding of their Rutherford hybrids in the 1920s; these were large-flowered evergreen, medium-sized azaleas, some scented, some frilled, intended for the conservatory and indoors, but happy enough outdoors in the South and in the San Francisco region. Joseph B. Gable of Stewartstown in Pennsylvania bred hardy rhododendrons and azaleas also in the 1920s and work started on the famous and fabulous Glenn Dale hybrids in the early thirties. These were part of a government-sponsored scheme, the work of B. Y. Morrison, head of the Plant Introduction Station at Glenn Dale, Maryland, entailing experiments with a wide variety of parents, impossible in anything but laboratory-like conditions, to produce thousands of seedlings (70,000 resulted from the breeding prior to 1940) and large-flowered evergreen azaleas, hardy in the mid-Atlantic states. In the South, the natural and manmade hybrids from Magnolia Gardens, those between the native azaleas and imported Ghent hybrids, were developed commercially through Berckmann's Nursery in Augusta, Georgia. These were but the tip of an azalea iceberg of importing and hybridising; other Kurume azaleas, that is, other than Wilson's Fifty that were but his personal choice, were imported 50 times over, and also the bonsai-like Satsuki hybrids and the Ryukyu Islands' strains. Indeed, it appeared that every Japanese island had its secret hoard.[40]

The north-west coast had been identified as rhododendron country as far back as the 1790s when the naval surgeon-botanist, Archibald Menzies (c. 1754–1842), accompanying the surveying and mapping trips of Captain George Vancouver, had found *Rhododendron macrophyllum* (meaning big-leaved) growing with *Arbutus menziesii*, the oriental strawberry, at Port Discovery on the Olympic peninsula south of Vancouver Island. Fifty years later the chief factor (and later governor), James Douglas, walked through fields of clover and tall grasses on the southern point of Vancouver Island looking for the site for the settlement of Fort Victoria; another 50 years on the land was laid out as Victoria's Beacon Hill Park, and planted with Waterer rhododendrons which came via the nursery of Thomas Meeham at Germanstown, Pennsylvania.[41] In 1908 Jennie Butchart began to transform the worked-out part of her husband's quarry at Tod Inlet outside Victoria into a garden of azaleas, maples and cherry blossoms with the help of a Japanese gardener; over the next 30 years the Butcharts extended their gardens, they entertained Frank Kingdon Ward, planted *Meconopsis baileyi* and large and small rhododendrons amongst thousands of other plants in their former limestone quarries. The Butchart Gardens, now 50 acres (22 ha.) and arrayed in seasonal planting schemes of great splendour, draw nearly three-quarters of a million visitors each year.[42] But the real rhododendron enthusiasts were tucked away in remoter places: George Fraser (1854–1944), a Scots gardener who had crossed Canada and settled at Ucluelet, halfway up the island's west coast, had imported Waterer hybrids for the Butcharts and other gardeners, and he reared the first widely recognised Canadian hybrid, *japonicum x canadense*, using a *canadense* seedling he found amongst a shipment of cranberry plants from Nova Scotia. *Rhododendron fraseri* has abundant rosy-lilac fragrant flowers; it spreads via underground stolons (and could undoubtedly get out of hand in too soft a climate) and occupies a place in the hearts of Vancouver gardeners. Fraser was one of a select sprinkling of enthusiasts in the backwoods, including the Buchanan-Simpsons and their Marble Bay Alpine Nursery, Ted and Mary Greig of Royston and the German nurseryman Richard Layritz, who imported from Exbury and had over 300 rhododendron varieties on his books. All these are fondly remembered pioneers who divined the rhododendron potential of *macrophyllum*'s homeland for long years before their popularity flowered.[43]

One of the motivations for the founding of the American Rhododendron Society by a group of enthusiasts in Seattle in 1944 was that the Second World War had put a stop to so much of the traffic in plants from Europe, and American gardeners had to stand on their own in a rather deferred post-colonial adulthood. In Australasia gardening was tied to Mother England's apron strings up until 1939 with a tautness hard to imagine now, some sixty years on. In Australia, as we know from the childhood of their Nobel Laureate, the novelist Patrick White, the smart Sydneysiders filled their retreat gardens in the Blue Mountains with English rhododendrons, and an interest in the possibilities of their native flora was only encouraged by the pioneering conservationists who formed the Sydney Bushwalkers in the thirties.[44] In New Zealand Edgar Stead at Ilam near Christchurch pioneered rhododendron growing with seeds and plants from Edinburgh and Exbury and Bodnant and he was the president of the New Zealand Rhododendron Association, also formed in 1944. Several 'Ilam' hybrids – two interestingly coloured 'Violet' and 'Apricot' – have international fame, as have the gardens at Pukeiti Hill at Taranaki on North Island, planted by enthusiasts in 1950. Pukeiti symbolises New Zealand's rhododendron independence.[45]

Self-sufficiency amongst the overseas customers did not mean that the aura of the Bagshot sands faded in the post-war world, for a new kind of 'nurseryman' – more worldly-wise, more sociable, dare I say it, more gentlemanly – came home from the war, looking for a job. Gone were the black bowlers and black waistcoats, buried along with the race of professional gardeners who had been their best customers; the new nurserymen were more likely dressed in check shirts and twill trousers, with countryish tweeds for show days. They were more relaxed, and tolerant of the fads and foolishness of an amateur gardening nation. Gomer Waterer died in 1945, and, after two years as a prisoner of war, his son Donald came home to run Knap Hill, where he was to stay until his retirement in 1976. They were wonderful years. Donald Waterer carefully unearthed the treasured plants that the two Anthony Waterers had reared and those that Frank Knight had secreted away for safety during the war. Stars such as 'Mrs Furnivall', rosy pink with dark crimson rouged petals, and her offspring, 'Furnivall's Daughter', paler but with more make-up, and the dainty, blushing 'Mrs J. C. Williams' were born.

At Bagshot they at last found a rhododendron with a catchy name: the brilliantly green-fingered Percy Wiseman, who had worked for Waterer's since 1925 and returned after the war to work on the seedlings from the island of Yakushima, mating them with 'Fabia Tangerine' and the Knap Hill dwarf red 'Doncaster' to create the 'yak' hybrids, or 'yaks'. Throughout the sixties the nursery introduced the Seven Dwarfs – the yaks 'Dopey', 'Grumpy', 'Sleepy', 'Bashful', etc, as well as 'Hoppy', meaning someone had misread the handwriting on the label because it should have been 'Happy'. Yak 'Percy Wiseman' opens apricot-coloured and fades to cream; but all the small, curly-leaved (though in some this charming characteristic has lessened in the hybridising), evergreen, garden-proof and large flowered yaks come in mouth-watering sorbet and soufflé colours.[46]

A parallel universe of rhododendrons had long existed, in a far less starry way than Knap Hill and Bagshot, at the Goldsworth Nursery in Woking, with an interesting but obscure beginning in the *ponticum* and *catawbiense* days of the early nineteenth century. Goldsworth was then owned by a character called Robert Donald, socially and Christianly conscientious and a bad poet. He serenaded his clients: to the Nobility and Gentry 'my respectful thanks are due, Likewise the Trade, and Flora's Friends so vast,/And an enlighten'd Public not a few', requesting their further trade in Woking and Dorking. Rhododendrons – standard bushes of *ponticum* – were but one of Donald's stocks in trade, but his son, also Robert Donald, planted the groves of pines and rhododendrons of Necropolis, the Brookwood Cemetery, which was opened in 1854.

In the early twentieth century the Slocock family had come to Goldsworth, and the second generation, the brothers Walter Ashley and Oliver Charles Slocock, took over in 1926. They were both great rhododendron men, with an astute eye for a good hybrid, strong voices in the political arena of the Royal Horticultural Society, and most importantly, solidly respectable nurserymen, staging fabulous exhibits at Chelsea and other shows and selling thousands of equally fabulous plants. Their stewardship included a farm-and-nursery integration, which allowed manuring and a rotation cropping for soil conservation – to replace the soil that went off with the 150,000 plants sold each year. The brothers were succeeded by their sons, the cousins John and Martin Slocock. John ran Charles Hill Nursery at Tilford, just down the hill from the Mangles' Littleworth Cross on the Surrey greensand, which specialised in rhododendrons, azaleas and camellias, until his death in 1986. Martin Slocock took over Knap Hill Nursery in 1976 when Donald Waterer retired. The Goldsworth Nursery land was covered with a housing estate.[47]

But the merry-go-round has not stopped yet. The South African-born Arthur George came out of the navy in 1956 and went to work for the Slococks at Goldsworth, paid 2*s* 11*d* an hour for seed sowing, propagating and grafting, but learning all the way. Rhododendrons were the premier plant of the late fifties Chelsea Flower Shows and he was duly captivated. Some likely rhododendron land, fifteen acres on Hydon Heath, south of Godalming, just down the hill from Gertrude Jekyll's legendary Munstead Wood, 'cropped up', as Arthur George puts it, in 1959, and he bought it, later adding another ten acres. It was covered in Christmas trees, which he worked to clear patch by patch, ready for his rhododendron stock plants. And then one of those serendipitous miracles happened. Arthur and Anne George knew Major-General Eric Harrison, who had bought Tremeer, an old garden at St Tudy, near Bodmin in Cornwall, where he had settled after the war, catching the rhododendron bug from the Magors at Lamellen and George Johnstone of Trewithen. In 1961 Eric Harrison married Roza Stevenson, the widow of John Barr Stevenson at Tower Court, Ascot. Roza Stevenson had remained at Tower Court in a bungalow she had built on part of her garden, after so many of her beloved big species plants had left for the Valley Garden at Windsor, but now she was leaving and there were still many good and young plants remaining at Tower Court. These fell Arthur George's way, and once a week for months he went over to collect them by the vanload, digging them into their new home at Hydon. One of the lovely plants that now flowers at Hydon is the *irroratum* hybrid 'Polka Dot', blush pink and carmine speckled, a returned ghost of the old German Wilhelma 'Württemberg' favourites.

The wonderful Roza Stevenson's happiness at Tremeer was short-lived. She died in 1967, but she is remembered with the greatest affection in the rhododendron world by the porcelain glow of the creamy-yellow bells of her name flower, a cross of Loderi 'Sir Edmund' and Kingdon-Ward's *wardii*.

Arthur George's first hybrid was *griersonianum x ponticum*, which he called 'Springbok'. He then crossed 'Springbok' with a yak to create his now famous Hydon yak hybrids, beautifully proportioned plants for the smaller garden, their pompoms of deliciously coloured flowers not too large for their rosettes of leaves, which retain the fascinating yak curls and deep veins.[48]

To return to the Bagshot sands. The legendary Standish and Noble, John Standish (1814–75) and Charles Noble (fl. 1840s–1880s), were a pair of youngish ex-gardeners who had set up in partnership in 1847, on the site of the old royal kennels opposite the gates of Bagshot Park (where Standish had been apprenticed in the royal garden renowned for its rhododendrons). They soon moved along the London road to a new plot with a deep peaty overlay, prepared by draining, trenching and manuring and cropping with potatoes and mangolds for their American shrubs. They called the business Sunningdale Nursery. Standish and Noble's was a brief but starry partnership as they netted not only the seeds and plants sent home by Robert Fortune, but also some of Joseph Hooker's haul from Sikkim, including a *thomsonii* seedling that was the first to flower in Europe at Sunningdale. Their large pinky-magenta 'Cynthia' was an early rival to 'Pink Pearl'. They parted in the late 1850s, ostensibly quarrelling over a hybrid, 'The Queen', which was denounced as an impostress, as an old flower under a new name. They shared out their plants, and John Standish, the best plantsman, went off to Ascot, from where he introduced 'Ascot Brilliant' and the white 'Standishii'. Charles Noble, the best businessman and also keen on rhododendrons (the only thing they seemed to have in common), stayed at Sunningdale, running his successful nursery for forty years until he retired in 1898.[49] When Sir Joseph Hooker retired from Kew he lived in a villa called The Camp at Sunningdale until his death in 1911, and it seems likely that Sunningdale Nursery acquired more plants through Hooker's influence.

For the following 40 years Sunningdale's plants were propagated and tended by the nursery manager, Henry 'Harry' White, a quietly distinguished rhododendron man, who reared 'Pink Drift' (*calostrotum x scintillans*) and – from the audacious marriage 'Pink Pearl' x 'Cynthia' – the 'Countess of Derby'. Sunningdale, a beautiful and stylish nursery, had by now become an investment, bought by the publisher Sir Hubert Longman, and when he died in 1939 it was sold to Major Herbert Russell MC and his cousin Neill Hamilton-Smith.

Enter James Philip Cuming Russell (1920–96), a soldier's son who preferred botany, was polished at Eton but missed Trinity

College at Cambridge because of the war, and took a commission in the Hertfordshire Yeomanry and was invalided out, recovered and came to run Sunningdale Nursery. Jim Russell and Sunningdale were well suited; he revelled in the stories of the rackety Standish and Noble history and of the wonderful plants, 'like superb pieces of garden furniture', the large bushes of *cinnabarinum roylei*, *thomsonii* and *campanulatum*, now centenarians.[50] He applied tremendously good taste to the planting of rhododendrons, which he felt needed a woodland background of bamboos, large ferns and carpeting plants to set off their beauty. He made himself a rhododendron expert, much sought after by a stylish gardening society set, who also enjoyed his amusing company and astounding skills at highland dancing. During the 1950s everything about Sunningdale was smart: the nursery itself was beautiful, more like a garden than a nursery; the catalogue was ornamental, well-designed, literate, friendly and informative; the displays at Chelsea and other shows were ravishing, and about one hundred and fifty smart people had Jim Russell discreetly lay out and plant their gardens, this last a Sunningdale service from the Standish and Noble days. Graham Stuart Thomas (1909–2003) joined the Sunningdale team and introduced his old shrub rose revival, and the old roses and rhododendrons were an unbeatable combination.

But the days of nurseries, even the most stylish and successful, were numbered. At Waterer's of Bagshot the managing director Gerald Pinkney had been to America and seen the idea of the 'garden centre', a marketing outlet with the plants potted into cheap, plastic pots as 'container plants' for lifting easily off the shelf and putting into the boot of the car. It seems so simple; how did we ever garden any other way? Real nurserymen could return to their quiet backroom lives, messing about in fields and potting sheds, and the garden centre would be a smiling face to the public world. Real nurserymen had never liked Joe Public anyway. But we are in a world of economics where might is right, and such a feat of reorganisation had to be done on a large scale, and Waterer Son &

Crisp of Bagshot and Twyford reinvented themselves as the Waterer Group, gobbling up Sunningdale and the famous seedsmen, Dobbie's of Edinburgh.

Graham Stuart Thomas had been head-hunted to be gardens adviser to the National Trust (and create his magnificent collection of old roses at Mottisfont Abbey in Hampshire for the Trust) and Jim Russell was being tempted away to make a rhododendron garden for George Howard at Castle Howard. So the world of the rhododendron on the Bagshot sands ends not with a whimper, but a bang, and migrates northwards to Maytime in the magnificence of Ray Wood.

Ray Wood is an historic feature of Castle Howard, surveyed as 'a fine young woodland' in 1563; some 150 years later it had been designed into a bosky wilderness of serpentine walks amidst leafery with ornaments and pavilions, and after another 130 years it was deemed to be outgrown and decaying. That was in 1849, when Joseph Hooker went to Sikkim, and whether by chance or calculation Lord Carlisle's agent suggested the wood should be planted with rhododendrons. He proposed asking Sir William Hooker – 'who has done Kew so admirably that he may be a good person' – or Sir Joseph Paxton, or George Fleming, head gardener at Trentham: 'it requires the knowledge of a woodman, a gardiner and a landscape gardiner combined'. Another 120 years passed and Lord Carlisle's descendant, George Howard, had found his rhododendron 'gardiner' at last.[51]

Jim Russell gathered his representative collection of species and hybrids throughout the gamut of rhododendron history – treasures brought from Sunningdale, layerings from the Hooker *thomsonii* and *cinnabarinum*, from known Forrest and Farrer plants, Joseph Rock's *basilicum*, Kingdon-Ward's *macabeanum*, the best of Wilson's Fifty Kurumes, *augustinii* hybrids, his own Sunningdale hybrid 'Malabar', seedlings from Ludlow and Sherriff's collectings and from more recent Sino-Himalayan expeditions, all to be planted with companionable camellias, hydrangeas, magnolias, roses and viburnums beneath the young oaks, chestnuts and beeches in the

33 acres (13 ha.) of Ray Wood. The microclimate of the wood was all important; it is on a north-facing slope, staying cool and making the most of the fairly limited rainfall in rhododendron terms, about 28 inches annually, on sandy soil with hundreds of years of accumulated leaves 'producing the almost mythical humus-rich, leafy, moisture-retentive but well-drained substrate, of a low pH, that could hardly be better designed . . .'[52] The plants were babies, six to nine inches high, set in slit trenches with no digging (the weeds had been chemically cleared), no fertiliser, only some netting to keep off the rabbits. Ray Wood was opened to visitors in 1989; the rhododendron sequence flowers from February until 'Polar Bear' fades in August, a living history that needs no more words because it is there to illuminate so much of what I have written up until now.

On the Bagshot sands there are garden centres now, and plenty of rhododendrons for sale. Notcutts' have taken over Waterer's Bagshot site, but as you enter the garden centre in spring you can still see, in the distance, on the old nursery land, the huge flowering rhododendrons, some the very same stock plants that gave these Surrey sands their worldwide fame.[53]

ABOVE Sergio Garcia of Spain at the 13th tee, 1st round of the 2003 Masters Tournament, Augusta National Golf Club, Georgia, USA, the photograph published (double-page spread for the rhododendrons!) in the *Guardian*, 12 April 2003.

RIGHT Simon James, Pink Azalea, from *Days Like This*, 2000.

Stanley Spencer (1891–1959) *Convoy Arriving with Wounded* – at the gates of the Beaufort War Hospital, Bristol, mural painting no. 1, 1927, at the Oratory of All Souls, Sandham Memorial Chapel, Burghclere, Hampshire, now owned by the National Trust.

TOP Rhododendron hybrid 'Roza Stevenson' at Kew.

ABOVE Species *Rhododendron griersonianum*, originally collected by George Forrest in 1917 and the most successful parent of many hybrids.

RHODORA canadenſis. *L.*

Pierre Joseph Redouté (1759–1840), *Rhodora canadensis* (*Rhododendron canadense*) from C.L. L'Héritier de Brutelle, *Sertum Anglicum* (observations of rare plants growing in Kew Gardens 1786–7), published in Paris, 1788–92.

Rhododendron fulgens, a presentation painting included in *The Garden* at Christmas 1905.

Leon de Smet (1881–1966), *Still Life with Azaleas*, oil on canvas.

Raymond Booth (b. 1929), *Rhododendron keiskei*, oil on paper.

Rhododendron 'Pink Pearl', the most popular hybrid of the twentieth century, introduced by Waterers in 1897.

Leaf variations of rhododendrons, faces and reverses, originally photographed by Harry Smith for C. E. Lucas Phillips and Peter N. Barber, *The Rothschild Rhododendrons: A Record of the Garden at Exbury*, 1967.

Graham Hillier (b. 1946) *The Rhododendron Path*, inspired by a visit to Clumber Park, with his wife Candia Hillier and the author, 2002.

CHAPTER SEVEN

The Ecologists' Tales

> We abuse land
> Because we regard it as a commodity belonging to us.
> When we see land as a community to which we belong,
> We may begin to use it with love and respect.
>
> Aldo Leopold (1886–1948)[1]

JOURNALISTS ARE TRICKSY DEVILS, always looking for a fight. *Gardener's World* asked Roy Lancaster, that most genuine of plant lovers and a Himalayan traveller, 'Is there a plant that you wish had never been introduced to cultivation?' 'There are many,' hedged Roy with his winning smile, 'but high on my list is *Rhododendron ponticum*.'[2] Shame on you, Mr Lancaster. *Ponticum* has gloriously played her part as a proud parent. From old hybrid classics 'Everestianum' and 'Cunningham's White' to Arthur George's Hydon beauties, she has started so many hybridisers – James Mangles for one – on their way, and was so often the only plant available to the enthusiastic beginner, that without her we would not have had perhaps one-third of our historic and beautiful hybrids and the rhododendron story would be much the poorer. And, after all, who are we *to blame the plant*?

The blame game might begin with William Wordsworth, defending his beloved Lake District from invasions of larches, tourists and exotics in his *Guide to the Lakes*. Wordsworth blamed the 'Ornamental' gardeners, the followers of the eighteenth-century Picturesque, who squealed in delight over rugged rocks and dashing torrents and yet thought not 'to inquire of themselves wherein that beauty which they admire consists' but found such places more delightful when overlaid with 'the whole contents of the nursery-man's catalogue jumbled together – colour at war with colour, and form with form? – among the most peaceful subjects of Nature's kingdom, everywhere discord, distraction and bewilderment'.[3] Before any rhododendron had reached the Lakes he averred that a house was best 'belonging' to its setting, that native-growing trees and shrubs, birch, holly, dogberry and thorns, a wilding cherry or two, gave any single spot 'sufficient dignity' to support its spirit of place. A few exotics might be allowed as long as they were kept close to the doors of the house, but this was an indulgence to our human feeling (or failing?) 'that prompts us to gather round our dwelling a few flowers and shrubs, which from the circumstance of their not being native, may, by their very looks, remind us that they owe their existence to our hands, and their prosperity to our care'.[4]

The next taste guru, John Ruskin, was wise enough to love his *Rhododendron ferrugineum*, 'the rubied crests of Alpine roses' in their homeland, but he too, writing of his travels in the 1860s in *Sesame and Lilies* (1865), ran into trouble. He recalled:

> I was staying at Montanvert to paint Alpine roses, and went every day to watch the budding of a favourite bed, which was rounding into faultless bloom beneath a cirque of rock, high enough, as I hoped, and close enough, to guard it from rude eyes and plucking hands . . . on the day it reached the fullness of its rubied fire, I was standing near when it was discovered by a forager on the flank of a travelling school of English and German lads – they swooped, threw themselves into it, rolled over and over, shrieked, hallooed, fought, trampled and tore it up by the roots. They left me much to think about.[5]

At home, at Brantwood on Lake Coniston, Ruskin made his hillside garden of native plants, but later in his life he did bring home some alpines (*ferrugineum* perhaps?) simply because he wanted them near him and could travel no more. When he became too ill to garden the gate was shut on his wild hillside; Ruskin died in 1900, leaving Brantwood to his niece, Joan Severn. Mrs Severn made additions to both house and garden, and she planted rhododendrons, seemingly from the best of motives – she remembered that Ruskin loved them – and she was given them by his friends. She planted *ponticum*, of course, and what are now red-flowering giants (possibly 'Broughtonii') and a mass of deciduous azaleas, including *luteum*, that scent Brantwood's terrace in spring.[6] Would Ruskin be shocked at this alien invasion, or smile at the good intentions that mistook the fashionable Victorian hybrids for little *ferrugineum*?

Rhododendrons have, I fear, been treated as a commodity (as have many of the lands where they grow). At first we were pleased enough to have the European species, but then the Americans came rushing in, and I confess that I did not know gardeners were still growing the Europeans until I was checking up on John Ruskin's favourite and discovered Ronald McBeath of Edinburgh Botanics writing on the Series *Ferrugineum* in Marianna Kneller's *Book of Rhododendrons*. He sees things the other way around, delighted to find in the wild the species that grew so well in his garden, *hirsutum* and *ferrugineum*. Interestingly in the wild, in favoured places from the Balkans to the Pyrenees, *ferrugineum* can be dominant, but in the garden it is well behaved, 'slow growing, neat and compact'.[7]

These alpines were quickly ousted by the Americans, especially *maximum* and *catawbiense*, much mated with the Turkish *ponticum*, until Hooker's Himalayans came along, and out went the Americans and *ponticum* as quickly as if they had developed a nasty smell. In truth it was really a nasty colour, that mauve that *ponticum*, *maximum* and *catawbiense* possess and that seems to dominate any hybrids of all three; it is questionable that it is an unpleasant colour, but it has those aniline chemical connections, it was overexposed in the Mauve Decades and perhaps there are just too many wild flowers in the mauve and purple spectrum for gardeners, who are such colour-snobs, to regard it as anything but common. Oddly, the Himalayan aristocrat *augustinii*, one of the most revered of rhododendrons with her fluttering papery bells, is also usually – if I am brutally truthful – mauve. But it has become customary to call her 'lavender-blue' or 'bluish', perhaps more in hope than expectation, for blue (the one colour rhododendrons are not) has long been the Holy Grail of hybridisers. Is it mischievous to suggest that *ponticum* might have bred a true blue had she been treated properly?

Instead *ponticum* – and to a lesser degree *maximum* and *catawbiense* – became unfashionable. The useful features of *ponticum* and *catawbiense* had been their toughness and their ability to tolerate rough treatment at the hands of a nation of bad gardeners, for after all the Catawba Indians had told of the impassable 'slicks' and 'hells' of their rhododendrons at home. Toughness was much needed; within twenty years of the arrival of Hooker's Himalayans Shirley Hibberd (1825–90), in *The Amateur's Flower Garden* (1878), opened his Chapter 10 with:

> The money spent on rhododendrons during 20 years in this country would nearly suffice to pay off the National Debt. If the reader fails to appreciate the force of this remark, its meaning may be reached through an inspection of all the villa gardens in the country ... in a considerable portion of them will be found numbers of perishing rhododendrons, inhabiting a common border and associated with laurels, aucuba, hollies ... all surviving *except* the rhododendrons ... going from their pristine buxom beauty to a condition of shrunken starved-ness ...

Despite, or because of this, horticultural innovation marched on, the reliable *ponticum* stock was ousted, and those nurseries with fields of sturdy *ponticum* seedlings had to offload – hence John

Waterer's advertisement in the *Gardeners' Chronicle* for 'strong plants for immediate planting', at 10s 6d, 15s or a guinea per hundred, of *ponticum* 'usually acknowledged as the best Evergreen' for 'under-cover'. The need for 'cover' was nothing to do with gardening or even forestry; it was caused by the pursuit of a far stronger passion, the Victorian country gentleman's craze for shooting, in particular 'shooting-flying' – the following of the birds on the wing through the gunsight and killing them in full flight – which had been made possible by Alexander John Forsyth's (1769–1843) invention of the percussion cap.

This Scots minister, and son of the minister of Belhevie in Aberdeenshire, was a keen wildfowler who found himself ever disappointed when the birds escaped, forewarned by the flash of his gun. He devised a small enclosed cap of explosive ignited by a hammer, which in turn detonated the cartridge without the giveaway flash, which was eagerly adapted into sporting guns (and eventually for the army). For the double-action shooting-flying the guns had to be out in the open field, or on the edge of a wood, meaning that small coverts of low evergreens were planted, so that the birds could be lured into 'cover' before they were finally driven into the air by the beaters. These plantings, clearly beyond the province of the gamekeepers, were seen as the job of the head gardener, with advice already given by (another) Alexander Forsyth (*c.* 1809–85), gardener to the Earl of Shrewsbury at Alton Towers (and afterwards to Isambard Kingdom Brunel at Watcombe Park, Torquay). Forsyth actually recommended a range of plants: pernettya, cotoneaster, cranberry, holly, gaultheria, mahonia (these providing berries for the birds), laurel, yew, gorse, box, privet and *Fuchsia discolor* as well as rhododendrons. He also proposed cherry and apple trees planted beside the farm roads, their fruits intended for game and wild birds (a tradition still retained by wise farmers and estate managers), and 'demi-dykes', earth banks planted on their sides and top. Rhododendron, fuchsia and gorse seedlings, a few inches high, should be planted in groups of five or so, and protected with a circle of large stones. Forsyth actually envisaged a completely fruitful countryside (or did he just wish to keep small boys from his orchards?), with bilberries on the heath, so that nowhere was a 'sinful waste'.[8]

Forsyth's horticulturally ambitious schemes never materialised. The pernettya, cranberry, mahonia, even cotoneaster and certainly fuchsia plants were just not available, none produced in the right kind of numbers nor at a cheap enough price. Rhododendrons were available, and they were so widely popular that the estate gardens could rear thousands of their own seedlings and layers, as the thousands of 'Altaclerense' (from her *arboreum x catawbiense x ponticum* parentage) at Highclere have shown. The parsimonious, or shrewd English landowner ran his vast estate on its inner resources, and the rhododendron seedlings were ready to hand or cheaply bought for planting by the thousand, as many as 40,000 at a time, into his groves and copses. Shooting-flying became an ubiquitous passion in the British Isles, amongst the aristocracy led by the Prince of Wales, later Edward VII, and for the gentry and farmers determined to keep up with their 'betters'. From Devon to Norfolk and Nottinghamshire, from Northumberland across to Snowdonia, moor, copse and grove reverberated to the sound of the guns.

What happened next? The swift answer must be that the dreadful cycle of depressions and wars set in with more than biblical force: the agricultural declines of the 1880s and after, followed by the overwhelming losses of young men in the First World War, the economic collapse of the landowning classes in the twenties, the thirties depression and finally the Second World War. Sixty years of depopulation and the rise of mechanised farming left a deserted, depleted and neglected countryside, especially in the uplands. It was not 'wild', for the whole of the British Isles, even in the most remote areas, had been thoroughly domesticated by sheep and man, but everywhere not directly cultivated for wheat or potatoes was untended, left to the law of the jungle. If the valuable timber was hauled out, only rutted earth and shattered branches were left behind. Gone, as if overnight in Nature's terms, were the careful woodland skills of coppicing, charcoal burning and the cutting of rides, not to mention the complementary skills of a vanished army of gardeners and keepers who tended the walks and woods, lakes and copses, watercourses and commons far beyond the garden walls. What remained, in deserted plantations and parks and gardens with broken walls, was a contrived plant community, left to its own devices. The hierarchy defined by Oliver Rackham as the *natives* (the oak and the fox) that 'arrived here by natural processes in prehistoric times', the *naturalised* (rabbit, pheasant, sweet chestnut, Oxford ragwort) 'originally introduced by human agency from overseas, but now maintaining themselves without further intervention' and the *exotics* 'dependent on domestication' (guinea pig, peafowl, walnut, horse chestnut and cannabis) buckled before the opportunistic.[9] Rhododendrons were third-class exotics but with ambitions to naturalise (and move up to second class), perhaps because their genetic memory told them that they had once been natives and first class (with box, hornbeam, spruce and fir, *ponticum* are known to have been natives in Ireland as well as parts of Britain before the glaciers advanced) and they meant to be 'first class' again.

In post-war Britain the very same landscapes in which the vigorous escapee rhododendrons were having their field day, including the Peak District, the Lake District, Snowdonia and parts of Northumberland, were pronounced untouchable, as they were designated as National Parks (the western highlands and islands of Scotland and western Ireland were so empty and neglected as to be virtually untouchable anyway). Though thousands flocked to enjoy these 'wild' landscapes, they were walkers and sightseers, not workers. Even those who bought up the cottages and barns and joined the indigenous farming population in the parks played no part in working the fabric of the landscape; they too just looked, admiring the rhododendron-girt countryside as it flowered in springtime. In fact, most people loved the 'free gardens' that the rhododendrons provided, on the Norfolk heathlands, in the Peak District's Goyt Valley, along Surrey roads and Dorset lanes. In neglected places, especially in mid and north Wales and around Lyndhurst in the New Forest, their flowers had a ghostly prettiness that spoke the romance of lost gardens.

In the sixties the nascent ecological revolution began to bite, and pioneers such as Aldo Leopold (quoted p. 213), George Perkins Marsh, Asa Gray and others came into their own, with the realisation that our world was not as it should be, and it was time to do something about it. Ernst Haeckel's 1866 term 'ecology' was brought out and dusted off, European Conservation Year of 1970 opened up the debate on habitats, plant communities and landscape quality, and ecologists ousted the tunnel-visioned botanists and cursed horticulturists for playing fast and loose with exotic floras and keeping no records of what was planted and where. Alien 'pests' were identified, including Japanese knotweed and Himalayan balsam; these two were generally invasive but *Rhododendron ponticum* had been more choosy, colonising the most precious landscapes, the 'inalienable' upland National Parks of the Peak District, Lake District (some probably escaped from Ruskin's Brantwood) and Snowdonia, as well as the oakwoods of Killarney where it was bullying the native *Arbutus unedo*, and the wilderness areas of western Scotland. *Ponticum*'s special crime seemed to be its preference for these high status landscapes, which it 'contaminated' with the surburban gardenesque; purists in their hiking boots seeking communion with wild nature clearly did not wish to be reminded of their mother-in-law's shrubbery.

It was an aesthetic argument that set the conservationists grumbling, an argument over Stourhead, Henry Hoare II's (1705–85) great eighteenth-century landscape garden in Wiltshire, a National Trust treasure. Hoare had a genius for understanding his landscape. He had lovingly set his lakes, his broad grassy sweeps and tree-clad slopes, with a long path meandering a circuit via temples and sculptures, bridges and follies. 'Why is Stourhead so successful?' questioned the Trust's consultant Lanning Roper in a lecture to the RHS in 1968: 'The setting is superb . . . the view across the lake . . . the bridge over the stream in the valley in the foreground, and the Pantheon on the distant hillside . . . or the Temple of Flora under huge beech trees, with a beautiful stone urn on the lower slope by the lake . . . All superb . . . no other garden possessed such a series of delightful pictures, which compose and recompose so successfully.' Stourhead was lovely at every season: 'the autumn colour was magnificent, in the winter [it was] equally satisfying, with the bold stems of the huge trees silhouetted against the carpets of russet leaves or snowy slopes with deep blue shadows . . . and in spring with the tender new greens of the beeches and oaks, the silvery greys of the willows and poplars and drifts of daffodils pouring down the banks . . .'[10] Spring – there is the rub, for springtimes posed a problem in that Stourhead was ablaze with rhododendrons, especially *ponticum*, deemed too Victorianly vulgar for this classical eighteenth-century conceit. How dare they intrude? There was a tremendous furore, arguments raged, the rhododendrons must be later plantings, they were out of keeping, and wrong. (In fact, they just might have been right: for Hoare was helped by Charles Hamilton (1709–86) of Painshill and could well have been a Bartram's box customer for *maximum* seedlings; also by the time of the Temple of Apollo, 1765, *ponticum* would have been available.) Researches revealed Stourhead not to have been a pioneering rhododendron garden (or rather they did not reveal that it was) and thus the *ponticum* was deemed a rogue. It must have come from hybrids grafted on to *ponticum* stock, which duly reverted. After a decade or more of debate Stourhead's plantings were calmed down, with just a few judiciously placed and trusted hybrids. Though, dare I say it, at least one – Koster's icy-lavender 'Mrs Charles E. Pearson' – has some *ponticum* in her blood.

The Stourhead furore sensitised the *ponticum* debate; it became fashionable to hate them. In fact, demonisation was something of a political necessity; for every purist's genuine sense of outrage there were half a dozen hard-pressed National Park officers and wardens who needed to raise funds and motivate teams of volunteers to fight 'those ruddy rhododendrons'. Their toxic shade spread through oakwoods, throttling the life out of the woodland floor plants, their relentless root systems choked rivers and streams, they exerted their sterile monoculture across hill and down dale and were useless to bird or beast. Commercial foresters hated them for similar vices, for depriving their planted rows of other alien species of air, water and light. Press and television played up the annual rhododendron-bashing forays, making the most of pictures of conservationists at war with a much-loved (in the public's eyes) plant.

Rhododendron wars were tainted with a bitterness from the decided rift that opened between the champions of natives and those of exotics, with very little logic on either side. The former hunted out copies of Robert Gathorne-Hardy's *The Native Garden* (1961) (despite the author's admission of 'make-believe' and of writing on the principle that the home-grown only becomes desirable when one is deprived of the rest) and tended native gardens. The latter talked up the heritage status of such plants as chrysanthemum and camellia cultivars, and formed the National Council for the Conservation of Plants and Gardens (NCCPG, 1980) to organise national collections of all the varieties, or cultivars, of favourite exotic species. Thankfully, occasionally – but none the less puzzlingly – an overgrown rhododendron jungle, choking with layered and self-seeded *ponticum*, was hailed as a magical, mysterious and romantic treasure, as at Heligan and Aberglasney.

When the ecologists examined the rather larger and equally (in terms of decades of neglect) lost woodlands and groves of the demonic rhododendrons, they found things to be equally perplexing. In the Peak District the shooting estates and their game cover seemed the chief culprits, and Errwood Hall was identified as the 'home of rhododendrons in the Peaks' – meaning the source of escapees – from 40,000 seedlings planted in 1850. Chatsworth, Wentworth, Renishaw and Broomhead Hall were equally culpable, but so was the modern landscaping scheme around Kinder Reservoir, just west of Kinder Scout, where rhododendrons were planted as screening. The National Parks authority, having spent inestimable energies and resources opposing reservoirs, now found that even the ameliorating efforts caused them trouble. And at Chatsworth and Clumber, where hundreds of thousands of visitors wore out the landscape each year, the rhododendrons played a useful role in protecting sensitive areas. Nor were the *ponticum* so completely sterile and useless: they provided winter roosts for robins, blackbirds, nightingales and warblers (blackcap and chiffchaff). The count of parasites and insects hosted by rhododendrons was rising, providing food as well as shelter for small birds. Badgers built setts in the thickets, deer were grateful for the cover and otters made use of waterside groves.[11]

'Death to the Menace' the headlines still scream. The immediate remedy is eradication, hauling the brutes out by the roots with a large, yellow machine that obliterates every other living thing and remakes the landscape as primordial slime. Defoliation is a possibility, though hopefully with something more refined than Agent Orange and its deadly dioxins that still contaminate the soils of Vietnam – a country rich in rhododendrons (which were, of course, not the actual enemy there, but the hiding places of the enemy). The bare stems have a potential market as biomass fuels. Cutting by machine or hand labour and burning – rhododendrons make excellent charcoal – and subsequently spraying new young growth with a systematic herbicide (glyphosate) is another tactic, tried successfully in a scheme in the west of Scotland.[12] It is absolutely essential to respray every three years to kill regrowths. More insidious and powerful herbicides are available but these pose risks by contaminating watercourses, and drifting to forestry plantations and other people's rhododendron gardens. Biological controls have been investigated by searching for native predators amongst wild *ponticum* in Portugal, but what the scientists call the 'exploitable mycota', the bugs found, are either ineffectual or a threat to garden hybrids. The Dutch have tested a stump-rotting pathogen but this turns out to be the same pathogen that causes silver-leaf disease in a number of woody plants, until recently a notifiable disease of stone fruits in Britain.[13]

Or is the rhododendron-threatening disease already here? This summer of 2003 has brought alarms about the presence of *Phytophthora ramorum*, a contagious fungal disease that withers leaves, amongst rhododendrons in Cornwall. Whilst it would seem tragedy enough that this fungus has been found in ancient specimens at Heligan and Caerhays Castle, when careless talk suggests it was also the source of sudden oak death in the woods of California, then panic is not far away: 'Sick Rhododendrons Threaten the English Oak,' scream the accusing headlines.[14] It really is time we stopped blaming the plants. Oaks and rhododendrons have been growing as companion plants since time immemorial, certainly before we arrived on Earth, and it is our interference that should carry a government health warning.

Where there are too many *ponticum* perhaps we could import some Yetis to feed on them? Certainly, equally fantastic notions have appeared the minute the newspapers look for an ecological angle: 'Mile after mile of Snowdonia National Park is covered with rhododendrons and controlling them costs millions,' whined *The Times* on 28 October 2000.[15] Well, someone should look into the park's bookkeeping then, because the eradication scheme in Scotland quoted above was budgeted at £140,000, of which 90 per cent went into paying local workers. Snowdonia seems cursed, not with *ponticum*, but faint-hearted residents; landowners 'buckling under the strain' and locals like the businessman who had walked up Craig y Llan regularly for twenty years and now complained that the *ponticum* barred his path. More energetic locals have formed the weightily named Beddgelert Rhododendron Ponticum Management Group, so it is to be hoped they are handy with machetes. People managing their landscape are the solution, not deadly chemicals and bugs.

The sad stupidity of the rhododendron wars is the tarring of the whole genus with the brush of *ponticum* 'menace'. In the *Guardian* of 29 March 2003, Paul Brown, the environmental correspondent, prompted by yet another government initiative to protect 'natives' (red squirrel = good, grey = bad; water vole = good, mink = bad), went for the rhododendrons: 'other plants, such as rhododendrons, are still popular garden centre plants but the wild version has been declared a menace ... where the shrubs form dense forests and crowd our native plants'.[16] The shy *dalhousiae* and delicate *williamsianum* are equally as 'wild' as *ponticum*, but they would never crowd out anything. Such careless reporting does untold harm and, in this global village that we now inhabit, *ponticum* herself has become a threatened native and in need of protection in her Turkish homeland. The naturalists confront the gardeners with a vengeance, begging the whole question of 'what is a native?' Is not this becoming as outdated a notion in plants and animals as it is in human beings? *Ponticum* is not the special devil; the problem is ours.

The rhododendron universe has become subject to 'revisionism', much as every other aspect of society has been. Botanists and biologists have joined hands with geologists and espoused Asa Gray's 1850s observations on the similarities of the floras of eastern North America and eastern Asia. Rhododendrons are prominent amongst the hundred species that these two regions shared and they have found themselves drafted into paper after paper in the very lively study field of the Tertiary relict floras, the survivors of plants that were distributed throughout most of the northern hemisphere some 65 to 15 million years ago. Gray's two areas have been extended to five 'refugials': western North America (California, Oregon, Washington and the Vancouver area), south-eastern North America (Maine to Louisiana), south-eastern Asia (China, the Himalayas and the Vietnam/Thailand/Burma peninsula), eastern Asia (Korea and the Japanese islands) and the eastern Mediterranean (Turkey and around the Caspian Sea). The great genus *Rhododendron*, of course, thrives in all these areas as a 'native' in a half dozen or a hundred guises. Korea (though Wilson went there) and Vietnam (the ancient Nam Viet, home of the sultry southern red azaleas in Chinese literature) have both been frequently visited by rhododendron hunters in the last twenty years. Science seems to have confirmed in one sentence our myopic fumblings of 250 years, which it has taken me more than six chapters to relate.

But the implications of the new science are intriguingly iconoclastic. A frequent pattern has emerged which shows that the Japanese species of the Tertiary relicts (including corylus, hamamelis, aesculus and rhododendron) are more closely related to American than Chinese species, despite the mere 600 miles of sea between China and Japan. These plants have older genetic memories and are presumed to have migrated from 'America' via the lost land of Beringia, the former link between Russia and Alaska, now below the shallow Bering Sea, or the (still hypothetical) Aleutian Islands land bridge. The lingering ghost would seem to be the mysterious *Rhododendron camtschaticum* recently (1996–7) seen on Chekhov Mountain on Sakhalin Island, a low-growing deciduous species with nodding flowers, hanging on to the limits of life in the chilly mists of pine and birch scrub, with vaccinium and ledum.[17] Does *camschaticum* suggest differences that are more than climatic between the Japanese species, predominantly smaller 'azaleas', and the big-leaved Chinese giants?

The North Atlantic land bridge remains a topic of debate, though it is now generally accepted that it was broken some 50 million years ago, with 'stepping stone' islands remaining to allow species to migrate. Liriodendron and magnolia were both known in Iceland during the Miocene, the fourth epoch of the Tertiary period, and scientists seem to generally agree that this land bridge was 'almost certainly' the principal connection between America and Eurasia for migrants. Imaginative leaps, which writers are allowed to take but scientists are not, send the rhododendrons lovers cheering to the barricades; for here is a rhododendron ring around the earth, confirmed by the existence of known species, which casts a sceptical aura around the concept of 'natives'. The island of Ireland presents a good illustration.

Interestingly Ireland, with the money in the north and around Dublin, and the best climate for rhododendrons in the far south-west, missed out on the *ponticum* phase of arrivals completely, and yet has a *ponticum* 'problem'. The novelist, educational pioneer and gardener, Maria Edgeworth (1767–1849) of Edgeworthstown, County Longford, was an early fan of rhododendrons. In June 1812 she wrote to thank John Foster (1740–1828) of Mount Oriel at Collon in County Louth, the last speaker of the Irish House of Commons and a friend of her father's, for his gift of twelve plants, with rather a profusion of embarrassment because she had asked for one rhododendron and been given twelve, and then left them behind and they had to be sent on to her. In 1829 she was pleased with a present from her mother, 'a little rhododendron which has a fine fat flower bud', and three years later she was admiring Lady Longford's rhododendron bank at Pakenham Hall, Tullynally in County Westmeath, though she did not take to her ladyship.[18] There was a strong Irish connection to the Hooker rhododendrons; *maddenii* was named for the Irish plant collector Lt.-Col. Edward Madden of Old Conna Hill, near Dublin (who sent the first *Lilium cardiocrinum* to Glasnevin along with buddleia, abelia, meconopsis and primulas), and *edgeworthii* for Michael Pakenham Edgeworth (1812–81) of the Bengal Civil Service, Maria's nephew, who had a garden at Anerley in south London. The Wilson/Forrest/Kingdon Ward plants were most widespread in Ireland, and especially planted in woodland gardens in the south-west, including Annes Grove near Castletownroche in County Cork, Derreen, County Kerry, and around the fabled Lakes of Killarney (Mrs Delany's 'enchanted place') at Muckross and Killarney House. It is here in what is now the Killarney National Park that they have a *ponticum* problem, but as *ponticum* were never planted this must come from reverted hybrid stock. Stranger still, these extreme south-west approaches belong to the Lusitanian flora (named, like the doomed liner, for the

Roman province that stretched to the Iberian peninsula). Killarney is famous for the *Arbutus unedo*, the Killarney strawberry tree, which grows around the lakes, and seems to grow equally well on both sandstones and limestones on either side of the geological fault that runs through the park. The arbutus was first noticed in the mid-seventeenth century, according to Geoffrey Grigson, growing at its northern limit in Kerry, Cork and Sligo, but much reduced by charcoal-burning. The 'gallant red' fruit were noted by John Gerard (1545–1612) in his *Herball* (1597) as harsh to the taste and 'hurt the stomach' but by John Pechey as excellent as an antidote to plagues and poisons (*Compleat Herbal of Physical Plants*, 1694).[19] Now, someone must stand up for the *ponticum*, for arbutus and rhododendron are *both* natives of the Iberian peninsula (to add insult to injury the 'demon' *ponticum* is usually quoted as being brought from Gibraltar to Kew in the 1760s), and both belong to the family Ericaceae; they are, in fact, sister plants, and arguably *ponticum* has just as much right in Killarney as the arbutus. Is it simply that the arbutus is more 'antique', that it was celebrated by Shelley, or is it that prejudice against *ponticum* has become habitual?

It would also seem that far too little attention has been paid to the question of plant communities. George Forrest had been adamant that rhododendrons were sociable plants, that they interleaved, literally, with plants of their own kind and others of the family Ericaceae in complex and complementary growing patterns. These, we may assume, as with humans, modified their more extreme tendencies. If Forrest's words were inadequate then Captain John Noel of the 1924 Everest Expedition was equipped with a camera modified to work in low temperatures, and he brought back coloured pictures showing plant communities: the tropical forests of rhododendrons tangling with bamboos, vines, giant ferns; the temperate zones at 7,000 feet, upland forests of spruce, pine, oaks, magnolias, splashed with blue iris and crimson, yellow and pink rhododendrons, and the 10,000-feet alpine pastures carpeted with gentian, saxifrage, primulas and low-growing rhododendrons.[20] To a rhododendron the community is all. As early (in terms of rhodo-dendron cultivation) as 1928, Hugh Armytage Moore, creator of Rowallane (now in the care of the National Trust for Northern Ireland), reviewed the wider scene – the company of arbutus, per-nettya, gaultheria, cassiope, andromeda ('bog rosemary'), calluna, daboecia, kalmia, ledum and many ericaceous others that rhodo-dendrons might keep. Not only were there so many 'garden worthy' denizens of these species, perfectly desirable in their own right, but they created the ecological landscape for the rhododendrons, and at ground level where it had most effect. Since then, though the owners of the great rhododendron gardens have done their best, it seems that there has been very little serious study and practice of planting communities, from the plants' rather than the gardener's point of view. The exception seems to have been Tony Schilling, that most restrained and sensitive of Himalayan travellers and plantsmen, who combined horticulture and ecology (coining the term hortecology) in his plantings at Wakehurst Place, with firstly the Himalayan Glade of the mid-seventies and then the Trans-Asian Heath Garden, which filled an area left 'vacant' by the 1987 Great Storm. The Trans-Asian Heath Garden fulfils exactly Hugh Armyt-age Moore's suggestions. We get there after about 60 years.

The logical conclusion to be drawn from the round-the-world rhododendrons would seem to be that if, as individual species, the American *catawbiense*, the Turkish *luteum*, the Chinese *grif-fithianum*, for instance, had spent millennia adapting themselves to the ecological niches in which they survived the endless glaciations, then it was foolhardy to bring them together again by hybridisation. Rather like the Sorcerer's Apprentice, we had not the first idea of what we were really doing. Overnight, in their timescales, we remixed their genes into those nineteenth-century hybrids, confused their chemistry and set them scrabbling for survival, which looks to us very like domination. Ecologists now say that natural hybrids are a very rare phenomenon, and that the frequent reports of them (of which the plant hunters were very fond) prove this in that when it does happen it is so rare that we notice it. The grafting of these desirable hybrids on to *ponticum* and *luteum* rootstocks for mass sales compounded the situation, something perfectly well evident (though perhaps expressed in rather small print) to that crafty old William Robinson, when he allowed a fellow gardener to tell of his troubles with suckers from his grafted hybrids: his *ponticum* 'with a small scraggy piece in the centre to show that once it was meant to be a hybrid variety of special beauty' – and worse – 'the older the plant the larger is the base from which the suckers spring, and consequently the larger is the number of suckers. With Ghent azaleas the trouble is nearly as bad; the common yellow form on which they are grafted, being a strong grower, soon makes short work in ejecting the less vigorous intruder . . . the labour and money spent in an endeavour to obtain some specially beautiful effect results in a commonplace arrangement of lilac and yellow.'[21] Add a dose of the aforesaid neglect, lack of gardening, and 150 years, and the progenitor of the 'rhododendron wars' is revealed as neither *ponticum* nor even *luteum*, but our own foolishness.

The early growers, the members of the Rhododendron Society, had the right idea in their 'notes' from individual gardens (these were so valuable that the scarce volumes of *Notes* from 1916–39 have been reprinted by the American Rhododendron Society). The species and early hybrids, large or small plants, reacted in highly individual ways (they were, after all, individuals) to their places of residence, differences in soil, aspect and company, their responses to a late snowfall or a prolonged drought and all the vagaries of the seasons. Now we know the best motto: 'Microclimate is All'. But in the timespan of the rhododendrons our time for observations has been infinitesimal, and certainties are few; indeed the challenge of growing rhododendrons, so vast and so uncertain, is the real excitement of this great genus.

To an ecologist the appearance of a mould or mite is evidence of a plant's response to its situation; to a gardener the arrival of an azalea leaf mining bug or a fungal bud blaster or leaf spotter is an incitement to warfare, and endless fruitless gossip in the gardener's special vein of gleeful misery. There is little evidence of any plant pathology on rhododendron diseases, perhaps because they are 'mere' ornamentals – a status to be challenged shortly. The bugs and fungi seem fairly manageable; the cause of the greatest contention is the growing medium, the lime and peat question. Despite the plant collectors', and most particularly George Forrest's, repeated assertions that they found both large and small species growing on limestone rocks, the plants in cultivation have a reputation of being determined calcifuges, lime haters. Gardeners, who make hasty judgements, virtually ignore the most ravishing flowers at a show with a disparaging 'They won't "do" with me' and not a second glance. Rhododendrons are shallow-rooted plants, their great enemy is drought (and wind, but this is a matter of microclimate) and the best advice was always to give them a heavy mulch to protect the roots from August drought. In the days of this advice the mulch would be compost, manure or industrial waste, the latter including peat, the loose crumbly layers that were a by-product of industrial peat cutting for fuels. As gardening became more popular, so did the peat as a clean, light, water-retentive and yet manageable medium for protecting root systems, as virtually foolproof in the nurseryman's eyes as anything could be, so that peat was always recommended. It was ladled into planting pits, whole beds and borders were made of it, and with the advent of garden centres in the 1960s it became the preferred medium for the potting of all container plants. Conservationists protested against the uncontrolled peat digging, first in Holland, then in Ireland, and a Peatlands Conservation Council came into being to act as a control, but the gardening juggernaut was only slowly halted. The RHS carried out trials of various peat-substitutes at Wisley in 1997 but in July 2001 The Garden had to report that 'peat usage by home gardeners increased by 50% in the 1990s despite the publicity given to the issue'.[22] The National Trust, the B&Q chain, David Austin Roses and others are all working towards peat-free mulching and

potting, with recipes of bark, wood fibre and loam; in March this
year (2003) I watched the rhododendron beds in the Savill Garden
being covered with their 'special mix', a chocolatey but peat-free
coating.

The peat habit must in part be responsible for the 'lime-hating'
mantra, though the endlessly complex and individual requirements
of differing species and hybrids cannot be overestimated. Rhododendrons are just as complicated as people. On matters of cultivation the ultimate authorities are the Cox dynasty; as long ago as
1956 E. H. M. Cox and Peter Cox wrote in *Modern Rhododendrons*
of experiments to test the alkalinity that the plants would withstand,
which found that calcium content in the soil was more critical than
pH value. 'In other words rhododendrons will grow in a soil that
is pH8 (slightly alkaline) provided that the alkalinity is caused by
magnesium and not by calcium' and the plants healthily flowering
for six years in pots of magnesium-induced pH8 soil proved this.
The Coxes' opinion was 'that it does not matter, with few excep-
tions, so long as there is plenty of humus present in the soil'. But
they did not end it there, for good drainage, soil quality and feeding
were all equally critical.[23]

Clearly leaching, the washing through of the calcium, is also
critical. In *The Garden* of March 1999 David Kinsman, a geologist
and geochemist, noted that gardeners could be successful on alkaline
soils by frequent watering with acid rainwater during the summer.
He also tested out Forrest's opinions, confirming them in the same
regions of Yunnan in 1996, by taking soil samples: 'Yet pH measure-
ments in the thin, often organic-rich soils overlying the limestones
almost always indicated the soils to be acid (pH4.5–5.9). Only *R.
primuliflorum* was found to have alkaline soil in its root zone
(pH7.4–7.9).' He concluded that the climate was critical, in that in
the cold, dry winter months the plant took little from its soil, but
in the summer, when the plant was 'active', the acid monsoon rain
(typically pH5) bathed the plant and its roots in acidic water.[24]

As a matter of interest, the species which will tolerate up to slightly alkaline soils include *fortunei, augustinii, racemosum, wardii, ciliatum, impeditum, sargentianum* and more than a dozen others. *Sargentianum* will develop yellow or chloritic leaves if the soil is too acid, and Peter Cox's remedy is a dressing of ground limestone. The old hybrid 'Cunningham's White' (also tolerant of pH6.5–8) has been used as a 'control' in trials of the new German Inkarho hybrids, first marketed in 1998 as 'the world's first lime-tolerant rhododendrons'.

Conversely, or nearly so, a metallurgist John Lancaster, growing a hundred or so rhododendrons from the Coxes' Glendoick nursery on Sussex sandy loam (pH5.5–6.5) found his plants getting in trouble. By serendipity two were moved, one to an area which had been treated with mushroom compost, one to where some lime mortar rubble had stood, and both thrived and flowered profusely, whilst their companions still sulked. Gradually, tentatively at first, the mushroom compost 'tonic' was given to *cinnabarinum, barbatum* and *thomsonii*, as well as *Viburnum x bodnantense*, a jasmine and a magnolia, and all were obviously improved in health and vigour. Again Peter Cox was quoted (*The Larger Species of Rhododendron*, 1979,) that 'many claims have been made on the startling effects lime can have on growth and leaf colour on certain soils', but there was no scientific proof. The Plant Research Institute in Victoria, Australia, has since done tests over six years with 'Cornish Red' hybrids, concluding that 'calcium is not toxic to rhododendrons unless there is a gross disturbance of the plant's general nutrition' and that all the test plants increased their growth rate by an average of 50 per cent over the control plant. Dr Lancaster asked again, 'Do rhododendrons hate lime?' and answered himself a qualified 'no'.[25]

Horticulturists and gardeners (and many botanists) are loath to deal in biochemistry, but now I am there it is essential to follow the genus Rhododendron into a different world, the world she first inhabited long, long before she became a garden ornament.

Stanley 'Cookham' Spencer (1891–1959) was a brilliant painter of flowers, capturing the line and presence of the wild flowers in his Thames-side meadows as well as the more exotic residents of greenhouses and gardens, but unfortunately his native Cookham is not rhododendron country. I have to move him just south of New-bury to the village of Burghclere in Hampshire, close enough to 'Altaclerense's' Highclere for there to be rhododendrons along the village roads. The leafy village is quiet after the roar of the A34, and that kind of instinctual directional guidance system that picks up the pilgrim trail in such villages does not fail me. Just as expected, here is the modestly gated entrance into the orchard garden in front of the Oratory of All Souls, the chapel memorial to Lieutenant Henry Willoughby Sandham, who died in 1919 as a result of serving in the Macedonian Campaign. The murals on the chapel walls, often called Spencer's greatest work, were commissioned by Lt. Sandham's sister and her husband, Mr and Mrs John Louis Behrend. Spencer's delighted response was 'What ho, Giotto!' His own war service had been in the Royal Army Medical Corps, and in Mace-donia; he had some privately horrific memories, and a professional ghoulishness for flesh and blood in painted form, just as he revelled in the textures of fabrics and flowers and lard-like flesh. In the Sandham chapel the flowers come as a blessed relief from the flesh and blood and traumatic rituals of war; an exquisite morning glory entwines through a rusty ploughshare in the corner of 'Map Reading on Route March' and the rhododendrons, in full flower, tumble in a flood through the opening gates of the Beaufort War Hospital at Bristol as a lorryload of wounded men arrives. It is said that Spencer painted the rhododendrons, from those growing along the roadside near the chapel, painstakingly, as a respite from the raw details of his other subjects.

The chemical constituents of rhododendrons can produce devas-tating hallucinations and all the breakdown of the human systems that, with startling similarities, fill the literature of 'shell-shock'. At the hospital gates they are an apt introduction to something of their medical history.

Most of the early rhododendron men were medics. Their botany was learnt as part of their medical training. It was Robert Graham, as Regius Professor at Edinburgh, who found that his students were more likely to pay attention if he included the wider world of other than medicinal plants and took them for botanical walks on Saturday afternoons, but Graham was still a practising doctor on every weekday afternoon. His successor John Hutton Balfour Regius Keeper and Queen's Botanist 1845–79, was also a medical man, but when he retired in 1879 the connection was weakened, and finally broken. The Hookers at Kew, father and son, were the coming breed of notably scientific and economic botanists, servants of imperial enterprise. But the Graham and Balfour legacy persisted in so many who went out to the Indian Botanic Gardens and became rhododendron men. Roxburgh, Wight, Falconer and Griffith have appeared long ago in this story; John Forbes Royle (1799–1858) was another, for whom *cinnabarinum roylei* was named, and he was superintendent at Sahranphur, returning to be Professor of Materia Medica at King's College London in 1837. (If any of these noted 'rhododendron' medics did any actual medical research on rhododendrons, other than making herbarium collections, it has not survived, or at least I have not found it.)

As the rapid industrialisation of Western medicine turned to distilled pharmaceuticals, the name 'Materia Medica' remained in the sphere of the vegetable drugs. The much-prosecuted pioneer of homoeopathy, Christian Friedrich Samuel Hahnemann (1755–1843), born at Meissen in Saxony, and a doctor unhappy with conventional practice, took to heart Hippocrates' dictum 'like cures like' and began to test doses of a tincture of cinchona bark (isolated in 1820 as the source of quinine) on himself. Finding that he developed ague and 'marsh fever' (the temperate climate name for malaria) he went on to 'prove' other drugs, and inspire others to his system. *The Encyclopaedia of Pure Materia Medica – a Record of the Positive Effects of Drugs upon the Healthy Human Organism*, edited by Timothy F. Allen, and published in America in 1879, has seventeen tightly printed pages of provings of a tincture of the Russian in-toxicant and anti-rheumatic 'yellow rosebay', *Rhododendron chrys-anthemum*. It immediately becomes clear that this is a powerful drug; collapse into sleep, awake to intoxication, confusion, vertigo, amnesia, delirium, visions (*frightful* visions), which as the dosage progresses settle into a stupefaction, – beating headaches that become 'tearing pain'; repeated doses multiplying and intensify the ills that assault all the senses – pains, pustules, burnings, buzzings, loss of senses, taste, smell and sight – soon spreading to all parts of the body. Nausea and vomiting cause the severe collapse of formerly stout party in a horrifyingly gruesome way.

Curiosity about *Rhododendron chrysanthemum* was rife in the early days of the Rhododendron Society (in the First World War) and Professor Isaac Bayley Balfour made extensive enquiries into the St Petersburg archives to find that it grew all along the mountain borders of Siberia, Mongolia and Manchuria, and up to Kamchatka and in the mountains of Japan. Since then the horticulturists have had little to do with it, but the species has gone on providing the tincture for the homoeopathic remedy. Within the last decade it has been used in notable developments in Germany and Austria in the treatment of psychotic illness, mainly through rhododendron-induced interpretation of dreams.[26]

Rhododendron maximum, the American pink rosebay, has been medically proven as an astringent and narcotic; evidence from American poison control centres in the early 1980s was that the majority of cases were of small children who had sucked the sweet-ness from the flowers or eaten whole flowers, and 10–15 flowers eaten was the worst case. Of 152 patients, 143 had no symptoms, eight had gastrointestinal upsets but these were not solely caused by the flowers, and one child had mild hypertension and was kept in hospital overnight. As these were small children, of the toddling, adventuring stage, it seems unlikely that they were out with truly wild species and must have ingested garden hybrids; *occidentale* (California and Oregon), *macrophyllum* (British Columbia to Cali-

Professor Sir Isaac Bayley Balfour (1853–1922)
lecturing at the Royal Botanic Garden Edinburgh,
rhododendron sprig in hand.

fornia) and *albiflorum* (California, Oregon and Colorado) are cited
as poisonous. However, the breakdown of the connection between
botany and medicine seems evident in the cavalier attitude to naming the species in actual case histories, in which 'rhododendrons'
are cited *en masse* in an unhelpful and confusing way.[27]

More specific are the legendary poison honey species, which have
been steadily investigated since the late eighteenth century, when
a paper was presented to the American Philosophical Society on
ponticum, *luteum* and the kalmias as a source of toxins. Not surprisingly most of the evidence comes from Trabzon, for between 1984
and 1986 the Karadeniz University School of Medicine reported 16
patients with honey intoxication – 14 men, 2 women, between 30–
48 years old – all dizzy, weak, perspiring and with nausea and
vomiting one hour after eating 50g of honey. There were various
complications but an intravenous saline drip (0.5mg atropine) was
given and after 24 hours all recovered. It is now known that the
offending elements are grayanotoxins (formerly called andromedo-
toxins and similar to alkaloids of the deadly veratrum and aconite,

for which there is no certain antidote). But not all rhododendrons produce these toxins.[28]

In an effort to pierce the mystery shrouding Chinese medical botany, Dr Emil Bretschneider compiled his *Botanicon sinicum* in 1895, unfortunately entirely from sources known in the West, and much of the mystery remained. The Austrian botanist Heinrich Handel-Mazzetti (1882–1963) was marooned in Yunnan and Sichuan during the First World War and published his very detailed memoir in 1927 (published in English translation by David Winstanley, 1996) and I have found a single reference to R. C. Ching, who collected in the chief timber-felling region of Gansu in 1923, finding two large-leaved species, *agglutinatum* and *anthopogonoides*, which though not new at least further attested to the native species growing in the north. Even present-day Chinese botanists admit that the references are few, and that nothing at all was done between 1911 and 1940 for lack of funds. But in the late thirties Dr Wen-pei Fang started studying the flora on the sacred Omei Shan and in the early years of the Second World War the University of Sichuan published his first volume, despite printing difficulties, 'on paper curiously soft and fibrous . . . the first set of fifty folio-sized botanical drawings included twenty rhododendron species, all described in English and Chinese . . .'[29] Dr Wen-pei was a pioneer and he continued working at Sichuan University until the 1980s, since when the Chinese botanists' views of their own flowers have filtered into the West. Their photographs of a gentle Yunnan countryside are softly affectionate; printed on matt paper they are very serene and inexact images by our standards, but all the more enchanting. Sturdy white ewes and rams with curled horns, carefully shepherded, graze in a meadow of pink flowered *racemosum* in Zhongdian county; pink *yunnanense* flower on the margin of a lake; woods of larch and firs with fringes of purple *rupicola* are seen in Lijiang county; tall tsuga and pink masses of flowers contrast with a weather-beaten but beautifully flowering *sinogrande* in a field.[30] The flowers are unremittingly lovely but the habitats are most interesting: *phaeochrysum*, white and lightly speckled, tucked under a mature fir in a plantation of young firs, *edgeworthii* literally hanging out of the roots of a tree perched on a cliff top, and wild species and wild horses along a peaty, rocky stream. Somehow they are more believable, too.

The Chinese botanists wish it to be known that things have changed since Forrest's day; if they are asked for their feelings about plant hunting they still usually respond with 'Please, don't do that.' But they also know that whereas the old ways meant a sustainable countryside, the modern pressures of logging, reafforestation, mechanisation and road building are too much for the rhododendrons. In 1995 a joint project between the Kunming Institute of Botany and Edinburgh Botanics set out to achieve the Chinese botanists' dream of re-establishing their lost botanic garden, and in March 1999 they inaugurated the traditional Naxi-style building and 62-acre (26 ha.) garden. They have two objectives: to rehabilitate the rhododendrons and the alpine plants of Lichiang, and to record and conserve the biodiversity of Tibet and the plants of the Hengduan range of mountains.[31] They know they have much to do.

The botanists would also like to return their culture of flowers to the people of Yunnan and Sichuan. They plan to develop the distillation of essential oils from many species, including *thymifolium*, *micranthum*, *aureum* (the old name for the remedy species *chrysanthemum*), *cephalanthum*, *racemosum* and the many other fragrant-leaved species. Distillation in bulk offers 'a bright prospect' for Chinese industry. They are digging out the old medical uses, wary of the potent poison of the hawk-cuckoo flower, the red *simsii*, which can cause skin diseases (some people are known to have steeped the roots in wine, drunk it and died). It is a powerful pain killer – 'the pill that can even tame a tiger' – and it takes little imagination to realise the possible development of drugs as well as compounds that can be used against rice pests and all kinds of galls and aphids. Toxic complexities clearly match those of fungi, for the villagers of central Yunnan collect flowers of species they know well; *decorum* and *siderophyllum* are two, which are boiled and steeped in cold water to remove the bitterness, then eaten as vegetables. The leaves and barks are tannin rich, though much more needs to be learned about this.

The Chinese Rhododendron Society held its first show, with due celebration, in April 1987 at Wuxi. After three red ribbons had been cut by three dignitaries the Wuxi town brass band struck up, firecrackers were thrown from rooftops and a flight of pigeons let loose from the centre of the crowd. Each province had its display in the courts and pavilions of an old monastery and the show was seen by some 300,000 people, many coming by special trains from Shanghai. Oh, for such chutzpah in Britain or by the American Rhododendron Society!

The British observers at the Wuxi show were Johnny Millais' nephew Ted and his wife Romy, owners with their son David of a distinguished rhododendron nursery, Crosswater Farm at Churt in the Surrey greensand hills. Even for the bearers of such a famous name in the rhododendron world, getting to Wuxi, and afterwards on to an extended tour of western Yunnan, was only by special invitation and lengthy negotiation. Their 24-hour train journey from Chengdu to Kunming (spectacular during daylight hours) was shared with a couple from Hong Kong, good company, 'very kind to us' and intrigued 'to find two English OAPs travelling alone in western China'. After their warm welcome at the Institute of Botany and a look round, the next day saw them spending eight hours in a bumping truck, drinking local beer to save boiling the water, driving through a countryside where the farmers still threshed the wheat with flails or simply laid it in the road to let the trucks do it, and seeing piglets going to market tied on to bicycle handlebars, ending up at the hotel which was their base for climbs up Cangshan and Ailao. There were plenty of rhododendrons: masses of *decorum* from about 7,000 to 10,000 feet, many single stems only six inches high with a flower on top; vast quantities of *neriiflorum*, *yunnanense*, *trichocladum* and others growing and flowering together, with many variations in forms and colours as they climbed higher, and from the main ridge of Cangshan they looked down on the yellow seas of *lacteum*, much as Frank Kingdon Ward had done. The layered, dark green *Abies delavayi*, beloved by Chinese landscape painters, made a wonderful background for *cyanocarpum* in many shades of pink; 'one form so much better than anything I have ever seen in England,' wrote Ted Millais. There was a cliff face 'plastered' with yellow *sulfureum*, only reachable by mountaineers or a helicopter; there were curiously broad-leaved *taliense*, their leaves curled with cold and half buried in the snow – 'one wonders where the English forms came from' with their much narrower leaves. Going to Mount Ailao, forty miles distant, the village children scattered at the sight of them, never having seen Europeans before, but soon came creeping back, often carrying exquisite flowers. Endless cups of green tea accompanied the parley with the headman as the Kunming botanists requested permission to climb his mountain. It was granted. On Ailao *decorum* was again different to those on Cangshan, the experts debated over other names, and they found a few *sinogrande* flowers left on plants near the top of the mountain, the *sinogrande* being their goal. After that there was the village feast and the long drive back to their hotel. Then it was 200 miles north to Lijiang (the old Naxi town, now a World Heritage Site, the new town presumably having eaten up the botanic garden which had existed from 1958–70) and three climbs on Yulongxueshan to about 12,000 feet. Primulas, daphne (a scented yellow *Daphne aurantiaca* mixing itself with a powder-blue *lapponicum* rhododendron) and *Cypripedium tibetica*, purple slipper orchids (which Kingdon Ward had found here), accompanied more rhododendrons – many species different again – culminating in 10 to 15-feet-tall *beesianum*, huge trusses of rose and salmon pink flowers, 'the finest . . . we saw on the whole trip'. The abiding impression from Ted Millais' account[32] was, besides the wonder of it all – 'the trip of a lifetime' – that with his great experience so many of the species that he saw were 'curious' and 'different' to those he was familiar with at home. I wonder if it is just possible that the rhododendrons in their homeland are in blissful ignorance of the systemised existence that we have concocted for them so far away?

What was also evident was the Chinese pride in their rhododendrons, the botanists' punctilious requests to local officials for permission to see 'their' flowers, and the complete ban on collecting plants and seeds (the Japanese have been too greedily collecting and one 'nameless Dane' had all the plants he had collected removed at the airport).

And what of rhododendrons in Chinese gardens, are they there now? Beyond the touristic and banal, books on China's gardens are still rare in the West, and even rarer are the travelling photographers such as Peter Valder, who venture to explore remote temple and tomb gardens, parks and botanical gardens and the gardens of 'ordinary' people. Valder's *Gardens in China* (2002) shows the healthy status of a favourite flower, carefully tended in temple gardens, a splendid unnamed species flowering in a farmer's garden, gorgeous species at Shenyang Arboretum in the north, which was founded in 1963 – one of many new provincial collections – and others flowering in Black Dragon Pool Park, next door to the Botanical Institute in Kunming. They are abundant in the courts of the gardens of old Suzhou, one aptly named the 'Joyful Garden', and in another court pink azaleas are dazzlingly displayed in grey slate containers.[33]

Perhaps, after all, the real understanding of the rhododendrons resides in the East, and their centuries of sojourn in the West have just been a brief interval. The most distinguished Western taxonomists now believe that their work has to be done in the field, where the rhododendron's variable responses to her neighbours and growing conditions reveal her true identity, whether species or natural hybrid. So, is the future in China, as her botanists and biochemists venture into a new rhododendron age? It would seem that there, from a basis of age-old instincts and clues, a wider understanding of the genus will be found.

CHAPTER EIGHT

Rhododendrons Now!

THE WORLD OF RHODODENDRONS has changed completely within the last 50 years – it has in truth been turned upside down – with the discovery of the equatorial Malesian species, which extend into the southern hemisphere and Queensland. Named for the French pharmacist Julien Joseph Virey, the vireyas are a sexually isolated section of the genus of around 320 species, though the number continues to grow as further discoveries and identifications are made. Even though their name dates from the 1820s, and they are a rediscovery, the vireyas are latecomers at the garden party, now very popular in Australasia and America but only tentatively known in Britain, and yet they constitute almost one-third of the known species of all rhododendrons. Apart from being tropical, many epiphytic, the vireyas are protected by scales that cover leaves, stems and sometimes even the flowers. These scales are visible and can be scraped off with a thumbnail; they seem to conserve moisture and may act as a sunscreen. Many vireyas have very long, narrow tubular flowers; the species *tuba* is well-named. At least the story of the vireya allows my text a respite from that word 'rhododendron' for a while.

Vireyas began with a flourish, or a commercial flyer, in the 1880s, when Veitch's Royal Nursery in Chelsea raised something like 500 hybrids – those sturdy seedlings that James Mangles had reported

on in the *Gardeners' Chronicle* – from the first half-dozen imported
species, which included Thomas Lobb's wondrous orange *javanicum*
and the white, scented *jasminiflorum*. It was a flyer that failed; the
tender vireyas could not compete with the hardy hybrids, and most
of them went the way of all flesh; the yellow and scarlet 'Souvenir
de J. H. Mangles' and 'Princess Alexandra' (named for the then
Princess of Wales) are among about eight survivors of Veitch's 500,
now all antiques that vireya experts like John Kenyon at Tauranga
in New Zealand's North Island and Christopher Fairweather
at Beaulieu in Hampshire pride themselves in keeping in their
collections.

Vireyas virtually disappeared from known cultivation for 60
years; they were seen in the wild, in the jungles of Malaysia and
Borneo, by botanists and gardeners who were soldiers during the
Second World War, and remembered when life resumed afterwards.
In the best of botanic traditions it was an Anglican priest, Norman
Cruttwell (1916–1994), who played a major role in their rediscovery;
he arrived as a bush missionary in Papua New Guinea in 1946 and
remained for 42 years. In his ceaseless travelling to his remote and
scattered flocks Canon Cruttwell came to know the island and its
people, and they knew him and could guide him to the best places
for flowers. In time, reminiscent of Brian Houghton Hodgson and
his Tibet, he could sketch the mountain paths from memory, he
could name the birds and many of the reptiles and insects, but his
chief loves were the flowers, the gentians of the high grasslands
above the 'moss forest' and the orchids and vireyas of the tropical
woodlands, which he located and described in his botanical diaries.
In 1961 Dr Hermann Sleumer of the Dutch national herbarium at
Leiden made an extensive tour to record the Malesian flora.
Sleumer, the first important name in vireya taxonomy, named the
elegantly white-trumpeted and scented *cruttwellii*, and the yellow-
orange *christianae*, this for the canon's mother, Christian Cruttwell,
who joined her son in mission work as a widow approaching 60
after her 'first' life as a vicar's wife in Hertfordshire.

The early sixties seemed to be the beginning of everything: 'every-one seems to be in mountaineering mood this year,' Cruttwell wrote in February 1962. He added, perhaps rather wistfully, 'for so long I've had these mountains to myself'. He was writing to John Latter, a vulcanologist, whom he had heard was tramping the Daga Ranges of the Owen Stanley Mountains in the extreme south of Papua New Guinea, looking for a reported volcano, which turned out to be a grass fire. Not much escaped Norman's 'bush telegraph': he learned that Latter was also a keen entomologist, and – being as interested in curious rocks and lava flows as in everything else – suggested they explore together the following August. John Latter still has his diary to remind him of the rigours of that trip with the indefatigable Norman, who 'looks over the top of his spectacles and chuckles' in a disarming way, and his dog Panda. 'I remember sitting down to rest on a beautiful slope studded with alpine flowers, and Norman saying "Don't sit there! You're sitting on *Gentiana cruttwellii*! Go and sit somewhere else!"' Norman kept up a running commentary of his infectious enthusiasms – for the "thrilling" birds, Princess Stephanie's bird of paradise and the crested gardener bird that weaves dendrobium orchids and other bright flowers into its house-building, for a rare lobelia, for the butterflies, and for Mount Goodenough, the home of vireya *goodenoughii*. Nineteen years and many botanists' trips later, the now Canon Cruttwell, curate at Goroka in the central mountain region, still managed to walk the Australian Rhododendron Society tour party off their feet, eight hours up and down the paths of the mossy forest on Mount Gahavi-suka. In his seventieth year he went island-hopping and found the lovely *luralense*, pure white and lily-like, growing near the limit of vegetation on a volcano, and within the sulphurous smells of its steam vents, on Bougainville Island. His final work at Goroka was as founding curator of the Lipizauga Botanical Sanctuary for wild orchids and vireyas in Mount Gahavisuka National Park. Canon Cruttwell left Papua New Guinea, after 'a wonderful life . . . richly blessed' in 1988; the following year saw the issue of a set of four

Papua New Guinea vireya stamps, each painted by him, and including *cruttwellii* and *christianae*.[1]

The mantle of vireya taxonomy has passed from Sleumer to Dr George Argent at Edinburgh Botanics. Dr Argent is quietly spoken, a modest man gracefully perplexed by the seemingly endless variations of his vireya universe, with so much waiting to be discovered. He has led expeditions to Sabah and the 'wonderful', rich hunting ground of the challenging Mount Kinabalu, which yielded 25 species, and to Irian Jaya (the Indonesian part of New Guinea). Since the 1960s the Edinburgh collection has grown to over 200 species, the supreme (indeed the only large) collection outside Australasia and North America. In the chill, grey north the vireyas fill their glasshouse with fluttering colours; the critical factor in their health is light, says their keeper, David Mitchell, 'vireyas are easily victims of SAD', the seasonal affective disorder. Another Botanics' staff member, Paul Smith, was a first-timer on the 1992 expedition to the Baliem valley of the Central Highlands of Irian Jaya, the home of the primitive Dani people. The Dani are gardeners and pig keepers, and the heavily laden botanists had to trudge for hours in the high-altitude heat through cultivated gardens and pig paddocks until they reached a narrow strip of woodland and Paul Smith caught sight of his first wild vireyas, the rich yellow *macgregoriae* and scented, white *inundatum*, quickly followed by others. He had expected them 'to look different in the wild from the ones we grow in glasshouses in Edinburgh, but I had not expected to see them festooned with lichens and mosses, sometimes damaged, often looking straggly and sickly. I should have realised they were competing with everything else around them and were not protected against passing people, insects or pigs!'[2] The vireyas, it seems, play a kind of Box and Cox with the Dani and their pigs, quickly moving into areas that are relinquished as the people move on: even so, Dr Argent feels logging has been replaced by cabbage growing as the chief threat to his vireyas.

Besides Papua New Guinea, Irian Jaya and Sabah, the New Zealand and Australian botanists have hunted vireyas in Kalimantan (Borneo), Sulawesi, the Bismarck Archipelago and the Solomon Islands. The discovery of *lochae*, a compact bush with pink bell flowers, as a native of northern Queensland, has given a proprietorial glow to the New World gardeners, a pride in their own: in their 1997 'practical gardening guide' on species and hybrids the nurseryman John Kenyon and garden writer Jacqueline Walker are resolutely honest about this independence:

> While the familiar temperate rhododendron and azalea hybrids, which for more than a century have been bred for Northern Europe, are steeped in horticultural tradition, the vireya hybrids now proliferating in nurseries draw upon a much smaller repository of practical and published expertise, whilst the gardens to which these vireyas are destined are also smaller. The large, landscaped parks of wealthy landowners of the past were fitting settings for those earlier temperate introductions, where sweeping driveways of imposing rhododendrons led to private estates and public parks that now swarm with tourists. By contrast, today's vireya growers are likely to garden on small plots, patios, or even just a balcony. Although large rural gardens are still not entirely beyond reach, enclosed urban properties of diminished dimensions are now the norm. Happily the vireya is perfectly suited to such sites. Limited space encourages intensive planting, especially vertical planting to which vireyas readily adapt. Provided their needs are met, vireyas can be grown in large numbers within relatively small spaces.[3]

So there you have it: the vireya revolution.

It has all happened so quickly, so unlike the painstaking and halting progress of the big rhododendrons and even the azaleas into widespread cultivation. A special trans-Pacific relationship has been established between New Zealand and eastern Australia with California, Oregon and Washington, via Honolulu, where there is a vireya collection at the Lyon Arboretum. Most of the species vireyas are already regarded as collectors' items and a large variety of hybrids, about 400, though that is a moving target – in shades of yellow, orange and scarlet, and sometimes all three together' – vie for gardeners' affections, often with faintly nauseating names: 'Lemon Lovely', 'Cherry Pie' or 'Pretty Cotton Candy'. Names apart, many of these hybrids are enchanting plants, retaining their glossy green rosettes of typically rhododendron foliage with frilled trumpety flowers, flowers and foliage in perfect balance in even young plants. The names Blumhardt and Jury figure prominently in New Zealand hybrids. Os Blumhardt, pioneering collecting and breeding since the 1950s, has produced 'Kisses' ('one of his best,' says John Kenyon, 'this bushy upright shrub bears magnificent heads of lolly-pink and cream') and the sun-gold and orange 'Ra', as well as the more delicate 'Silver Thimbles', an aptly named miniature bush with reddish stems. Felix Jury introduced the orange species *macgregoriae* to New Zealand and used it for successful hybrids, work now carried on by his son Mark Jury at North Taranaki. The flowers of healthy vireyas have a luminous quality that shows to perfection amongst glossy green leaves and ferns in dappled shade. 'Popcorn', generally acknowledged the best pure white, lights a dark setting, but so do 'Dawn Chorus', blushing salmon-apricot, and the vivid 'Ra' or 'Simbu Sunset' in their turn. In containers or hanging baskets, for deck living in a warm town garden, on their own, or with strong foliage or light grasses, the smaller vireyas with their vivid scented trumpets are an easily acquired habit. They are (as yet) free from serious disease, some can tolerate light frosts, but most would need wintering inside in eastern North America and northern Europe.

Vireyas are work in progress; theirs is a story on the move. The best places to see them (apart from the scientific collection at Edinburgh, which is not normally open to visitors) are at the Pukeiti Rhododendron Trust at New Plymouth on New Zealand's North Island, the Adelaide Botanic Garden, the Australian National Rhododendron Garden at Olinda, Victoria, the Strybing Arboretum at San Francisco and the Rhododendron Species Foundation near Seattle.

All the vireya people seem to agree that their plant has a great future, as a pot plant for outdoors and conservatories, for cut flowers (wonderful for arranging), as 'brighteners' for swimming pool surrounds and even beside fishponds, where the vibrant colours are enhanced by the light reflected from the water. There must be something in all this, for the wily Dutch nurserymen have started producing vireyas in their thousands.

In England, Christopher Fairweather at Beaulieu (working in his own nursery and in some of the Exbury glasshouses) has been patiently rearing and testing his vireya seedlings, which he is now putting on the market. Are they easy to grow? By following a few rules the answer would seem to be 'Yes'; with good drainage, the correct feeding and watering (they like to be moist but not too wet) and an unheated conservatory for the winter (at 8–10°C/ 46–50°F) but going outside as soon as frosts are past into a position with sun and shade, then vireyas are happy in Hampshire. White 'Popcorn', the old Veitch hybrid 'Pink Delight' and the oranges 'Java Light' and 'Just Peachy' are recommended.[4] And, interestingly, further proof of vireya happiness in Hampshire comes with *Rhododendron rushforthii*, a new species collected in Vietnam in 1992 by Keith Rushforth. It has small yellow flowers and bluish-green curling pointed leaves (it is taxonomically *Pseudovireya*) and has thrived in the Rushforth garden in Fareham, wintering in an unheated, east-facing conservatory.[5]

I am left with a slightly uncomfortable prompting from the distant past over this short, sharp and apparently effortless vireya history. All the collectors in the tropical wilds have observed that vireyas love to colonise disturbed ground. During the Second World War islands were occupied by the Japanese and the people took to the hills; when the war ended the vireyas moved in after they had returned to their villages. The vireyas established themselves behind the Dani people's peripatetic cultivation, and Dr Sleumer noted that they colonised after landslides. He states: 'the production of seeds in large quantities and their distribution by wind makes possible such initial settlements. The same thing occurs when natives burn down trees'. He found one species growing in a most unlikely habitat, 'where it had survived frequent grass fires'.[6] Vast quantities of seed, widely scattered, a phoenix-like persistence to survive fires – have I not written these things before? In the context of *ponticum* wars? For the sweet little delicate vireyas are rhododendrons inside, and perhaps they have some recolonising to do away from their tropical islands? The cleverly induced hybrids are getting hardier and hardier; will the last enemy, Jack Frost, soon be defeated? Will we have trees all over the world playing host to roguish epiphytic rhododendrons?

Back in Britain the old guard with the rhododendron-girt drives were picking up the pieces after the war. Edmund de Rothschild returned to Exbury in 1946 and took a look around; he had been discouraged in any interest in the rhododendrons during Lionel's lifetime but now found himself, as he has confessed, 'moved by the beauty of my father's legacy. Although I could see that there would be a huge task ahead – acres of brambles and weeds to be cleared, hundreds of dead branches to be cut away and many sickly plants in need of uprooting – I decided, there and then, to try to restore the garden.' The head gardener, Francis Hanger, who had taken over when Arthur Bedford died and seen Exbury through the war, coping with the Nissen huts on the lawns and an invasion of thousands of military personnel, had been lured away to be curator at the RHS Wisley garden. It later transpired that everyone thought that Exbury was lost beyond recall, or that no one would be mad enough to try (a state of mind that the RHS has pursued with vigour in the succeeding decades, always preferring new gardens to old ones; and they have also exhibited a somewhat dubious loyalty to rhododendrons as we shall see). Likely head gardeners were rare birds in those days but these things often turn out well. Eventually Fred Wynniatt, who had worked at Exbury before the war (and spent two years as a prisoner of war incarcerated in a salt mine), settled in, and Francis Hanger came down to help him at weekends.

At Whitsun 1955 Exbury was opened to visitors; on the Bank Holiday the line of cars stretched all the way back to Beaulieu and the great age of garden visiting had dawned.[7]

In the Exbury woods a quieter magic was working, and is working still, as the seedling treasures that Lionel de Rothschild had planted in quiet corners came into the light. Fred Wynniatt found a turkey-red species under a great *ponticum*, which turned out to be Forrest seedling 25601 from his 1924–5 expedition, flowering unseen until it was brought out and exhibited in 1959. The white, crimson-eyed and -spotted 'Kathmandu' was found in 1965 on the far limit of the woods, and the huge, brilliant crimson 'Rouge' suddenly 'appeared' in the woods in 1950, a surprise on a morning walk. Best of all was a plant that had been growing at the back of the estate yard for more than a dozen years before it bloomed in 1954, two days before the Rhododendron Show. It had 'huge trusses of deep, rich cream, enlivened by the ruddy eye of *lacteum* (for all the world as though a bumble bee were sitting in it)', and was taken to the show, duly awarded a prize, and named 'Lionel's Triumph'.[8]

The Exbury charisma, or Lionel's long-reaching ghost, or what you will, still rustles the foliage of the rhododendron world. The famous Exbury 'Carita' was originally registered in 1935, and her sister followed, named 'Golden Dream'. Some 40 years later, in far away Tasmania, a group of enthusiasts led by a local dentist and naturalist, Dr Noel Sullivan, founded the Emu Valley Rhododendron Society with the intention of making a community garden. By 1981 they had their site, about 30 acres (12 ha.) set in a natural amphitheatre of blackberry swamp and scrubland on the west bank of the Emu River in north-west Tasmania. As an act of faith some society members climbed through the dense undergrowth to a small knoll and planted 'Carita Golden Dream'. The plant did not survive, but in the folklore of the society 'the plant died but the dream persists'. The replacement plant now flowers every spring, as does the whole garden, open every day of the year, with a collection of over 17,000 azaleas, rhododen-drons and companion plants and native flora.[9]

At Exbury Fred Wynniatt (maize-yellow flowers, *fortunei* x Exbury 'Jalisco') was succeeded as head gardener by Douggie Betteridge, who is still around to offer support, when asked, to Exbury's first woman head gardener, Rachel Foster; appointed in 1998, a young and starry personality, in whom an affection for her 'Exbury Beauties', as she calls them, is strongly evident. Behind the sheer glamour of the flowers Rachel Foster's Exbury still has the power to absorb and surprise. For the past dozen years Lear Associates of Oxford have been painstakingly cataloguing the rhododendrons, entering them on a custom-built database, which had 17,500 accessions by May 2002. The methods devised for identifying plants, for which Exbury has better paper documentation than any other garden, are to benefit other collections.[10] In another part of the wood, a former physics teacher, Dr Michael Robinson, who collects rhododendrons in East Sussex, regularly haunts the further recesses of the Exbury woodlands looking for Lionel de Rothschild's late-flowering hybrids. 'Late' flowering means July, August and even September; perpetuating his beloved rhododendrons into the late summer was one of Lionel de Rothschild's dearest ambitions, one he never lived to see flower, and Mike Robinson is finding this legacy. The many *auriculatum* hybrids of differing kinds that he finds still flowering each September upset our accepted notion that rhododendrons are merely spring flowers.[11]

Seen retrospectively, the decision of Edmund de Rothschild (rich red 'Kilimanjaro' x 'Fusilier') to restore Exbury on a strictly commercial basis was a natural act of filial affection and family pride; is not all gardening a process of constant renewal after disasters, be they natural or man-made? But perhaps the Exbury factor and Rothschild flair (a film of the garden by Edmund's elder son Nicholas has attracted the sobriquet 'heaven, with the gates open') have obscured the role of the rhododendrons themselves in the social revolution of garden opening.

Garden visiting has become one of the great British 'lifestyle' innovations of modern times. Other Europeans and certainly

Americans are much more shy of opening their gardens to all-comers, but in Britain this has become a vital ingredient of tourism and a leisure activity that attracts more of the natives on almost any given weekend (with winter openings now popular) than a major sporting event. Gardens, however, are fickle, like life they rise and fall, come and go; rhododendrons, on the other hand, are phenomenally long-lived, far outlasting our human span, and they lurk in forgotten gardens, tempting any passers-by with an atom of sensibility to return and rescue them.

Trebah, the nameplace of Gill's 'Trebah Gem', is a case in point. It is on the Helford estuary, pretty near to heaven itself, and one of the many gardens planted by the Fox family, Cornish Quakers of legendary status, in the early nineteenth century. For over a hundred years Trebah flourished, each owner planting pines, rhodo-dendrons and dicksonias (the tree ferns famously used as ships' ballast). In 1939 the estate was broken up and sold, and during the war, along with so many other Cornish coves, Trebah's ravine shielded the secret preparations for the Normandy invasion of June 1944. After the war the Fox mansion burned down but the eighteenth-century wing remained; for forty years Trebah changed owners 'on average every six years' until it was bought in 1981 by Tony and Eira Hibbert for their retirement. They imagined drinks on the sunny terrace and afternoon strolls down through the flowery jungle to their beach for a little leisurely sailing. But their timing was bad. The value of historic gardens, not as private inheritance but as public 'heritage', had been argued by the Garden History Society since its founding in 1965; this was dismissed as socialist twaddle by many owners of large, and especially rhododendron, gardens, who much preferred – like the Aberconways of Bodnant – to arrange adoption by the National Trust, a gentrified institution with which they could share a common language. The GHS per-suaded county councils to investigate and list their historic gardens, and in 1980 the National Council for the Conservation of Plants and Gardens (NCCPG) was founded under the patronage of the

Prince of Wales to do much the same for garden plant species and hybrids. As the Prince of Wales is also Duke of Cornwall, Cornwall was quick off the mark, looking into its especially rich legacy of imported plants. The Hibberts were soon asked, 'How are you getting on with the restoration of your famous historic garden?' Their immediate reaction was to sell up and 'retire' somewhere else, but 'Trebah Gem' had already exerted her power and netted them, and as they were the kind of people who had never shirked a challenge in their lives, they started work, helped by their family. Trebah opened to visitors in 1987. 'This is no pampered, pristine, prissy garden with rows of clipped hedges, close-mown striped lawns and daily raked paths,' warns the garden guide. 'You are going to see a magnificent old, wild and magical Cornish garden – the end product of 100 years of inspired and dedicated creation, followed by forty years of mellowing and ten years of love and restoration.'[12]

In another part of the wood other people were fighting their way through other rhododendrons. Early in 1982 Walter Magor (1911–95) of Lamellen, the son of one of the pioneers of the Rhododendron Society, had visited Heligan for the first time with Damaris Tremayne and Alan Clark. 'I think I have seen most of the original Indian rhododendrons still growing in the British Isles,' he wrote afterwards, 'but nothing to compare with those at Heligan, where *arboreum*, *falconeri*, *grande*, *niveum* and *griffithianum* must all be thirty feet or more, and were in full flower when I paid my first visit'. He continued with a detailed account of the plants he had seen and the history of the garden, which was well known in Cornwall, and concluded that the plants were of great interest and well worth conserving. In 1950, he had learned, the tenant, Commander Thomas, had confided to a botanical visitor that 'because of the vast size of some of the rhododendrons he expected – or hoped – that they would be given the status of *national monuments*'. 'What a hope!' commented Walter Magor, 'but what a chance for the NCCPG, or the Garden History Society, to show its mettle.'[13]

This was unlikely as both societies had a broad brief that prevented them concentrating on a single garden, and anyway I am convinced that a garden responds best to the force of a single personality rather than to a committee. In Heligan's case the forceful personality and management and media skills belonged to Tim Smit, who formed a team to bring the 'Lost Gardens' back to life, into books and television series and into the highest visitor ratings. The Svengali behind the scenes was Tony Hibbert, who discovered that his own escape from the Germans after his capture at Arnhem had been assisted by Tim Smit's grandfather's Resistance group; to gather Cornwall's support for the Heligan venture was by way of a thank-you. Walter Magor's high opinion of Heligan, not usually quoted as far as I am aware, is particularly interesting, as there have been many doubters that Heligan was worth all the fuss; in rhododendron terms it clearly was. Since Heligan Tim Smit has marched on to the even greater challenge of the Eden Project (where vireyas are a feature), with even greater success. The advent of Eden galvanised the Cornish gardens, almost all rhododendron gardens, into greater efforts than ever before in advertising their attractions to visitors. As the Cornwall Gardens Trust map shows, there are effortlessly 28, all down England's foot. A weekend or even a week's tour is hardly enough; six months' exploration might be nearer the mark. And still they come. The Boscawens' Tregothnan on the Fal estuary – with the tender *Rhododendron lindleyi* as its emblem – has camellia trees cut for florists' greenery and is going into English tea production. The connoisseur's choice, chosen for the Rhododendron Group Tour in May 1997, based at Budock Vean near Falmouth, was Caerhays, Trebah, Glendurgan, Tregothnan, Trewithen, Tremeer and Pencarrow. They also visited Lamorran House in St Mawes, a garden made in the last twenty years.

I know that gardens are, like most of the good things in life, a matter of personal chemistry; with too many at a viewing it is easy to overindulge and constant admiration is an absolutely exhausting exercise. But when a garden comes spiralling out of history and

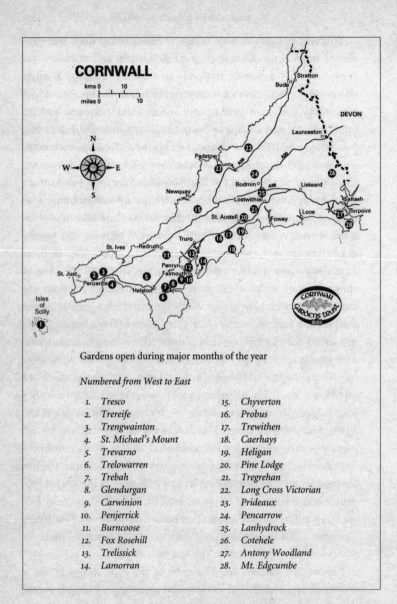

CORNWALL

kms 0 — 10

miles 0 — 10

N W—E S

DEVON

Gardens open during major months of the year

Numbered from West to East

1. Tresco
2. Trereife
3. Trengwainton
4. St. Michael's Mount
5. Trevarno
6. Trelowarren
7. Trebah
8. Glendurgan
9. Carwinion
10. Penjerrick
11. Burncoose
12. Fox Rosehill
13. Trelissick
14. Lamorran
15. Chyverton
16. Probus
17. Trewithen
18. Caerhays
19. Heligan
20. Pine Lodge
21. Tregrehan
22. Long Cross Victorian
23. Prideaux
24. Pencarrow
25. Lanhydrock
26. Cotehele
27. Antony Woodland
28. Mt. Edgcumbe

The Cornwall Gardens Trust's map of rhododendron gardens
open to visitors.

into the rhododendron spectrum, then there are refreshing layers
to peel away. Sheringham Park was Humphry Repton's (1752–1818)
swan song, his 'favourite and darling child in Norfolk'. Repton
was 60 when he started work there in 1812, a garrulous and kindly
man who had become something of a social engineer as well as the
doyen of landscapers, and he was concerned that his clients had
the right attitude to the countryside, to whom many were newcomers. He liked, indeed he said he loved, the Abbot Upchers on
sight, and recommended that they should let the local poor gather
wood in the park; they should improve the local workhouse and
organise community fishing competitions on the beach. With his
son, John Adey Repton (1775–1860), he built them a low and colon-
naded house, artfully sited behind a knoll to shelter it from the sea
winds, and designed them a lilting landscaped park, full of variations and surprises, woods and groves. Sheringham is generally
thought Repton's masterpiece. Abbot Upcher died in 1817, followed
by Repton a year later. But the Upchers remained at Sheringham,
and through the nineteenth century they planted rhododendrons
of Hooker and Veitch introductions, and then hardy hybrids,
including 'Purple Splendour', 'Sappho', 'Gomer Waterer' and good
old 'Britannia'. Quite how many generations of Upchers planted I
am not sure, but in 1952 Thomas Upcher wrote of his collections,
of magnolias, pieris, eucryphias and other exotic trees besides his
30 different hybrids and 65 species of rhododendrons – these in
spectacular thickets, three-quarters of a mile long each side of the
drive to the house, and viewed from purpose-built towers. When
he died in 1986 Sheringham passed to the National Trust. A plant
survey identified rather a lot of *ponticum* from old rootstocks, but
also noted that it was providing shelter from the cold and the
wind, so it was treated moderately. So gradually, with the clearing,
50 of Thomas Upcher's species have been found and identified,
including his 40-year-old *macabeanum* that he so hoped would
survive, and also many of the old hybrids which we can no longer
name.[14]

The story of John Holms, how he marched along Princes Street with his *sinogrande* umbrella and on to the Edinburgh Botanic Garden to general acclaim, has already been told; now Holms reappears in connection with Glenarn, at Rhu just north of Helensburgh on the shore of Gare Loch. Glenarn was built in the 1840s on 15 acres (6 ha.) of land, and its first owner was Andrew MacGeorge, advocate and friend to William Hooker whilst Hooker was at Glasgow University and after he went south to Kew.

MacGeorge was apparently 'not interested in gardens' but – possibly with Hooker's encouragement – he had paths made through the oak and birch woodland and planted hybrid rhododendrons around the lawn.

Because of MacGeorge the present owners, Michael and Sue Thornley, who think of their *falconeri* in the guise of a 'huge buddha', also hope that it is a Joseph Hooker Sikkim seedling. Glenarn became most distinguished as a rhododendron garden in the hands of the Gibson family, especially Archie and Betty Gibson and Archie's brother Sandy. After a tremendous storm in 1928, which felled 60 trees, the Gibsons began remaking their garden, with a great deal of help from John Holms. Holms had by that time spent his father's fortune from Paisley mills (on an Arts and Crafts house and garden by the great Scottish architect Robert Lorimer as well as his rhododendron garden at Larachmhor, near Arisaig). As he ran into ever greater debts and eventual bankruptcy in the ten years until his death in 1938, Holms passed his best plants and his knowledge on to the Gibsons, introducing them to other Scots rhododendronophiles at Pollok, Lochinch, Dawyck and Blackhills. The Gibsons collected and bred their own large-leaved hybrids, and Glenarn found its place amongst the glorious gardens of the 1950s.

Then, once again, comes the stark reality that the rhododendrons may be in their prime but we humans are fading: Betty and Archie Gibson died in 1975, followed by Sandy in 1982. The following year, on a chilly March day, the Thornleys saw it for the first time; 'by the time we had reached the top of the drive we had decided that we would try to restore Glenarn'. They demolished half the house and made themselves comfortable indoors, and outdoors they started on a seven-year jigsaw of their plant finds, recording them all in an accession book. There have been surprises and setbacks, there are plenty of other flowers besides the rhododendrons, the tasks are all perennial and cyclical, but with evident affection and enjoyment the Thornleys are building the history of Glenarn and making it anew.[15]

The cycles of decline and restoration could fill the rest of my book, for there is a gently thriving underground of rhododendron gardening that never reaches the headlines, nor wishes to, going on up and down Britain, on, for instance, the small sandstone ridge through Tetworth and Everton near Sandy in Bedfordshire. I am also certain that this is happening in Europe. But there are other stories to be gathered in, not least the rhododendron politics.

The Rhododendron Association, successor to the Rhododendron Society, did not survive the Second World War and the death of Lionel de Rothschild; his personal zeal backed by undreamed-of resources had launched the modern passion for the plants, but in 1946 the Association found themselves with overwhelming private problems with their own neglected and ruinous gardens. They were also leaderless; Edmund de Rothschild had quite enough to do with N. M. Rothschild's role in overseas economic development as well as restoring Exbury, and the other likely candidate, Lord Abercon-way of Bodnant, was president of the Royal Horticultural Society. The best that could be done was to take the rhododendron gardeners under the RHS wing as the Rhododendron Group, a perceived takeover which caused a lot of grumbling in the shrubberies. In April 1949 an international conference planned for before the war was held in London, at Vincent Square; it was actually an Anglo-American conference with precious few of the latter, and there was trouble in the air. Dr Hermann Sleumer had published his conclusions on the necessary revisions of rhododendron classification, having managed rather miraculously to put his evidence together after his papers had been virtually destroyed during the Allied bombings of Berlin. The Americans knew of Sleumer's work but the British, in that sensitive post-war atmosphere, did not. Edinburgh Botanics began their revisions of Professor Bayley Balfour's classifications almost as if Sleumer did not exist, but the Americans were interested in the German work and thought the matter should at least be discussed. The ensuing 'debate', which frankly meant many differences of opinions, carried on for years and through several international get-togethers; as classification is a generational thing the detailed arguments have worked themselves through as new 'lumpers or splitters' – the way taxonomists themselves define their skills – have reorganised rhododendrons into differently composed subgenera and sections. Anglo-American differences are now forgotten; during the 1990s the botanists collaborated on their revisions, the papers were collated and published at Edinburgh, the classifications and the identifications of the living collections at the Botanics and at the outstations at Benmore, Logan and Dawyck – all stored on a computer database.

The Rhododendron Group has soldiered on, despite a certain and understandable peevishness at being a 'subgenus' of the RHS; they are the enthusiasts who organise annual tours and produce and edit the annual yearbook, which has been continuously published since 1946. It is now *Rhododendrons with Camellias and Magnolias*, but aficionados – though they are often the same person – insist upon separate garden tours and separate international conferences, so life amongst these lovelies can be exciting. There is also an RHS Rhododendron Committee (as there are RHS Rose, Lily, Daffodil etc. committees) that organises and judges shows and produces the *Rhododendron Handbook* – the 'stud book' – and the *Rhododendron Register*, which records hybrids and their pedigrees.[16]

The American Rhododendron Society is more a state of mind than a mere replica of the British or any other national group. It was refounded in 1960 and now has 70 chapters, including those in Canada, Denmark and Scotland as well as the more predictable Massachusetts, New York, Piedmont, Cascades and Portland, Oregon. The north-west, Washington and Oregon, is the prime rhododendron country, the home of famous nurseries such as James Barto of Eugene, Oregon, and Bovees of Portland (raisers of the hybrid 'Goldbug'). The society has a garden established – with a ceremonial planting of 40-year-old 'Cynthia' bushes – during the 1950s at Crystal Springs Lake at Portland. Enshrined in the society is the belief in hybridising, which it corporately feels to have taken over from the 'big British estates', though I doubt that any of the individual members see themselves in quite that way. Harold Greer (joint author with Homer Salley of the current bible of *Rhododendron Hybrids*) has influenced this philosophy with his expressed view that 'hybridizing is open world-wide to growers of rhododendrons, and I am thankful that with rhododendrons there are no country boundaries, only people throughout the world that love rhododendrons!' Consequently even such a guru as Mr Greer, asked to name the best hybrids, does not know; however, he begins usefully with some that have been awarded the ARS's accolade, the SPA or Superior Plant Award, first given in 1971 to 'Lem's Cameo' ('Dido' x 'Anna') and 'Trude Webster' ('a huge and perfect pink', a self-hybrid of 'Countess of Derby'). After a gap of eleven years (more I suspect due to a blip in administration rather than an absence of superior plants) along came pink 'Ginny Gee' (*keiskei* 'Yaku Fairy' x *racemosum*), yellow 'Patty Bee' (*keiskei* 'Yaku Fairy' x *fletcheranum*) and 'Party Pink'. Rather late in the day, in 1991, the SPA was awarded to 'Scintillation', a survivor from Charles Dexter's hybrids of the 1920s; I suspect that few of the present spate, more an avalanche of hybrids, will last a quarter of that time.

From the beginning the ARS has also harboured a group of species fanciers, led by David Leach, whose classic *Rhododendrons of the World* was first published in New York in 1961. The species' people were keen to establish a living museum for the hybridising as well as a botanical collection, which has now settled into corporate status under the wing of the Weyenhauser Corporation in Federal Way (business park heaven?) between Seattle and Tacoma. It is the Rhododendron Species Foundation that tends to talk classification with the botanic gardens of the world, whereas the ARS is full of gardening enthusiasts and nurserymen.

If the concept of universality and the complexity of it all leave the individual gardener (let alone the chronicler) gasping for an exit, then that escape is in the local and particular. It is paradoxical that world-scale marketing on the one hand, and the micro-achievements of individual gardeners on the other, both serve the world of the rhododendron. As a world-class plant it now attracts 'How to Grow Them' manuals of an ubiquity that leaves the internet looking a model of specificity, and I can only imagine is the revenge of the Antipodeans for half a century and more of being bombarded with English gardening books. *Growing Rhododendrons and Azaleas* is originated and copyrighted by David Bateman Limited in Auckland, New Zealand (1995) and it is evidence of the global village of gardening. It specifies that the best climatic areas, the new heartlands, are the Pacific north-west, the south of New Zealand's South Island and the mist-sodden Celtic fringes of northern Europe. As very few gardeners of any kinds (not enough for marketing purposes) live in these places, likely growing regions are extended to North Island, New Zealand (the location of Pukeiti, New Zealand's most famous rhododendron garden), south-eastern Australia and Tasmania, the southern United States and southern England. *Growing Rhododendrons and Azaleas* continues with brief paragraphs on ways to grow, which at last produces something I have long been curious about, the climbing rhododendron: upright azaleas 'Fielder's White' and 'Orchid Gem', and 'Fragrantissimum' and some *maddenii* hybrids will all tie to espaliers or trellis and some produce better foliage for this treatment. After recipes for soils and fertilisers, the major part of the book is filled with lists of likely plants; this a test of enthusiasm and how far you will travel to find them. This slim paperback, selling at under £10, holds all the anomalies that I feel beset the modern rhododendron grower. It lists something like 50 of the most glorious species, those whose names are indispensable from these rhododendron tales, and including *ponticum*. Amongst larger hybrids the 'Naomi', 'Fabia' and 'Loderi' clans are still all in favour and Halfdan Lem has clearly succeeded Exbury as the world's favourite hybridiser. Is the Australian or Oregonian grower something of a hybrid, too, torn between the legendary British 'classics' and the party-frilled and multishaded modern flowers? *Growing Rhododendrons and Azaleas* runs through the deciduous Ghent azaleas (about twenty still grown), the still growing strong *Mollis* azaleas ('Anthony Koster' yellow/orange blotch, 'Orange Glow' and the orange/red 'Winston Churchill'), the fragrant *occidentale* hybrids (creamy white flushed pink 'Delicantissima', white flushed pink 'Exquisita', pale apricot 'Graciosa' and white flushed darker pink 'Irene Koster'), and gives sixteen names from the long history of Knap Hill, Exbury and Ilam hybrids (Stead's work at Ilam continued by Dr J. S. Yeates until his recent death). The Girard and Carlson hybrids are thought the most important new ones, which leaves the evergreen azaleas intended for the conservatory or indoor plant market: the new striped and spotted Glenn Dales, and a new generation of Morrison hybrids with contrasting frilled edges to petals. Vireyas are not forgotten.

I am left slightly exhausted by this glimpse into the mind of the modern fancier, but also with some understanding of the frustrations of the New World for 'old Europe' and matters of dispute that have rumbled beneath the surface of jovial international gatherings from the days of George Bush to George W. Bush. It was started by the American enthusiasm for the British traditions, when the Pacific Rhododendron Society, concerned at the scarcity of the *Rhododendron Notes* from 1916–1939, wanted to print facsimiles and applied to the RHS Lindley Library to borrow some missing years. They were refused, nor were any photocopies permitted; Edinburgh supplied the necessary texts and, surely for the only time, rhododendron spats featured in *Private Eye*. To easygoing Americans, especially those having to live here, the lack of encouragement to newcomers was icy. There were no arrangements at shows for informal meetings, nor means of any kind for plants or seeds to be available to keen gardeners. There was a distinct wrapping of secrecy around the names and addresses of the members of the Rhododendron Group, access was difficult, there were no 'local' clubs nor any 'newsletters'. Their were charges of nepotism and favouritism, that rhododendron propagation was looked upon as an arcane subject beyond the grasp of normal gardeners, and that many of the great gardens kept their hybrids (Bodnant had registered no less than 300) for themselves.

These charges were laid by an extremely distinguished American rhododendronophile, also a member of the Pukeiti Trust, the Sierra Club, the Save-the-Redwoods League, who happened to live in Sussex. It was the time-honoured clash between the open dispositions bred in the 'home of the brave' and the more reserved natives of 'perfidious Albion'. To be fair to the latter it was perhaps retrenchment against a real sense of gloom that pervaded the last fifteen years or so of the twentieth century. Were the great days gone for ever now that the independence of the Rhododendron Society, born 1916, had been subsumed as a 'group' within the Royal Horticultural Society? Why were there so few exhibitors at the shows and, worst of all, what could be done about the blindly anti-rhododendron press? Some things have to be put down to changing times, and they may change back again. The Rhododendron, Camellia and Magnolia Group is open to members of the RHS, the 'Notes' are still published annually as a yearbook and the Wessex Area of the group, covering most of southern England, is particularly active with garden visits, lectures, plant sales and seed distribution. In some parts of Britain, notably north-west England and Scotland, rhododendronophiles have a chapter of the American Rhododendron Association. If the New World growers seem to have an almost manic enthusiasm and boundless ambition then these do seem to be rushing into the void of a lethargic mood in Britain, where the rhododendron world lacks charismatic leadership.

On the ground some of the American gardeners are wizards at the manipulation of microclimates, which is really what growing rhododendrons is all about. In her *Rhododendrons in the Landscape* (2000), Sonja Nelson describes her visit to Walter Ostrom in his windy (an almost unrelenting nor'easter replaced by a wet southerly) seaside garden, near Halifax, Nova Scotia. He uses boulders and sand to raise the planting level above the high water mark, adds a thick layer of planting mix, and grows *yakushimanum* and azaleas and small-leaved lepidote species (the scales providing protection) with cranberry and other natives. He has planted a windbreak of stewartias, styrax and birch.

In Washington State the rise in population has extended housing into the woods; 'second-growth stands of Douglas fir, western hemlock and western red cedar' are a typical western Washington garden. In two acres of woodland garden Jeanine and Rex Smith have created underlayers of more human proportions, with cherries, cornus and white-barked birches and large hybrid rhododendrons, 'Apricot Fantasy' and the white with red splashes 'Phyllis Korn'. They mix natives, mahonia and gaultheria, and juggle shelter and aspect to achieve a rhododendron theme, from *impeditum* and *williamsianum* with hardy geraniums and heathers on the rockery to a giant *macabeanum* among ferns and other woodland ground covers. (I begin to realise that these 'amateurs' do grow a wide variety of species.) Sonja Nelson again: 'the woodland garden of Dave Hinton near Orono, Ontario, stretches . . . cold hardiness to the limit . . . in the midst of rolling farmland . . . where temperatures routinely drop to minus twenty degrees Fahrenheit [−29°C] in winter'. With a canopy of red pine and white spruce and windbreaking hedges he has an informal woodland of *dauricum*, *smirnovii* and home-bred very hardy hybrids, northern native American azaleas, with viburnums, peonies and Solomon's Seal.

In the mid-continental cold winters and hot summers of Urbana, Illinois, Donald Paden juggles hedges of yew and Korean box and sheltering oaks, spruce, hollies, sour gums (Nyssa spp.) and yellow-wood (*Cladrastis lutea*) to accomplish a garden of his own *dauricum* and *carolinianum* (the native Piedmont rhododendron) series hybrids, with *yakushimanum* hybrids and the deciduous Northern Lights azaleas, these bred for cold-hardiness at the University of Minnesota Landscape Arboretum.[17]

The pioneering spirit has lingered with American gardeners, of which there are thousands of such enthusiasts, all members of ARS. Hot off the press as I finished my tales was a ravishing book, *The American Woodland Garden*, subtitled 'capturing the spirit of the deciduous forest', written and photographed by Rick Darke of Land-enberg, Pennsylvania, a much-published expert on grasses and former taxonomist and curator at Longwood Gardens. This is a celebration of an American habitat in which rhododendrons and azaleas come into their own. Rick Darke's photographs reveal the natural beauty of the American natives: Pinxterbloom, with blush flowers and their extended stamens of darker pink, blooming at the sunny edge of a Delaware wood; delicate white *alabamense*, with her egg-yellow blotch, at Winterthur; green rosettes of *arborescens*, the Sweet Azalea, with witch hazel along a Pennsylvania river bank; pink 'Roseshell', *prinophyllum*, flowering in dappled light in Vir-ginian woodlands, and the rich yellow, orange and 'flame' azaleas still flowering on Gregory bald in the mountains of North Carolina where William Bartram found them. The ghost of Professor Charles Sargent would applaud this book; it is a recognition, 'a portrait drawn from the ethos, the aesthetic, and the ecology of the eastern deciduous forest', the backdrop for lives from Nova Scotia to Florida. It is for gardeners 'who tend a modest piece of ground that is part of the larger forest' and for those who design larger landscapes and look to the conservation of 'nearby nature'. At last the American rhododendrons are returning to the company of the dozens of species from which they were culled.

It might be said that the American gardeners have at last arrived where the British were well over a century ago with William Robinson's 'the wood wild garden' in his *Wild Garden* of 1870. The incremental approach to knowledge and the quiet dispensation of the same are encapsulated in the story of a quiet corner of Perthshire, a place that has had far too little attention so far. The name of the place is Glendoick. Ah! Glendoick. The spark of recognition lights up throughout the rhododendron world. I have spoken earlier of Euan Cox's expedition with Reginald Farrer, a horticultural anointing for a young man in his twenties. Cox was captivated by many of the plants he saw but perhaps mostly by the rhododendrons. At home in Glendoick he planted every one he could beg or buy, 'hopefully, but with little knowledge . . . I soon found that many of the species are tricksy plants in our part of the country, and what with climate and lack of experience it was a case of the survival of the fittest.' He set out to learn, putting what he learned into a little book, *Rhododendrons for Amateurs*, published in the 1920s. When *Wild Gardening* (1929), a small green book of 122 pages of almost pocket-size, was published it took a detailed and friendly but imaginative and practical approach, written out of his experiences with his own four and a half acres (2 ha.) at Glendoick. If you are lucky enough to be making a wild garden today, this still makes cheering reading. The rhododendrons and primulas and plenty of other things thrived, but in terms of allegiance the former won out. Euan Cox's son Peter was trained as a horticulturist and nurseryman and after a spell of plant hunting he set up the specialist rhododendron nurseries at Glendoick. Father and son wrote *Modern Rhododendrons* (1956); it was dedicated to 'our long suffering wife and mother who listens without complaint to hours of "rhododendron" talk, so long as it is strictly forbidden at mealtimes'. *Modern Rhododendrons*, with illustrations by Margaret Stones, is a period piece, the absolute proof that the best of British mid-twentieth-century know-how resided elsewhere than along the rhododendron-girt drives of the 'big estates'. In due course, Peter and Patricia Cox (also a horticulturist) reared a third generation, Kenneth, who now manages the nursery at Glendoick and its stock of a thousand species and cultivars.[18] Peter Cox, a reserved and rather shy man, is the quiet doyen of the rhododendron world; his is the voice of sanity in what can seem an overwhelmingly complex world. His books are carefully attuned to plant size; *Dwarf Rhododendrons* (1973), *The Larger Rhododendron Species* and *The Smaller Rhododendrons* (both 1988) are the 'port in a storm' for anyone wanting to know about rhododendrons now. Kenneth Cox is already a prolific author, enmeshed in the lore and reality of plant hunting that is his heritage. In 1995 he and David Burlinson led an expedition to the high passes of Tibet, discovering that Frank Kingdon Ward's *Riddle of the Tsangpo Gorges*, published in 1926, was the only 'guidebook' available. In 2001, in collaboration with Ian Baker, a resident of Kathmandu and Himalayan explorer, and Kenneth Storm Jr., American anthropologist and Himalayan mountaineer, Kenneth Cox edited a reprint of *Riddle of the Tsangpo Gorges*, the text as the original, the book adorned with hundreds of their photographs from recent expeditions, of the fantastic landscape and the flowers. There are photographs of primulas, gentians, iris, clematis, yes, but primarily the rhododendrons: *campylocarpum* 'Yellow Peril' hanging from a cliff on the Doshong La; *wardii* fringing a mountain torrent; bright purple *oreotrephes* filling a pinewood below Sirchem La; a meadow of little mauve *nivale* with *Primula alpicola*, and many, many more.

This, I feel, is where I came in, and with Kingdon Ward's 'rhododendron fairyland' of the Doshong La, *Tales of the Rose Tree* has come full circle. It has been only one among many possible orbits of history for 'this race of giants on a global scale', but I hope an exhilarating journey none the less. Far from being of the 'triffid' tendency, with an agenda for taking over the planet, the genus would seem in need of our care and protection in many of its native habitats. I know now that I am firmly a rhododendronophile and am very near to regarding them as one of the wonders of the world. They are, as a genus, surely the most curious, beautiful, intriguing and glorious of living things with whom we share our small planet. Maybe, perhaps, we could change their name?

ACKNOWLEDGEMENTS

My books increasingly reflect my life, and *Tales of the Rose Tree*
is no exception. My acknowledgements go back through at least
twenty five years and the following rhododendron memories: to
my first enchantment with Adam and Pamela Gordon's woodland
of Mangles' hybrids in the late seventies, to a visit to Jim Russell
at The Old Dairy at Castle Howard, to the 1987 New York Botanic
Garden's 'circus' tour of American cities when John Bond dazzled
the audiences with slides of his rhododendron charges in the Savill
and Valley Gardens, and to my subsequent return visits to the
Arnold Arboretum with Nan Sinton, Kerry Walter and Peter del
Tredici and to other old gardens of New England with Mac
Griswold. This quickly brings me full circle for Kerry Walter left the
Arnold to work on the taxonomic database for plant distributions
at the Royal Botanic Garden, Edinburgh, and RBGE's *The Genus
Rhododendron, its Classification & Synonymy* (Chamberlain, Hyam,
Argent, Fairweather and Walter, 1996) has been one of my 'rocks'.
The other has been the wisdom of Mr Bean, whose third volume
of *Trees and Shrubs Hardy in the British Isles* (8th edition 1976) is
made into a weighty tome by his generosity to rhododendrons.

My gratitude to these and my other sources is unbounded. I have
made every endeavour to credit my quoted sources adequately and
accurately in the text or in the notes, and would like to add my
particular thanks to the following: to Cynthia Postan for her encouragement and help, to Sally Beamish at Brantwood, to Nicholas de
Rothschild, Lionel de Rothschild and Rachel Foster at Exbury, to
T J Binyon author of *Pushkin* (2002) for the Fet poem, to John

Drake for his expertise on the Turkish flora, to Brenda McLean (whose biography of George Forrest is soon to be published), to Fiona Cowell for her researches on Thorndon Park, to those resourceful booksellers Anna Buxton and Mike Park, to Miranda Gunn for the Gauntlett catalogue, to Arthur and Anne George at Hydon Nurseries, to the Millais family at Crosswater Farm, and Juliet Barker for directing me to Wordsworth. My thanks also go to Faith Raven for the Ardtornish report, to Dr Trevor Smith for homeopathy references, to Mary Bartlett and John Latter for memories of Norman Cruttwell, to Libby and David Allen and Warren Boyles for an insight into Tasmania and to Shirley Evans and Cornwall Gardens Trust.

The colour illustrations for *Tales of the Rose Tree* are quite simply 'the pick of the bunch' and I feel very proud of them as a fitting tribute to the genus Rhododendron. My thanks go especially to Marianna Kneller, Peter Aldington, Mac Griswold, Richard Bisgrove, Kate Marr of Titley & Marr, Simon James, Chris Linnett and Graham Hillier. My admiration and thanks go to Caroline Hotblack who has miraculously located the archive illustrations, including for the cover and endpapers; these sources are all duly acknowledged on pages 285–288 but I would like to add my thanks particularly to the Royal Botanic Gardens at Kew and Edinburgh and the Royal Horticultural Society. My congratulations and thanks go to Vera Brice for her design of the book as a whole and for her enchanting treatment of the illustrations.

As ever libraries have been my vital resource, and for this book my appreciations go to staff members at the London Library, the University Library and Needham Institute library in Cambridge, and the Wellcome Institute library. I am also grateful for an Authors' Foundation grant which assisted with my research expenses.

As to my literary agent Caradoc King at A P Watt, this is our fourteenth book in twenty years or so and we are entering the realms of anniversaries! My special thanks go to his assistant agent Martha Lishawa. At HarperCollins Caroline Michel is refreshingly supportive and this is my second book for Michael Fishwick, the most empathetic of editors (and there is another to come!) My appreciative thanks to them and especially to Kate Hyde and Carol Anderson for their expert handling of my manuscript.

Tales of the Rose Tree is very intentionally titled: it cannot purport to be a history of the genus *Rhododendron*, a vast and immeasurable subject, even during the minute prism of time since about 1753 when it has been named 'rhododendron'. I pray that my august sources will not be overly infuriated or ashamed at my trespass into their territory. My gratitude is to everyone, those named above and other friends, acquaintances and relations who helped me this far. For my readers I earnestly wish that *Tales of the Rose Tree* is the key to an enchanted world.

JANE BROWN, *Elton, January 2004.*

NOTES

All places of publication are London unless otherwise noted.

FOREWORD

1 George Argent and Marjory McFarlane, eds., *Rhododendrons in Horticulture and Science, Papers Presented at the International Rhododendron Conference, Edinburgh, 2002*, Royal Botanic Garden, Edinburgh, 2003.

2 Richard Dawkins, *Climbing Mount Improbable*, 1997, p. 238.

3 Jane Brown, *Lanning Roper and his Gardens*, 1987.

4 Lanning Roper, *The Sunday Times Gardening Book*, 1967.

5 Jane Brown, *Beatrix; a Gardening Life of Beatrix Jones Farrand, 1872–1959*, New York, 1995.

CHAPTER ONE A Rose by Another Name

1 G. Argent, M. Mendum and P. Smith, 'The Smallest Rhododendron in the World', *New Plantsman*, 6(3), September, 1999.

2 Charles Lyte, *Frank Kingdon Ward: The Last of the Great Plant Hunters*, 1989, p. 109.

3 M. Rothschild, K. Garton and L. de Rothschild, *The Rothschild Gardens*, 1996, 2000 edn, p. 60.

4 A. S. Byatt, *The Biographer's Tale*, 2000, p. 116.

5 Norman G. Brett-James, *Life of Peter Collinson*, 1925, p. 240.

6 Byatt, *The Biographer's Tale*, p. 116.

7 John Ruskin, *Complete Works*, ed. E. T. Cook and A. Wedderburn, 1903, vol. 7, *Modern Painters V*, p. 129, and vol. 25, *Proserpina*, p. 367.

8 Ruskin, *Complete Works*, ed. Cook and Wedderburn, 'Splügen' in *Poems*, pp. 370–1.

9 Afanásy Fet, 'Rhododendron' in *Polnoe sobranie sochinenii*, Leningrad, 1959, p. 468.

10 John Betjeman, 'Pot Pourri from a Surrey Garden', in *Collected Poems*, 1958, pp. 50–1.

11 Kenneth Cox, ed., *Frank Kingdon Ward's Riddle of the Tsangpo Gorges*, 2001, p. 142.

12 William and Melva Philipson, 'The Taxonomy of the Genus', in *The Rhododendron Story*, ed. C. Postan, 1996, pp. 22–37.

13 Ray Desmond, *Sir Joseph Dalton Hooker: Traveller and Plant Collector*, 1999, p. 178.

14 W. Blunt and W. T. Stearn, *The Art of Botanical Illustration*, 1994, p. 265.

15 Michael and Sue Thornley in Marianna Kneller, *The Book of Rhododendrons*, 1995, p. 22.

16 J. D. Hooker, *Indian Letters 1847–51*, letters 5 and 23 June 1849, quoted in Desmond, *Sir Joseph Dalton Hooker*, p. 167.

17 J. H. Mangles in *Gardeners' Chronicle*, 9 April 1881.

18 Algernon Swinburne in *Images and Insights: The Catalogue of the Hugh Lane Municipal Gallery of Modern Art*, Dublin, 1993, p. 16.

19 Laura Ponsonby, *Marianne North at Kew Gardens*, 3rd imp. 1999, p. 15.

20 Ibid.

21 Sven-Ingvar Andersson and Steen Hoyer, *C. Th. Sørensen: Landscape Modernist*, Copenhagen, 2001, p. 56.

CHAPTER TWO *Sinogrande's* Story

1 See P. H. Davis, ed., *Flora of Turkey and the East Aegean Islands*, vol. 6, Edinburgh, 1978, pp. 90–4, Andrew Byfield, 'Adventures in the Pontic Mountains', *The Garden*, October 1996, pp. 624–6, and Andrew Byfield, 'Flowers that Made Men Mad', *Cornucopia: Turkey for Connoisseurs*, 3(13), 1997, pp. 56–9.

2 Rose Macaulay, *The Towers of Trebizond*, 1956, 1986 edn, p. 76.

3 Ibid., p. 138.

4 John Freely, *The Redhouse Guide to the Black Sea Coast of Turkey*, Istanbul, 1996.

5 John Larner, *Marco Polo and the Discovery of the World*, 1999, p. 23.

6 Ray Desmond, *European Discovery of the Indian Flora*, 1992, p. 189.

7 Desmond, *Joseph Dalton Hooker*, p. 144.

8 Ibid., p. 148.

9 Stephen A. Spongberg, *A Reunion of Trees: the Discovery of Exotic Plants and their Introduction into the North American and European Landscapes*, 1990, pp. 143–5.

10 Armen Takhtajan, *Floristic Regions of the World*, trans. T. J. Crovello, Berkeley/Los Angeles, 1986.

11 Richard Mabey, *Flora Britannica*, 1996, p. 158.

12 W. J. Bean, *Trees and Shrubs Hardy in the British Isles*, 8th rev. edn. 1976, p. 540.

13 Ibid.

14 Maggie Keswick, *The Chinese Garden: History, Art and Architecture*, 1978, p. 29.

15 From the Proclamation of the First Emperor *c.* 221 BC, *Selections from Records of the Historian Yang Hsien-yi and G. Yang (trans.)*, Beijing, 1979, pp. 170–2, quoted in 'Preface' to *The British Museum Book of Chinese Art*, ed. Jessica Rawson et al., 1992.

16 Po-chu-I, 'The Five Gates, Climbing the Terrace of Kuan-Yin and Looking at the city of Chang-an, AD 827', in *Chinese Poems*, trans. Arthur Waley, 1946, p. 178.

17 Ibid.

18 Ibid., p. 125.

19 Edward Schafer, 'Li Te-yu and the Azalea', *Asiatische Studien*, 18/19, 1965, p. 105 (in Botany box VI, Needham Institute Archive, Cambridge).

20 Feng Guomei, ed., *Rhododendrons of China*, vol. 1, Beijing, 1988, p. 3.

21 Ibid.

22 Ibid.

23 Ibid.

24 Bai Juyi, 'Recalling the South', quoted in Feng Jin, 'Jing, the concept of scenery in texts on the traditional Chinese garden; an initial exploration', *Studies in the History of Gardens and Designed Landscapes*, n.d., p. 342.

25 Po-chu-I, 'The Flower Market', in *Chinese Poems*, trans. Waley, p. 132.

26 'A Dream of Mountaineering', in *Chinese Poems*, trans. Waley, p. 189.

27 Arthur Waley, *The Life and Times of Po-chu-I, 772–846*, 1949.

28 Percival Yetts, 'Notes on the Flower Symbolism in China', *Journal of the Asiatic Society*, January 1941 (Needham Institute Archive).

29 John Makeham, 'The Confucian Role of Names in Traditional Chinese Gardens', *Studies in the History of Gardens and Designed Landscapes*, v. 18(3), 1998, p. 194.

30 Jack Goody, *The Culture of Flowers*, 1993, pp. 358ff.

31 Edward H. Schafer, *The Vermilion Bird: T'ang Images of the South*, Berkeley/Los Angeles, 1967, p. 260.

32 Kang-I-Sun Chang and Haun Saussy, eds., *Women Writers of Traditional China*, Stanford, CA, 1999, p. 39.

33 Richard M. Barnhardt in Barnhardt et al., *Three Thousand Years of Chinese Painting*, 1997, p. 39.

34 Joseph Needham, *Science and Civilisation in China*, vol. 6, part 1, *Botany*, 1986, p. 438.

35 Craig Clunas, *Fruitful Sites: Garden Culture in Ming Dynasty China*, 1996, pp. 108–11.

36 Clunas, p. 168.

37 Ibid., p. 72.

38 Hsu Hung-tsu quoted from Ch'ên Shou-yi, *Chinese Literature: A Historical Introduction*, New York, 1961, pp. 557–8.

39 Keswick, *The Chinese Garden*, pp. 10–13.

40 Maldwin Drummond, 'Dam the Flowerpots: Early Difficulties of Importing Plants by Sea' in *Pleasure Grounds*, ed. Gill Hedley and Adrian Rance, Southampton Art Gallery and Hampshire Gardens Trust, 1987, pp. 63–71.

41 Robert Fortune, *Three Years' Wanderings in the Northern Provinces of China*, 1847, p. 67.

42 Ibid., p. 155.

43 Ibid., pp. 152–3.

44 Hazel le Rougetel, 'The Fa Tee Nurseries of South China', *Garden History*, 10(1), 1982, pp. 70ff.

45 See Schafer, *The Vermilion Bird*.

46 Spongberg, *A Reunion of Trees*, p. 182.

47 Sheila Pim, *The Wood and the Trees: A Biography of Augustine Henry*, 1966, p 85.

48 Spongberg, *A Reunion of Trees* p. 183.

49 Ibid., pp. 188–190.

50 Brenda McLean, *A Pioneering Plantsman: A. K. Bulley and the Great Plant Hunters*, 1997, p. 23.

51 J. Macqueen Cowan, ed., *The Journeys and Plant Introductions of George Forrest VMH*, 1952, p. 36.

52 Ibid., pp. 12–14.

53 These photographs are in the library of Edinburgh Botanic Garden; some were published in Henry J. Noltie, 'Snapshots of China', *The Garden*, May 1996, pp. 274–7.

54 Cowan, *The Journeys and Plant Introductions of George Forrest*, pp. 18–20.

55 Bean, *Trees and Shrubs Hardy in the British Isles*, p. 773.

CHAPTER THREE The King's Botanist's Tale

1 See Sibylla Jane Flower, *A Walk Round Fulham Palace and its Garden*, The Friends of Fulham Palace, 3rd rev. edn., 1995. The garden is open every day.

2 See Edmund Berkeley and Dorothy Smith Berkeley, *The Life and Travels of John Bartram*, 1982, p. 13.

3 Betsy C. Corner and Christopher Booth, eds., *Chain of Friendship: Selected Letters of Dr John Fothergill of London, 1735–1780*, Cambridge, MA, 1971, Dr Fothergill to John Bartram, letter 19 February 1740/1.

4 Ibid., Dr Fothergill to William Bartram, letter 22 October 1772.

5 Peter Collinson to John Bartram, letter 20 January 1751, quoted in Mark Laird, *The Flowering of the Landscape Garden: English Pleasure Grounds 1720–1800*, Philadelphia, 1999, p. 72.

6 Norman Brett-James, *Life of Peter Collinson*, 1925, p. 126.

7 Laird, *The Flowering of the Landscape Garden*, p. 17.

8 Corner and Booth, eds., *Chain of Friendship*, Fothergill to Bartram, 13 January 1770, pp. 318–19.

9 Ibid., Fothergill to Humphry Marshall, 1772, pp. 18–19.

10 Berkeley and Berkeley, *The Life and Travels of John Bartram*, pp. 85–6.

11 Ibid.

12 Laird, *The Flowering of the Landscape Garden*, p. 73.

13 Thorndon Country Park is on the A128 south of Brentwood, 3 miles from Brentwood Station. It is open daily from 8 a.m. till dusk. Managed jointly by Essex County Council and Brentwood Borough Council; enquiries to Essex Ranger Service: 01277 211250.

14 In *The Flowering of the Landscape Garden*, Mark Laird describes how this colourful planting style was revealed during his researches for the restoration of Painshill Landscape Garden (at Portsmouth Road, Cobham, Surrey, KT11 1JE, www.painshill.co.uk). Seasonally variable opening times (01932 868113).

15 David P. Miller, ' "My favourite studdys": Lord Bute as a Naturalist,' in *Lord Bute: Essays in Re-interpretation*, ed. Karl W. Schweizer, Leicester, 1988, pp. 213–39.

16 Brett-James, *Life of Peter Collinson*, p. 53.

17 Ibid., p. 136.

18 Laird, *The Flowering of the Landscape Garden*, p. 76.

19 Ibid., p. 72.

20 Brett-James, *Life of Peter Collinson*, p. 137.

21 Gregory A. Waselkov and Kathryn E. Holland Braund, eds., *William Bartram and the Southeastern Indians*, Lincoln, NB, 1995, pp. 79–80.

22 Ibid., p. 81.

23 William Bartram, *Travels Through North and South Carolina, Georgia, East and West Florida*, fac. 1792 edn., Savannah, GA, 1973, part 3, chapter 3, p. 334.

24 F. P. Lee, *The Azalea Book*, 2nd edn., Princeton, NJ, 1965, p. 146.

25 David Solman and Graham Douglas, *Loddiges of Hackney: The Largest Hothouse in the World*, ed. Jane Straker for the Hackney Society, 1995.

26 John Harvey, *Early Nurserymen*, 1974, pp. 129–30.

27 Ibid., p. 84.

28 R. Todd Longstaffe Gowan, 'A Proposal for a Georgian Town Garden in Gower Street: The Francis Douce Garden', *Garden History*, 15(2), 1987, pp. 136–43. Mark Laird and John H. Harvey, 'The Garden Plans for 13 Upper Gower Street, London: A Conjectural Review of the Planting, Upkeep and Long-term Maintenance of a Late Eighteenth Century Town

Garden', *Garden History* 25(2), 1997, pp. 189–211.

29 James Lees-Milne, *William Beckford*, Montclair, NJ, 1979, p. 59.

30 Peter Hayden in *The Oxford Companion to Gardens*, eds G. Jellicoe, P. Goode and M. Lancaster, Oxford, 1986, p. 490.

31 Walter Schmalscheidt, 'Hybrids for a Cold Climate: The Seidels', in *The Rhododendron Story*, ed. C. Postan, 1996, pp. 109–14, and Walter Schmalscheidt, *Rhododendron-Zuchtung in Deutschland*, Cramer-Druck, Westerstede, *c*. 1980.

32 Lionel de Rothschild 'Hybrids in the British Isles: The 19th Century', in *The Rhododendron Story*, ed. C. Postan, 1996, pp. 115–35.

33 Mac Griswold, *Washington's Gardens at Mount Vernon: Landscape of the Inner Man*, Boston and New York, 1999, p. 143.

34 Mac Griswold and Eleanor Weller, *The Golden Age of American Gardens: Proud Owners Private Estates 1890–1940*, 1991, p. 194.

35 Ibid., p. 159.

36 Ibid., p. 171. The Royal Botanic Garden, *Edinburgh Journal of Botany*, 50(3), 1993, has twenty closely printed pages of citations, i.e. locations and collectors of American species – *calendulaceum, alabamense, austrinum, arborescens, canescens, periclymenoides, prinophyllum* and *viscosum* – that have joined their Asian cousins in Section Pentanthera.

37 Griswold and Weller, *The Golden Age of American Gardens*, p. 167.

38 Marion Cran, *Gardens in America*, 1932, pp. 174–80.

39 Ibid., p. 177.

40 Quoted in ibid., p. 178.

41 Quoted in ibid., p. 179.

42 Henry John Elwes, *Memoirs of Travel, Sport and Natural History*, ed. E. G. Hawke, 1930, pp. 176–9.

43 Andrew Jackson Downing, *A Treatise on the Theory and Practice of Landscape Gardening*, 6th edn., New York, 1859, pp. 40–1.

44 Stephen A. Spongberg, 'C. S. Sargent: Seeing the Forest and the Trees', *Orion* (New York), Autumn 1984, 5–11.

45 Griswold and Weller, *The Golden Age of American Gardens*, pp. 164–5.

46 Spongberg, *A Reunion of Trees*, pp. 171–4.

47 Stephen A. Spongberg, 'C. S. Sargent: Seeing the Forest and the Trees', *Orion* (New York), Autumn 1984, 5–11.

48 Mariana van Rensselaer, 'A Suburban Country Place', *Century Magazine*, May 1897.

49 Hollis Hunnewell, ed., *Life, Letters & Diary of H. H. Hunnewell 1810–1902*, Boston, privately printed, 1906.

50 See Brown, *Beatrix: The Gardening Life of Beatrix Jones Farrand*. The Asticou Azalea Gardens at Northeast Harbor, Maine, on Route 198, are open May to October.

51 See Roy W. Briggs, 'Chinese Wilson': A Life of Ernest H. Wilson 1876–1930, 1993. The author is Wilson's great-nephew.

52 See S. B. Sutton, *Charles Sprague Sargent and the Arnold Arboretum*, Cambridge, MA, 1970.

53 Griswold and Weller, *The Golden Age of American Gardens*, pp. 142–3.

CHAPTER FOUR What James, Harry and Clara Did

1 See Schuyler Cammann, *Trade Through the Himalayas: The Early British Attempts to Open Tibet*, Princeton, NJ, 1951.

2 Clements R. Markham, ed., *Narratives of the Mission of George Bogle to Tibet and of the Journey of Thomas Manning to Lhasa*, 1876.

3 Sir George Staunton made his garden at Leigh Park, Havant in Hampshire, in imitation of what he saw; this is now the Staunton Country Park, open daily, and some of the Chinese features remain.

4 H. J. Noltie, *Indian Botanical Drawings 1793–1868 from the Royal Botanic Garden Edinburgh*, 1999, pp. 18–20.

5 Ibid., pp. 20–2.

6 See *Political Missions to Bootan Comprising the Reports of Hon. Ashley Eden, 1864, Capt. R. B. Pemberton 1837, 1838, with Dr W. Griffith's Journal and the Account by Baboo Kishen Kant Bose*, Calcutta, 1865.

7 Rebecca Pradhan, *Wild Rhododendrons of Bhutan*, Kathmandu, 1999, and Rebecca Pradhan, 'Wild Rhododendrons of Bhutan', in *Rhododendrons in Horticulture and Science*, ed. George Argent and Marjory McFarlane, Edinburgh, 2003, pp. 37–41.

8 Desmond, *Joseph Dalton Hooker*, p. 161.

9 Bean, *Trees and Shrubs Hardy in the British Isles*, p. 731.

10 George Argent, 'The Vireya Story', in *The Rhododendron Story*, ed. C. Postan, 1996, p. 87.

11 Ibid.

12 H. R. Fletcher and William H. Brown, *History of Royal Botanic Garden, Edinburgh, 1670–1970*, 1970, pp. 126–7.

13 Desmond, *Joseph Dalton Hooker*, p. 97.

14 J. D. Hooker, Foreword to *Rhododendrons of Sikkim-Himalaya*, 1849/51.

15 Desmond, *Joseph Dalton Hooker*, p. 114.

16 See Mark Cocker and Carol Inskipp, *A Himalayan Ornithologist: The Life and Work of Brian Houghton Hodgson*, 1988.

17 Desmond, *Joseph Dalton Hooker*, p. 117.

18 Bean, *Trees and Shrubs Hardy in the British Isles*, p. 684.

19 Michael and Sue Thornley in Kneller, *The Book of Rhododendrons*, p. 22.

20 Noltie, *Indian Botanical Drawings*, pp. 22–4.

21 The *Botanical Magazine* plates have now been published in one volume, *The Ilustrated Rhododendron: Their Classification or Trade through the Artwork of Curtis' Botanical Magazine*, ed. P. Halliday, Kew, 2001.

22 Mary Forrest, 'Hooker's Rhododendrons: Their Distribution and Survival', in *The Rhododendron Story*, ed. C. Postan, 1996, pp. 55–70. In *Rhododendrons of Sikkim-Himalaya* (1849), p. 13, Hooker notes the enthusiasm of Florence Nightingale of Embley Park in Hampshire. As the home of the Crosfields in the 1920s and 1930s Embley Park was famous for its dwarf Japanese azaleas.

23 Edna Healey, *Emma Darwin*, 2001, p. 181.

24 Forrest, 'Hooker's Rhododendrons', pp. 55–70.

25 Elwes, *Memoirs of Travel*, p. 71.

26 Ibid., p. 119.

27 Alice M. Coats, 'Forgotten Gardeners III: The Mangles Family', *Garden History*, 1 (6) 1973, pp. 42–6.

28 Martin Mulligan and Stuart Hill, *Ecological Pioneers: A Social History of Australian Ecological Thought and Action*, 2001, pp. 25–7.

29 Earl A. Kives, ed. *Tennyson at Aldworth: The Diary of James Henry Mangles*, Athens, OH, and London, 1984. See also W. R. Trotter, 'The Poet and the Plantsman: Tennyson's Conversations with James Henry Mangles', *West Sussex History*, no. 26, September 1953.

30 James Mangles' articles were gathered together and reprinted as a tribute in the *Rhododendron Society Notes*, no. 2, 1917. (The early volumes of the *Notes* have been reprinted by the American Rhododendron Society.)

31 Mangles, *Rhododendron Society Notes*, no. 2, 1917.

32 Sir Edwin Lutyens' Foreword to Francis Jekyll, *Gertrude Jekyll: A Memoir*, 1934.

33 Jane Brown, *Gardens of a Golden Afternoon: The Story of a Partnership: Edwin Lutyens and Gertrude Jekyll*, 1982 and subs. edns.

34 See J. G. Millais, *Wanderings and Memories* 1919, n.d., and personal reminiscences of the Millais family as told to the author.

35 The following text is based upon

Violet Gordon's notes for a talk about her gardening, copy in the author's possession, by kind permission of Lady Adam Gordon.

36 Jane Brown, *Lutyens and the Edwardians: An English Architect and His Clients*, 1996 and subs. edns.

37 See Fulbrook, 'A house you will love to live in': The Sketchbook, Letters, Specification of Works and Accounts for a House by Edwin Lutyens 1896, 1899, Foreword by Mary Lutyens, ed. Jane Brown, limited edn, Marlborough, 1989.

38 Violet Gordon's notes for a talk about her gardening.

39 Lady Adam Gordon, 'The Restoration of the Mangles Garden at Littleworth Cross', *Rhododendrons 1976*, pp. 13–17, and Lady Adam Gordon, 'The Mangles Garden Today', *Rhododendrons 1993*, pp. 16–18.

40 Letter to the author.

41 Robin Loder in the *Leonardslee Gardens*, 2000. The garden is open from 1 April to 31 October, daily 9.30 a.m. to 6 p.m. Contact the Secretary, Leonardslee Gardens, Lower Beeding, Horsham, West Sussex, RH13 6PP, www.leonardsilee.com.

42 Bean, *Trees and Shrubs Hardy in the British Isles*, pp. 869–71.

43 Ibid., p. 825.

44 McLean, *A Pioneering Plantsman*, p. 122.

45 Ibid., p. 120.

46 Tom Holzell and Audrey Salkeld, *The Mystery of Mallory and Irvine*, 1986, p. 164.

47 John Hunt, *The Ascent of Everest*, 1953, 4th imp. 1954, pp. 66, 72 and 119.

48 Charles Stonor, *The Sherpa and the Snowman*, 1955, pp. 178–9.

CHAPTER FIVE Power Flowers

1 Desmond, *Joseph Dalton Hooker*, p. 144.

2 Cynthia Postan, 'Rhododendron Lovers in the British Isles', in *The Rhododendron Story*, ed. C. Postan, 1996, pp. 87–200.

3 William Arkwright to Charles Eley, collection of Mr and Mrs Rupert Eley, East Bergholt Place, Suffolk.

4 This text owes much to Douglas Ellery Pett's *The Parks and Gardens of Cornwall*, published by Alison Hodge, Bosulval, Newmill, Penzance, 1998, which is encyclopaedic in scope, but rhododendrons alone could fill another volume of garden and plant history, as I imagine it retold around Cornish firesides.

5 Pett, *The Parks and Gardens of Cornwall*, p. 330, on the Williams family and individual entries. Caerhays Castle has variable openings from March until May, www.caerhays.co.uk. Tel. 01872 501310. It is 9 miles south-west of St Austell.

6 Tony Russell and Derek Harris, *Westonbirt – A Celebration of the Seasons*, Woodland Publishing, Wakerley, Oakham LE15 8NZ.

7 Julian Williams on Subsection Williamsiana in Marianne Kneller, *The Book of Rhododendrons*, 1995, p. 56.

8 Cowan, *The Journeys and Plant Introductions of George Forrest*, p. 36.

9 Ibid., pp. 38–9.

10 Letter from Forrest to J. C. Williams quoted in ibid., p. 40. The photographs of Rhododendrons growing on limestone were published in the *Gardeners' Chronicle*, 82, 1927, p. 427. Verbatim report of George Forrest's address and debate 16 November 1920 published in *Rhododendron Society Notes* for 1920.

11 P. D. Williams to Charles Eley, collection of Mr and Mrs Rupert Eley.

12 Lionel de Rothschild in Rothschild, Garton and Rothschild, *The Rothschild Gardens*, p. 50.

13 See C. E. Lucas Phillips and P. N. Barber, *The Rothschild Rhododendrons: A Record of the Garden of Exbury*, 1967, rev. edn, 1979.

14 Miriam Rothschild in Rothschild, Garton and Rothschild, *The Rothschild Gardens*, 1996, p. 130.

15 Lionel de Rothschild in ibid., p. 48.

16 Miriam Rothschild in ibid., p. 23.

17 Phillips and Barber, *The Rothschild Rhododendrons*, p. 8.

18 Quoted in Bean, *Trees and Shrubs Hardy in the British Isles*, p. 829.

19 Nevil Shute, *Requiem for a Wren*, 1955, pp. 82–3.

20 See Jane Brown, *Lanning Roper and his Gardens*, 1987.

21 Brent Elliott, *Victorian Gardens*, 1986, p. 190.

22 The National Trust guide to Cragside, 1992. Cragside is north of Rothbury on the B6341, open daily but see current NT schedule, www.nationaltrust.org.uk or tel. 01669 620150. Rhododendrons are at their best in late May.

23 Lea Gardens, owned by the Tye family, is 3 miles south-east of Matlock in Derbyshire, off the A6. Open daily from mid-March till 30 June. Tel. 01629 534380.

24 Rebecca Dunbar, 'Rich Inheritance (the Christie Family and Blackhills)', *The Garden*, May 1999.

25 See 'Kingdon Ward and Cawdor', in *Frank Kingdon Ward's Riddle of the Tsangpo Gorges*, ed. Kenneth Cox, fac. reprint with additional material, 2001, pp. 23–5ff.. Cawdor Castle, Nairn, IV12 5RD, 11 miles north of Inverness by the A96 and B9090, is open May till October, tel. 01667 404615, www.cawdorcastle.com.

26 Quoted in Lanning Roper, *The Gardens in the Royal Park at Windsor*, 1959, pp. 96–7.

27 Roy Strong, *Royal Gardens*, 1993, p. 55.

28 Olwen Hedley, *Queen Charlotte*, 1975, p. 113.

29 Ibid., p. 180.

30 Jane Roberts, *A Royal Landscape: The Gardens and Parks of Windsor*, 1997, p. 226 and see also *Frogmore House and the Royal Mausoleum*: The Royal Collection, 2nd edn, 2001.

31 Elliott, *Victorian Gardens*, p. 72.

32 'A Day in the Royal Gardens, Sandringham', *The Garden*, 2 September 1905, article signed E. Hobday, Cambridge.

33 Roberts, *A Royal Landscape*, pp. 449–56, for a detailed history of Fort Belvedere.

34 Sarah Bradford, *King George VI*, 1989, p. 171.

35 Philip Ziegler, *Edward VIII: The Official Biography*, 1990, p. 189.

36 Ibid., p. 202.

37 Ibid.

38 Ibid., p. 203.

39 Bradford, *King George VI*, p. 130.

40 Ziegler, *Edward VIII*, p. 262.

41 Bradford, *King George VI*, p. 180.

42 Lanning Roper, *The Gardens in the Royal Park at Windsor*, p. 44

43 Ibid., pp. 102–4.

44 Russell Page, *The Education of a Gardener*, 1962, 1985 edn, seven indexed refs to gardening for the Duke of Windsor.

CHAPTER SIX 'Pink Pearl' Queen of the Bagshot Sands

1 John Harvey, *Early Nurserymen*, 1974, was published long before such histories became fashionable but remains a vital source.

2 E. J. Willson, *Nurserymen to the World: The Nursery Gardens of Woking and North-West Surrey and the Plants Introduced by them*, 1989, p. 16. Waterer's Bagshot Nursery is now part of Notcutts Garden Centre and visits to the mature stock plants in flower are arranged each May at London Road, Bagshot, tel. 01276 472288, www.notcutts.co.uk

3 Donald Waterer, 'The Waterers', in Bean, *Trees and Shrubs Hardy in the British Isles*, p. 935.

4 John Betjeman, 'A Subaltern's Love-Song', in *Collected Poems*, comp. and ed. by Lord Birkenhead, 1958, 1961 edn, pp. 97–9. Also 'Camberley': 'When sunset gilds the Surrey pines . . .', ibid., pp. 10–11.

5 Willson, *Nurserymen to the World*, p. 9.

6 Waterer, 'The Waterers', p. 937.

7 Ibid.

8 Willson, *Nurserymen to the World*, p. 27.

9 Waterer, 'The Waterers', pp. 936–7.

10 Willson, *Nurserymen to the World*, pp. 29–31. See also Alan Leslie, 'Rhododendron Pink Pearl', *The Garden*, May 1996, p. 291.

11 Quoted by Stephen Anderton in 'Ravines and Rhododendrons (Belsay Hall)', *The Garden*, June 1997, p. 420.

12 See 'Notes of the Week', Rhododendron 'Pink Pearl' and other varieties, in *The Garden*, 11 February 1905, p. 82.

13 Gertrude Jekyll on rhododendrons, *Wood & Garden*, 1899, May chapter, and Gertrude Jekyll, *Colour Schemes for the Flower Garden*, 1908, indexed refs.

14 Susan W. Lanman, 'Colour in the Garden: Malignant Magenta', *Garden History*, 28(2), 2000, pp. 209–21.

15 Philip Ball, *Bright Earth: The Invention of Colour*, 2001, pp. 240–1.

16 Ibid.

17 Richard Bisgrove, *The Gardens of Gertrude Jekyll*, 1992, p. 147.

18 Ibid., p. 110.

19 Plan for Folly Farm, Sulhamstead, Berkshire. Excellent copies of the Reef Point Collection of Jekyll drawings can now be seen at Godalming Museum, High Street, Godalming, Surrey, GU7 1AQ, tel. 01483 426510, email: museum@godalming.ndo.co.uk

20 V. N. Gauntlett's catalogue kindly lent to the author by Mrs Miranda Gunn of Ramster.

21 Ramster is on A283 south of Chiddingfold in Surrey, 20 acres (8 ha.) of shrub and woodland garden open in spring. The garden has a developing collection of hardy hybrid rhododendrons collected by the Wessex Rhododendron Group. See Miranda Gunn and John Bond, 'The Hardy Hybrid Collection', *Rhododendrons with Camellias and Magnolias*, 2000. Winkworth Arboretum is owned by the National Trust and open daily during daylight hours; it is on B2130 south of Godalming, tel. 01483 208477.

22 E. H. M. Cox, *Farrer's Last Journey: Upper Burma 1919–20*, 1926, p. 98.

23 Ibid., p. 94.

24 Margaret Fitzherbert, *The Man who Was Greenmantle: A Biography of Aubrey Herbert*, 1985, p. 20.

25 Fitzherbert, *The Man Who Was Greenmantle*, p. 20.

26 Reginald Farrer, *My Rock Garden*, 1907, p. 1.

27 E. H. M. Cox, *Plant Hunting in China*, 1945, p. 178.

28 Reginald Farrer, *The English Rock Garden*, 1920, p. xvii.

29 Fitzherbert, *The Man who Was Greenmantle*, p. 223.

30 Frank Kingdon Ward quoted in Judith Berrisford, *Rhododendrons and Azaleas*, 1964, p. 20, and in Charles Lyte, *Frank Kingdon Ward: The Last of the Great Plant Hunters*, 1989, pp. 86–7.

31 See Cox, *Frank Kingdon Ward's Riddle of the Tsangpo Gorges*. See also Frank Kingdon Ward, *Plant Hunting on the Edge of the World*, 1930, particularly chapter 5, 'Hanging Gardens of the Forest'.

32 Kingdon Ward, *Riddle of the Tsangpo Gorges*, fac. reprint 2001, pp. 142–3.

33 Russell Page, *The Education of a Gardener*, 1962, 1985 edn, p. 263.

34 Ibid., pp. 335–42.

35 Walter Schmalscheidt, 'Hybrids for a Cold Climate: The Seidels', in *The Rhododendron Story*, ed. C. Postan, 1996, pp. 109–14, and W. Schmalscheidt, *Rhododendron-Zuchtung in Deutschland*.

36 Robert Mallet, *Renaissance d'un parc (Awakening Beauty)*, trans. Bryan Woy, Varengeville-sur-Mer, c. 1996. Le Bois des Moutiers, Le Centre d'Art Floral, has a Lutyens house and formal garden as well as the rhododendron woodland. Four miles south of Dieppe, open daily from mid-March to mid-November, tel. 02 35 85 10 02.

37 Bodnant Garden, south of Llandudno by the A470, signed from the A55, open daily from March till November,

tel. 01492 650460, www.bodnantgarden.co.uk

38 Bean, *Trees and Shrubs Hardy in the British Isles*, p. 892.

39 Jenny Hendy, ' "Bowl of Brilliance": The Dorothy Clive Garden', *The Garden*, May 1998, pp. 314–17. The garden is on the A51 between Nantwich and Stone, at Willoughbridge, nr Market Drayton; open daily end March to end October, tel. 01630 647237.

40 For the 'azalea iceberg' see Frederic P. Lee, *The Azalea Book*, American Horticultural Society, Princeton, NJ, 1958, 2nd edn, 1965.

41 Leslie Drew and Frank Drew, 'Furs, Gold and Rhododendrons', in *Rhododendrons on a Western Shore*, Victoria (Vancouver) Rhododendron Society, ed. Alec McCarter, 1989, pp. 4–14.

42 Ibid. and Sylvia Farrer-Bornarth, 'Benvenuto! Welcome to the Butchart Gardens', in *Historic Gardens Review*, Historic Gardens Foundation, London, Summer 2001.

43 Stuart Holland, 'Rhododendron Fraseri', in *Rhododendrons on a Western Shore*, ed. Alec McCarter, 1989, pp. 30–1.

44 Mulligan and Hill, *Ecological Pioneers*, p. 151 and indexed refs. to Patrick White and Sydney Bushwalkers. See also David Marr, *Patrick White*, 1991.

45 Graham Smith, 'Growing Rhododendrons at Pukeiti', in *Rhododendrons in Horticulture and Science*, ed. George Argent and Marjory McFarlane, 2003, pp. 195–202. Pukeiti is open all year except Christmas Day; 2290 Carrington Road, RD 4, New Plymouth, Taranaki, New Zealand, email: *pukeiti@pukeiti.org.nz*. Website: pukeiti.org.nz

46 Mark Flanagan and David Millais, 'A Rhododendron for All Seasons (R. yakushimanum)', *The Garden*, April 2000, pp. 256–61.

47 Willson, *Nurserymen to the World*, p. 37 ff.

48 Arthur and Anne George, correspondence and in conversation with the author; Hydon Nurseries, Clock Barn Lane, Hydon Heath, nr Godalming, Surrey, GU8 4AZ, tel. 01483 860252.

49 Notes on Standish and Noble in Bean, *Trees and Shrubs Hardy in the British Isles*, pp. 938–40, and Willson, *Nurserymen to the World*, pp. 57–64.

50 Obituary, *The Times*, 13 May 1996 and James Russell, *Rhododendrons at Sunningdale*, 1960.

51 Lin Hawthorne, 'The Castle Howard Collection', *The Garden*, October 1997, pp. 742–7.

52 Ibid.

53 Frederick Street (of Heathermead Nursery, Woking), *Hardy Rhododendrons*, 1954, gives a vivid picture of the breeding of mid-twentieth-century hybrids.

CHAPTER SEVEN The Ecologists' Tales

1 Aldo Leopold, *Sand County Almanac*, 1949, quoted by Frank Fraser Darling in *Wilderness and Plenty: BBC Reith Lectures*, 1969, p. 83.

2 Roy Lancaster, *BBC Gardener's World*, quoted by Ian Rotherham, in appendix to 'The Ecology and History of Rhododendron ponticum as an Invasive Alien and Neglected Native with Impacts on Fauna and Flora in Britain', in *Rhododendrons in Horticulture and Science*, ed. George Argent and Marjory McFarlane, 2003, pp. 233–46.

3 William Wordsworth, *Guide to the Lakes* (5th ed, 1835) ed. and introd. Ernest de Selincourt, 1906, 1977 edn, pp. 83–4.

4 Ibid.

5 John Ruskin, *Sesame and Lilies* in *Complete Works*, ed. Cook and Wedderburn.

6 Brantwood, near Coniston, John Ruskin's home from 1872–1900, is open all year. www.brantwood.org.uk, tel. 015394 41396.

7 Ronald McBeath, 'Series Ferrugineum', in Marianna Kneller, *The Book of Rhododendrons*, 1995, pp. 84–5.

8 Alexander Forsyth, 'Game Preserves and Fences', *Journal of Horticulture*, 1846, p. 201.

9 Oliver Rackham, *The Illustrated History of the Countryside*, 1994, p. 16.

10 Lanning Roper, 'Landscape Design', a lecture to the Royal Horticultural Society, 24 September 1968, quoted in Brown, *Lanning Roper and his Gardens*, pp. 10–11.

11 Ian D. Rotherham, 'The Introduction, Spread and Current Distribution of *Rhododendron ponticum* in the Peak District and Sheffield Area', *Naturalist*, 111, 1986, pp. 61–7.

12 Angus Robertson, *Ardtornish Estate, Eradication of Rhododendron ponticum: Sustainable Land Management on a Demonstration Estate*, 1999. Further details from Angus Robertson, Ardtornish, Morvern, Oban PA34 5UZ, email: *angus@ardtornish.co.uk.*

13 Harry C. Evans, 'Biological Control of Invasive Alien Weeds Using Fungi, with Particular Reference to Rhododendron ponticum in the British Isles', in *Rhododendrons in Horticulture and Science*, ed. George Argent and Marjory McFarlane, 2003, pp. 8–19.

14 Simon de Bruxelles, 'Sick Rhododendrons Threaten the English Oak', *The Times*, 30 July 2003, and Paul Brown, 'Killer Fungus Spreads to Britain's Historic Gardens', *Guardian*, 30 July 2003.

15 Andrew Morgan, 'Those Ruddy Rhododendrons', *The Times*, 28 October 2000, p. 14.

16 Paul Brown, 'New Strategy to Combat Alien Invaders', *Guardian*, 29 March 2003, p. 14.

17 Richard I. Milne and Richard J. Abbot, 'The Origin and Evolution of Tertiary Relict Floras', *Advances in Botanical Research*, 38, 2002.

18 Christine Colvin and Charles Nelson, 'Building Castles of Flowers: Maria

Edgeworth as Gardener', *Garden History* 16(1), 1988, pp. 58–70.

19 Geoffrey Grigson, *The Englishman's Flora*, 1987 edn, p. 259.

20 J. B. L. Noel, *Thru' Tibet to Everest*, 1927.

21 W. Robinson, *The English Flower Garden*, 1893 edn, p. 626.

22 Editorial, *The Garden*, July 2001, p. 501. An RHS leaflet 'Peat and the Gardener' is on the website at www.rhs.org.uk/science/ horticultural-themes/mn-peat.asp

23 E. H. M. Cox and Peter Cox, *Modern Rhododendrons*, 1956, pp. 11–12.

24 David Kinsman, 'On Neutral Ground', *The Garden*, March 1999, pp. 158–61.

25 Peter Cox, *The Larger Species of Rhododendron*, 1979, p. 72, quoted in John Lancaster, 'Rhododendrons Hate Lime', *The Garden*, November 1991, pp. 584–7.

26 Peter Konig and Ute Santos, 'Dream Proving of Rhododendron chrysantum (in Austria)', *Homeopathic Links*, no. 4, 1995, pp. 19–20.

27 Kenneth F. Lampe et al., 'Rhododendrons, Mountain Laurel, and Mad Honey', *Journal of the American Medical Association*, 259, 1988, p. 2009.

28 Jean Bruneton, *Toxic Plants Dangerous to Humans and Animals*, trans. from French by Caroline K. Hatton, Technique & Documentation (Editions Tec. & Doc.), Paris, 1999. Valuable section and bibliography (predominantly veterinary) on rhododendrons, unlike most sources on poisonous plants, which are brief and rely on ancient references.

29 Judy Young, 'Introduction', in *Rhododendrons of China*, trans. J. Young and Lu-sheng Ching, Portland, OR, 1980, p. xv.

30 Feng Guomei, *Rhododendrons of Yunnan* (Chinese text), 1981.

31 Li De Zhu and David Paterson, 'Rhododendron Conservation in China', *Rhododendrons in Horticulture and Science*, ed. George Argent and Marjory McFarlane, 2003, pp. 171–7. Mark Nicolson, 'Bouquets for Blooming Chinese Connection', *Financial Times*, 19 November 2002.

32 E. G. Millais, 'A Visit to the Mountains of Western Yunnan', *Rhododendrons with Magnolias and Camellias, 1988–9*', 1988, pp. 13–19.

33 Peter Valder, *Gardens in China*, Timber Press, Portland, OR, 2002.

CHAPTER EIGHT Rhododendrons Now!

1 Information on Canon Cruttwell kindly given to the author by Mary Bartlett of Dartington and John Latter of Bargara in Queensland, Australia. *The Two Lives of Christian Cruttwell: Her Autobiography*, is published by Papua New Guinea Church Partnership, 157 Waterloo Road, London SE1 8XA.

2 Paul Smith, '*Vireyas in Irian Jaya*', *Rhododendrons with Camellias, and Magnolias 1994*, 1993, pp. 37–40. See also George Argent, 'The Vireya Story', *The Rhododendron Story*, ed. C. Postan, 1996, pp. 86–92, and George Argent, 'Species Patterns in Rhododendron Section Vireya from Sea Level to the Snow Line in New Guinea', in *Rhododendrons in Horticulture and Science*, ed. Argent and Marjory McFarlane, 2003, pp. 160–70.

3 John Kenyon and Jacqueline Walker, *Vireyas: A Practical Gardening Guide*, Timber Press, Portland, OR, 1997, p. 17.

4 Christopher Fairweather, 'Commercial Production of Vireya Rhododendrons', in *Rhododendrons in Horticulture and Science*, ed. George Argent and Marjory McFarlane, 2003, pp. 154–9.

5 George Argent and David Chamberlain, '*Rhododendron rushforthii*: A New Species from Vietnam', *The Garden*, December 1996, p. 776.

6 Quoted in Kenyon and Walker, *Vireyas*, p. 29.

7 Edmund de Rothschild, *A Gilt-Edged Life: Memoir*, 1998, p. 158 and the whole of chapter 6, 'Exbury'.

8 C. E. Lucas Phillips and Peter Barber, *The Rothschild Rhododendrons*, rev. edn 1979, pp. 42–3. See also Lionel de Rothschild, 'Hybrids in the British Isles: The 19th Century' in *The Rhododendron Story*, ed. C. Postan, 1996, pp. 115–35, and Lionel de Rothschild, chapter 3 on Exbury, in Rothschild, Garton, Rothschild, *The Rothschild Gardens*, 1996.

9 Terry Shadbolt and Warren Boyles, 'The Remarkable Emu Valley Rhododendron Garden', *40 deg. South, Tasmania and Beyond*, no. 18, spring 2000, pp. 32–4.

10 Michael Lear and Rachel Martin, 'Putting a Name to Garden Hybrids: Deciphering and Cataloguing Rhododendrons at Exbury', *Rhododendrons in Horticulture and Science*, ed. Argent and Marjory McFarlane 2003, pp. 178–85.

11 Michael Robinson, 'Late Flowering Elepidote Hybrids with Reference to Exbury and Other Gardens in Southern England', in *Rhododendrons in Horticulture and Science*, ed. George Argent and Marjory McFarlane, 2003, pp. 115–20.

12 Tony and Eira Hibbert, *Trebah Garden Guide*. Trebah Garden is on the Helford River south of Mawnan Smith, open every day. Contact the Trebah Garden Trust, Trebah, Mawnan Smith, nr Falmouth, TR11 5JZ, tel. 01326 250448.

13 Walter Magor, 'The Garden at Heligan in Cornwall', *Rhododendrons 1982/3 with Magnolias and Camellias*, 1982, pp. 1–3.

14 Keith Zealand, 'Sheringham Park – A Further Fifty Years', *Rhododendrons 2001 with Magnolias and Camellias*, 2001, pp. 36–8, and Thomas Upcher, 'Rhododendrons in East Anglia – Sheringham Park', *Rhododendron Yearbook 1951–2*, 1951.

15 Michael Thornley, ' "Glenarn": A Scottish West Coast Rhododendron Garden' in *Rhododendrons in Horticulture and Science*, ed. George Argent and Marjory McFarlane, 2003, pp. 86–94. Glenarn is off the A814 2 miles north of Helensburgh; open mid-March to mid-September; tel. 01436 820493, email: *mast@dial.pipex.com*. For further information on west coast gardens tel. 01499 600261, www.gardens-of-argyll.co.uk

16 The latest edition of the *Rhododendron Handbook* is the 6th edn, RHS, 1990. Supplements to the *Rhododendron Register* have been produced since the 1958 edition and the new register is 'on its way' under the direction of Dr Alan Leslie at the RHS Wisley Garden, Woking, Surrey, GU23 6QB, tel. 01483 224234.

17 Sonja Nelson, *Rhododendrons in the Landscape*, Portland, OR, 2000.

18 Glendoick Gardens Ltd, Glendoick, Perth, PH2 7NS, Scotland. Nursery open regularly. Tel. 01738 860205, www.glendoick.com

LIST OF ILLUSTRATIONS

COLOUR PLATES:

Section 1

Page 1 *Chamaerhododendros lauri-folio semper virens* (*Rhododendron maximum*) by George Ehret. (With kind permission, Royal Botanic Gardens, Kew (RBG, Kew))

Page 2 *Azalea pontica* (*Rhododendron luteum*), the poison honey azalea, by Sydenham Teast Edwards. (RBG, Kew)

Page 3 *Rhododendron dalhousiae* by Walter Hood Fitch (1817–1892), hand-coloured lithograph based on Hooker's sketch. (RBG, Kew)

Page 4 *Rhododendron ferrugineum* by Marianna Kneller for *The Book of Rhododendrons*, 1995. (Reproduced by kind permission of Marianna Kneller)

Page 5 Larachmhor, Inverness-shire, the remains of John Holms' house. (Photographs by Peter Aldington)

Pages 6 & 7 Alessandro Sanquirico (1777–1849), *Interno di una serra* (Inside a Hothouse). (The Metropolitan Museum of Art, Harris Brisbane Dick Fund, 1939. (39.54) Photograph © 1994 The Metropolitan Museum of Art)

Page 8 *Rhododendron falconeri* by Walter Hood Fitch (1817–92), lithograph from Hooker's pencil and watercolour sketch. (RBG, Kew)

Section 2

Page 1 (top) *Rhododendron williamsianum* by Emily Sartain (1903–90) for the illuminated autograph of King George VI. (Royal Horticultural Society, Lindley Library)

(bottom) Queen Elizabeth the Queen Mother photographed at

Royal Lodge, Windsor, by Cecil Beaton (1904–80), 1970. (Camera Press)

Page 2 Albert Moore (1841–93) *Azaleas*. (Dublin City Gallery, The Hugh Lane Collection)

Page 3 Sir Lawrence Alma-Tadema (1836–1912) *Unconscious Rivals*. (Bristol City Museum & Art Gallery/Bridgeman Art Library)

Page 4 Marianne North (1830–90), foliage and flowers of *Rhododendron grande*: the artist painted many rhododendrons, which had a special affinity with her flamboyant style. (RBG, Kew)

Page 5 (top) Flowers of Papua New Guinea drawn by N. E. G. Cruttwell and I Lowe for Papua New Guinea stamps. (Reproduced with Permission, courtesy of Post PNG Ltd)
(bottom) *Rhododendron brookeanum* (orange) and *Rhododendron apiense* (yellow) in the vireya house at the Royal Botanic Garden, Edinburgh. (The author)

Page 6 Marion Dorn (1896–1964) surrounded by some of her fabric designs, photograph by Horst, 1947. (© Corbis. All Rights Reserved)

Page 7 (top) The Harry Mangles hybrid Rhododendron 'Gertrude Jekyll' flowering in his garden, now Hethersett, at Littleworth Cross, Surrey. (The author)
(bottom) Gertrude Jekyll (1843–1932), planting scheme for Frant Court, Kent, 1914. (Illustration by Liz Pepperell, copyright © Frances Lincoln Ltd 1992, taken from The Gardens of Gertrude Jekyll by Richard Bisgrove. Reproduced by kind permission of Frances Lincoln Limited, 4 Torriano Mews, Torriano Avenue, London NW5 2RZ)

Page 8 Titley & Marr's 'Rhododendrons' fabric, originally designed by William Pearman in July 1860 and printed by Stead McAlpin in Carlisle for Daniel Walters & Company, London. (By kind permission of Messrs Titley & Marr)

Section 3

Page 1 (top) Sergio Garcia of Spain at the 13th tee, 1st round of the 2003 Masters Tournament, Augusta National Golf Club, Georgia. (David Cannon/Getty Images)
(bottom) Pink Azalea illustration from *Days Like This*, by Simon James. (© 1999 Simon James. Reproduced by kind permission of Walker Books Ltd., London SE11 5HJ)

Page 2 Stanley Spencer (1891–1959) *Convoy Arriving with Wounded* – at the gates of the Beaufort War Hospital, Bristol, Mural painting no. 1, 1927. (© Estate of Stanley Spencer 2004. All Rights

INTEGRATED ILLUSTRATIONS

Page 76 Rhododendron catawbiense, named for the Catawba Indians in whose Appalachian country it was found.

Pages 80–81 Richard Twiss (1747–1821), plan for the garden of 13 Upper Gower Street, London. (Bodleian Library, University of Oxford. MS. Douce c.11, fols 20v-21r)

Page 95 Rhododendron kaempferi, named for the German Engelbert Kaempfer. (RBG, Kew)

Page 96 Holm Lea, Charles Sprague Sargent's home in Brookline, an engraving of the 1890s showing the rhododendrons as the chief feature of the large and splendid garden.

Page 98 Beatrix Farrand (1872–1959), plan for the azalea border at the Arnold Arboretum carried out in the late 1940s and published in *Arnoldia*, 15 April 1949.

Page 99 Ernest 'Chinese' Wilson (1876–1930) on the left, and Charles Sprague Sargent (1841–1927) in front of *Prunus subhirtella*, 1915. (Photographic Archives of the Arnold Arboretum. Copyrighted by the President and Fellows of Harvard College, Harvard University, Cambridge, Massachusetts, USA.)

Page 127 John Guille Millais (1865–1931), artist, adventurer, sportsman and prime mover of the Rhododendron Society in 1915.

Page 145 Rhododendron fictolacteum flowering in mixed forest in Yunnan, photographed by George Forrest. (RBG, Edinburgh)

Page 149 (top) George Forrest's caravan resting in the shade. (RBG, Edinburgh)
(bottom) Forrest and two (unknown) companions on a day's hunting. (RBG, Edinburgh)

Page 178 A frequently featured advertisement by Waterer's of Knap Hill Nursery in the *Gardeners' Chronicle* in the 1890s.

Page 179 Pennell & Sons, advertisement from *The Garden*, 28 October 1905.

Page 184 Rhododendron nobleanum, an early hybrid, illustrated in William Robinson's *The English Flower Garden*, 1893 edition.

Page 186 Rhododendron indicum at Coolhurst in Sussex, illustrated in William Robinson's *The English Flower Garden*, 1893 edition.

Page 199 The spotted Wilhelma hybrid introduced in the nineteenth century by the Seidel Nursery of Dresden.

Page 237 Professor Sir Isaac Bayley Balfour (1853–1922) lecturing at the Royal Botanic Garden Edinburgh. (RBG, Edinburgh)

Page 256 The Cornwall Gardens Trust's map of rhododendron gardens open to visitors. (Cornwall Gardens Trust)

SOME OF THE BEST PLACES
TO FIND RHODODENDRONS

Note: Information for visitors to many of the places described in the text has been included in the Notes. The following are *Tales of the Rose Tree* essentials:

ARNOLD ARBORETUM of Harvard University, 125 Arborway, Jamaica Plain, Massachusetts, MA 02130–3500, is a public park and open daily.

BODNANT GARDEN, south of Llandudno by the A470, signed from the A55, open daily March until November. Tel. 01492 650460. www.bodnant.garden.co.uk

CAERHAYS CASTLE, nine miles south-west of St Austell, Cornwall, has variable openings between March and May. Tel. 01872 501310. www.caerhays.co.uk

CASTLE HOWARD, north-east of York, signed from A64 near Malton, has James Russell's collection of species and hybrids in Ray Wood. Tel. 01653 648444. www.castlehoward.co.uk

DARTINGTON HALL GARDEN, near Totnes in South Devon on the A384, is open every day, with fine mature rhododendron and camellia walks, originally planted by Beatrix Farrand for Dorothy Elmhirst, and Percy Cane's magnificent azalea steps.

DOROTHY CLIVE GARDEN is on the A51 between Nantwich and Stone, at Willoughbridge, nr Market Drayton, and is open daily from the end of March until the end of October. Tel. 01630 647237.

EDINBURGH ROYAL BOTANIC GARDEN, 20a Inverleith Row, Edinburgh EH3 5LR, open daily from 9.30 a.m. excluding Christmas Day and 1 January. Tel. 0131 552 7171. www.rbge.org.uk. Includes LOGAN, BENMORE AND DAWYCK BOTANIC GARDENS, which all hold part of this world-famous collection.

EXBURY GARDENS, Hampshire, signed from M27 junction 2 near Southampton, open daily, early March until early November. www.exbury.co.uk

HYDON NURSERIES, Clock Barn Lane, Hydon Heath, nr Godalming, Surrey GU8 4AZ, specialist nursery open all year, but not Sundays and closed for lunch. Tel. 01483 860252.

LEA GARDENS is three miles south-east of Matlock in Derbyshire off the A6. It is open daily from mid-March until 30 June. Tel. 01629 534380.

LE BOIS DES MOUTIERS, Le Centre d'Art Floral, four miles south of Dieppe, open daily from mid-March until mid-November. Tel. 02 35 85 10 02.

MILLAIS NURSERIES, Crosswater Farm, Crosswater Lane, Churt, Farnham, Surrey. Tel. 01252 792698. www.rhododendrons.co.uk includes an additional list of rhododendron nurseries.

MUNCASTER CASTLE, south of Ravenglass, Cumbria; gardens open all year, rhododendron walks at best mid-March to June. A collector's garden. www.muncastercastle.co.uk

NOTCUTTS GARDEN CENTRE (formerly Waterer's Bagshot Nursery), London Road, Bagshot, Surrey, arranges visits in May to the mature stock plants in the nursery ground. Tel. 01276 472288, www.notcutts.co.uk

OXFORD UNIVERSITY ARBORETUM, Nuneham Courtenay, south of Oxford on A423. 'Outstation' of Oxford Botanic Garden so check opening times. Tel. 01865 286690.

PUKEITI, 2290 Carrington Road, RD 4, New Plymouth, Taranaki, New Zealand, is open daily, except Christmas Day. Rhododendrons are in flower every month, but especially September to December. www.pukeiti.org.nz

RAMSTER is on the A283, one and a half miles south of Chiddingfold, Surrey, open daily from mid-April until July. Tel. 01428 654167. www.bigfoot.com/~ramster

SAVILL GARDEN, Windsor Great Park, signed from the A30 at Englefield Green, open daily except 25 and 26 December. Tel. 01753 847536.

SIR HAROLD HILLIER GARDENS, Jermyns Lane, Ampfield, Romsey, Hampshire; a collectors' garden made by the owner of Hilliers' Nurseries. Tel. 01794 368787. www.hillier.hants.gov.uk

VALLEY GARDEN, Windsor Great Park, is open every day from dawn to dusk, admission free but charge for car parking at Virginia Water on A30.

WESTONBIRT ARBORETUM, 3 miles south of Tetbury, Gloucestershire, with rhododendrons playing a significant part in the Holford collection. Open all year. Tel. 01666 880200.

WINKWORTH ARBORETUM, on the B2130 south of Godalming, is owned by the National Trust and is open daily during daylight hours. Tel. 01483 208477.

WISLEY GARDEN (Royal Horticultural Society), nr Woking, Surrey GU23 6QB, is 1 mile south of junction 10 of the M25 on the A3. Tel. 01483 224234. The Wisley collections are easily overlooked amidst the other glories of the garden but they are unique – modern hybrids, recently introduced species, tender rhododendrons under glass, rock garden plants and larger species and hybrids in the Wild Garden and on Battleston Hill.

ADDITIONAL RESOURCES

Membership of the Rhododendron, Camellia and Magnolia Group is open to members of the Royal Horticultural Society resident in the UK: for residents outside the UK membership of the RHS is not mandatory. Further information from www.rhodogroup-rhs.org or from the RHS membership hotline 0845 130 4646.

The Australian Rhododendron Society Inc., welcomes members for $25.00 Aust. See www.eisa.net.au/~mirra or apply to The Secretary, PO Box 21, Olinda, Victoria 3788, Australia.

The American Rhododendron Society, of which the Scottish Rhododendron Society is a chapter, can be contacted at 11 Pincrest Drive, Fortuna, Ca 95540 or via www.ars.org

INDEX

Page numbers in *italic* refer to the illustrations